THE IPSWICH BOOK OF DAYS

RACHEL FIELD

To Mervyn, with best wishes from Rachel Field, Ipswich, 2015

The History Press

With many thanks to Paul Field, Sheila Hardy – who gave me my chance –
Cathy Hunt, Sarah Rixon, and my sister, Linda Appleby.

First published 2014

The History Press
The Mill, Brimscombe Port
Stroud, Gloucestershire, GL5 2QG
www.thehistorypress.co.uk

British Library Cataloguing in Publication Data.
A catalogue record for this book is available from the British Library.

ISBN 978 0 7524 9012 0

Typesetting and origination by The History Press
Printed in India

– January 1st –

1904: On this Friday a 20hp Mercedes car, owned by William Pretty of Fonnereau Road, was given the registration number DX1 – the first car number plate to be issued in Ipswich. (John F. Bridges, *Early Country Motoring*)

1989: Sergei Baltacha became the first Soviet footballer to play professionally in Britain when he joined Ipswich Town from Ukrainian club, Dynamo Kiev.

Sergei came to England knowing just two phrases. The first was 'fasten your seat belts', which he had mastered on the flight over from Moscow, and the second was 'no problem', which he used in all circumstances, and which was why his team-mates ended up calling him 'Sergei No-Problem'. (Mark Gilbey, *Never Mind the Bolsheviks*)

1997: An all-day protest party marked the beginning of a sit-in which became known as the 'occupation of Ipswich airport'. Ipswich Borough Council owned the airport and wanted to close it to build a housing estate. Businesses and other airport users were given notice to quit and issued with writs when they refused to move out. Several protest marches followed, and there was a lobby at the House of Commons. But, by June, the Pitts Bar had closed, and the occupation ended early in 1998 when the very last aircraft left. (Ipswich Airport Association website: www.ipswichairport.info/)

~ January 2nd ~

1794: By January 2nd of this year the Royal Mint had nearly stopped producing coins. Coppers in particular were in short supply, so to help trading to continue the Government allowed some commercial firms around the country to mint and circulate their own tokens.

In Ipswich, James Conder, draper and haberdasher, seized the opportunity and issued several varieties of halfpenny and penny. Some showed Cardinal Wolsey's profile, while others featured the market cross or St Mildred's church. On the obverse were Conder's initials and an indication of where the tokens could be used (which was usually at Conder's warehouse).

James Conder was also an avid collector of trade tokens in general and was the first person to collect and catalogue them. Hence they became known as 'Conder's Tokens', especially in the United States.

Strangely, nearly seventy years later, a hoard of ancient coins was found buried deep under the doorstep of Condor's house in the Buttermarket. No one ever worked out why they were there. (William Conder, *Conder Family Ipswich*)

1824: On his walking tour of Suffolk, the antiquarian David Elisha Davy noted a pungent agricultural smell and wrote: 'I this morning walked from Martlesham to Waldringfield church, … I found a farmer near the church manuring his land for barley with sprats and was a good deal annoyed by the smell.' (David Elisha Davy, *Journal of Excursions*)

— JANUARY 3RD —

1794: The *Ipswich Journal* reported that cold, dry, windy weather in the previous summer had led to a poor harvest of peas and beans – one of the main field crops in Suffolk and a staple of the local diet:

> Cold north winds in June brought swarms of green and black lice, which destroyed great quantities of beans and peas all over the county.
>
> Where the lice did not destroy them, the drought that followed prevented them in general from being more than one fourth of a crop. In many parts of Suffolk no rain fell for 11 weeks.

(*Ipswich Journal*, 1794)

2013: Mick Sanderson, Rolling Stones fan extraordinaire, went into Ipswich to get his latest 'tongue and lips' tattoo done. His body was already pretty much covered in tattoos – a shrine to his favourite band of all time. Nothing, though, could beat the portrait on his right leg of former Stones bassist, Bill Wyman, which he would proudly show to anyone interested enough to ask.

When Bill Wyman and his band came to the Regent in 2008, Mick Sanderson met him after the gig and showed him the tattoo. Bill was tickled and took a photo of it. Imagine Mick's amazement a few years later when he bought Bill's new album Live Communication and there, on the insert, was the photo of his leg! (Thanks to Mick and Ann Sanderson)

January 4th

1906: Nina Layard (1853–1935), an Ipswich archaeologist, visited an excavation near the junction of London and Hadleigh Roads (later called Allenby Road). She had been on holiday in Scotland and had read about the dig in the newspapers. Realising that something significant was being unearthed, she hightailed it back to Ipswich to have a look. To her horror she saw that the land was being levelled by unskilled, unemployed men on a work-creation scheme. The site was not being explored – it was being destroyed.

Miss Layard set to work organising and supervising the dig. A sixth-century Anglo-Saxon cemetery was uncovered with over 150 burials and associated jewellery, beakers and weapons. Miss Layard saw to it that everything was properly recorded – although one of the finds, listed as 'an iron instrument in a silver case', turned out to be the key and rolled metal strip from a tin of corned beef! As she was a woman, she was not allowed to read her excavation report to the Society of Antiquaries. It was read for her by a male friend.

Miss Layard lived with her companion, Miss Outram, at Rookwood in Fonnereau Road for many years. (Steven Plunkett, *Nina Layard, Hadleigh Road and Ipswich Museum*)

— JANUARY 5TH —

1994: Tim Yeo, MP for South Suffolk (including the Shotley peninsula), resigned as a minister in John Major's government.

Late the previous year, the Major government had launched a 'Back to Basics' campaign. Its high moral tone had sparked intense media interest in MPs' private lives. Tim Yeo, a married man, let the side down almost immediately when a tabloid newspaper revealed he had fathered an illegitimate child by Conservative councillor Julia Stent. The scandal broke on Boxing Day, a quiet news period, and grabbed the headlines all over the New Year. To add to Yeo's misery, he was forced to admit publicly that this was his second illegitimate child. He had fathered his first when a student in the sixties.

Yeo's words of three years earlier, spoken to a branch of Relate in Sudbury, now sounded rather hollow. He had pronounced: 'It's in everyone's interests to reduce broken families and the number of single parents. I have seen from my own constituency the consequences of marital breakdown.' (*Express Newspaper*, January 4th 2014)

———

2012: The birthday of Guru Gobind Singh was celebrated at the Gurdwara in Bramford Road, the place of worship for most of Ipswich's 4,000-strong Sikh community. He was the tenth Guru and is honoured by Sikhs for giving them their five distinguishing symbols, which include wearing an iron or steel bracelet and having uncut hair.

On this Sunday, the Sikh holy book was read aloud by a team of readers without any break from beginning to end, and free vegetarian food was available for everyone. (Guru Nanak Temple website: http://ipswichgurdwara.com)

~ January 6th ~

1972: Lancelot de Giberne Sieveking, the pioneer BBC producer, died in Ipswich, having lived near Snape for many years.

His exotic name was fitting. He was German on his father's side, and related to Gainsborough and Gerard Manley Hopkins on his mother's. In 1924, Sieveking joined the BBC as a producer and playwright and worked there until retirement in 1956. He wrote many plays for *Saturday Night Theatre* on the Home Service and even C.S. Lewis himself enjoyed his wireless adaptation of *The Magician's Nephew*.

Sieveking produced the first BBC live football coverage. To help commentators he devised a plan of the pitch divided into eight numbered squares. It was also published in the *Radio Times* so that listeners at home could use it to follow the game. This may be where the phrase 'back to square one' came from.

In 1930, Sieveking produced the first ever British television play – a short Pirandello drama of two men having a philosophical discussion outside a café. Sieveking ended the programme by playing a recording he had made for sixpence on Southwold pier. It consisted of Sieveking making an explanatory announcement, clapping, and then humming *God Save the King*. (Derek Brady, *The Man with the Flower in his Mouth*; Tony Copsey, *Suffolk Writers Who Were Born Between 1800–1900*; Steve Hawley, *Artists, Film and Video*)

~ January 7th ~

1892: The Eagle Iron Works held its works' annual supper at the Friar's Head Tavern. After the meal, the evening was given over to entertainment. In traditional East Anglian style, there was some 'capital step-dancing'. Each man who wanted to dance got up in turn to do a few steps on the stepping flagstone in the bar room floor, accompanied by singing and a Mr Lanedell on the piano. (*Ipswich Journal*, 1892)

1897: William Flory, cab proprietor, died on this Thursday, aged 85. According to his headstone in Ipswich Old Cemetery, he was an active member of the Ipswich Memnonian Society for fifty years and much loved by his fellow freemasons.

The Memnonian Society was a musical club for freemasons. It was founded in 1832 by twelve men at the Dove Inn, St Helen's Street. They had a simple set of rules, a password and a secret grip, and their aim was to enjoy musical evenings together. The following year they moved to the Cock & Pye Inn and then on to the Fox, where they decorated their room with an Egyptian theme and bought their own piano. Ipswich's most prominent citizens became members and no doubt carried out behind-the-scenes business at meetings. Among other philanthropic work, members helped establish Ipswich Museum and the Fore Street public baths. (Thanks to Simon Knott)

~ January 8th ~

2010: Ipswich artist John Rixon curated a show called Quiet Voices at Tate Britain in central London. John, who worked for the Big Chill Festival and Suffolk New College, collaborated with other artists and musicians to explore the nature of quiet in video and sound. His starting point and inspiration was the phrase 'listen to the quiet voice', an aphorism suggested by Brian Eno to help break a creative block.

Alongside the large centrepiece video of icebergs floating in a glacial lagoon, John also showed a mesmerising film of parkland before and after snowfall. John said:

> The event was wonderful. The Tate agreed straightaway to the idea and I was lucky to work with the techno-musician Jon Hopkins who has since become so famous I couldn't possibly afford to work with him now! His music complemented the images I'd created perfectly.
>
> We left Ipswich after work and went to the Tate by train. It was snowing heavily, I remember. When we got to the gallery the atmosphere was so quiet and peaceful – even though people were wandering around talking with glasses of wine in their hands – and the setting was just right for the show. It was the perfect gig.

(Thanks to John Rixon)

~ JANUARY 9TH ~

1194: On or about this day, men and ships from Ipswich set sail in a flotilla from Dunwich and Orford carrying a ransom to free King Richard I (1157–99) from captivity.

Richard had been captured near Vienna two years before as he travelled home from the Third Crusade. At first he was held by his enemy the Duke of Vienna, who then passed him on to Henry VI, the Holy Roman Emperor, who demanded 150,000 marks for his release (£2bn at 2011 prices). Back in England, it took nearly a year to raise this enormous sum. His brother (the future King John) was reluctant to do anything to set Richard free. It was their elderly mother and the Archbishop of Canterbury who collected the ransom by levying taxes and confiscating church treasures.

By early January 1194, with all the money gathered in, the little fleet set off from the East Anglian coast carrying 'a king's ransom'. Richard was released a month later. (Rowland Parker, Men of Dunwich)

~ January 10th ~

1799: Elizabeth Edwards (*née* Kealy) was born on or about this day in Ipswich. She became a successful businesswoman, which was quite unusual for women in this period. She set herself up as a corsetière, making and selling stays and corsets from her shop in Tacket Street. She also sold garments from a cottage in Crown Street, as well as through agents in other Suffolk towns, such as Miss Oxberrow of Framlingham.

She offered to visit women at home if they invited their friends round for fittings – a corset party, perhaps the precursor of the Tupperware party?

One of her specialities was making corsets that were suitable for young ladies to wear for their deportment exercises and physical drills.

When her husband died in 1840, leaving her with a large family, Mrs Edwards was able to support them from her business. About the same time, she became a corsetière 'by appointment to Queen Victoria', which gave added kudos to her business in Suffolk.

In the early 1850s, Mrs Edward sold up to a Miss Todd of St Matthew's parish and emigrated from Ipswich with her adult children to live in South Australia. (*Ipswich Journal*, various dates; www.ancestry.co.uk)

– January 11th –

1965: Lady Blanche Cobbold became the honorary president of Ipswich Town Football Club. Simon Knott wrote:

> She was the first and, in her lifetime, the only female president of a professional football club. This was at a time when the Cobbold family virtually ran the club … and Lady Blanche followed Town through their finest years.
>
> In 1978, Ipswich Town won the FA Cup at Wembley, beating Arsenal 1–0, the only East Anglian team ever to win the trophy. A guest of honour that day was the new leader of the Conservative Party, one Margaret Thatcher. The Cobbolds were nothing if not Conservative, but the parvenu qualities of the Iron Lady would not have appealed to Lady Blanche … Anxious to assert the correct and appropriate protocols, an official of the Football Association approached Lady Blanche, and invited her to meet Mrs Thatcher. 'Mrs Thatcher?' said Lady Blanche. 'You mean – Margaret Thatcher?' The FA official confirmed that they were one and the same. 'Good God,' replied the grand old lady. 'I'd much rather have another gin and tonic.'

(Thanks to Simon Knott and Ralph Morris)

~ January 12th ~

1800: Soup at a penny per quart with a slice of bread was made available for the Ipswich poor on this winter Monday. A subscription to pay for the food was raised among public-spirited families such as the Ransomes, the Alexanders, the Byles and the Cobbolds. The soup kitchen was open between 12 p.m. and 1 p.m. in the yard of the Coach & Horses in Tacket Street. (*Ipswich Journal*, 1800)

1823: On or about this day, Lord Wellington accidentally shot his host, Lord Granville, in the face. They were near Hill Covert near Wherstead, shooting on Granville's land, when the accident happened. A Dr Bartlett of Ipswich was called and he extracted the pellets, or most of them, as two or three could not be removed. Lord Wellington was deeply upset, with tears streaming down his face.

In later years, the Vicar of Wherstead enjoyed recalling that he once saw the Lords Canning and Wellington at one of Granville's house parties. They were acting a charade in which the Iron Duke appeared as a nurse wearing a white cap and holding a pillow dressed as a baby in his arms. (Freda A. Fryer, *Wherstead*; *East Anglian Magazine*, 1951)

~ January 13th ~

1706: Judith Hayle, the only seventeenth-century teacher of needlework whose name is known, was buried in St Stephen's parish. She was nearly 60 years old and had spent most of her adult life in the area.

Between 1691 and 1711, Judith taught young middle-class women from Ipswich how to stitch samplers. These samplers were quite distinctive, as Judith's name or initials were always incorporated into the design to show that they were made under her tuition. One from 1691 made it even clearer: 'Elizabeth Meadows is my name and with my needle I wrought the same and Juda Hayle was my dame.'

The fifteen or so surviving samplers made by Judith's pupils form the largest group known from the period. Individual items eventually went into public collections such as the Victoria and Albert Museum. (Ipswich Women's History Trail; *Costume Historian*, June 2012)

———

1931: Ian Hendry, 'the actor who should have been a star', was born at his parents' house in Tuddenham Road on this Tuesday. One of his major successes was as Dr David Keel, the starring role in the first series of *The Avengers*. He left at the end of the series to concentrate on films, and it was only then that the bowler-hatted John Steed became the main character. (*East Anglian Daily Times*, 2013)

– January 14th –

1736: George II stayed overnight at the Great White Horse in Tavern Street to break his journey from Lowestoft to London. To mark the occasion, the nearby Cock and Pye Tavern put on performances by the Royal Company of Artificial Actors, a troupe of puppeteers who operated marionettes that were up to 5ft tall. (Carol Twinch, *Ipswich Street by Street*)

1940: Trevor Nunn was born in Ipswich. Educated at Northgate Grammar School, he threw himself into drama. One teacher in particular was an inspiration. Nunn recalled:

> He just had this incredible ability to unlock the texts. Every year he directed the school play. Wanting to impress him, and wanting to emulate him, was very much part of growing up. In the sixth form he would do Friday night extra Shakespeare sessions. We would all bicycle out to his windmill.

Nunn took his first steps in the acting profession as an assistant stage manager at the old Ipswich Arts Theatre and then, between school and university, he formed the Ipswich Youth Drama Group. Nunn aimed high even then – their first production was *Hamlet*! (*Ipswich Star*, 2012; *Guardian*, 2011)

~ January 15th ~

1905: In mid-January this year, Edward Ardizzone, the award-winning illustrator, writer and war artist, moved to Constable Road from his grandmother's house in East Bergholt. He was 5 years old and lived with his mother, brothers and sisters. His father had stayed to work in Indo-China, where Edward was born. Edward went to Ipswich Prep School where he struggled with his schoolwork and was bullied by other pupils. In fact, he was too scared to walk home across Christchurch Park, as a group of boys used to lie in wait for him there.

Although Ipswich held some deeply unhappy memories for him, what he saw in the 'rough and tough' town influenced him for life. He loved wandering around the docks which inspired the illustrations for his Little Tim series. When he was 10, he came across a scene that fired his imagination. In a rough part of town, he witnessed the spectacle of two barefoot women brawling outside a pub. They were wearing only torn nightdresses and 'were shrieking like cats'. Pub customers watched out of the window but did nothing. Ardizzone wrote that it was a formative moment in his career and he included a sketch of the scene in his autobiography, *Those who will not be Drowned*. (Susan Gardiner's blog; Edward Ardizzone, *The Young Ardizzone*)

‒ January 16th ‒

1789: It was one of the coldest winters on record throughout Europe and today Charles Berner of Woolverstone Park, ordered 15 guineas to be distributed to the poor living in the Shotley Peninsula parishes of Holbrook, Harkstead and Erwarton, to help them through the frostiest days. In Woolverstone, his own parish, he also arranged for flour to be distributed weekly to families. (*Ipswich Journal*, 1789)

‒‒

1875: The *Ipswich Journal* reported that a fire had broken out that week at the Reform Club in Tacket Street. Attempts to tackle it were risible. The fire brigade was late arriving at the scene and the nearby hydrants only produced trickles of water. The size of the blaze drew crowds, who jeered at the police and fire-fighters as they struggled in vain to save the building. After this shambles, the corporation was compelled to set up a new, properly organised fire brigade under new leadership. (Henry Reynolds Eyre, *History of Ipswich Fire Brigade*; *Ipswich Journal*, 1875)

‒‒

2010: The unappealing headline 'Ipswich Stink Back Again' appeared in the *Ipswich Evening Star*. (*Ipswich Evening Star*, 2010)

— January 17th —

1583: Everyone in Ipswich was ordered to keep a sturdy stick at home so that they could help put down any street disturbances. (Nathaniell Bacon, *Annalls of Ipswich*)

—————

1842: The lock at the new wet dock was used for the first time, but the ceremony was a fiasco.

Late in the afternoon of this gloomy day, a handful of people joined the mayor, the chief engineer and the dock commissioners to watch the lock in operation. No one had made arrangements for a ship to come through, so a grain carrier bound for Rochester was persuaded to use the lock just to mark it open.

After that, a brig laden with coal showed up unexpectedly. As the tide was low, the crew did not think they would be allowed into the lock. When they realised that they would be, they made a mess of the awkward turn needed to come in through the gates from the new cut. The ship crashed into a side wall and damaged it.

The *Ipswich Journal*, which had always opposed the scheme, concluded rather sarcastically: 'After no inconsiderable delay and bungling, the Town may be considered to enjoy the advantages of a wet dock.' (*Ipswich Journal*, 1842; Robert Malster, *Ipswich: An A to Z of Local History*)

– January 18th –

1297: Princess Elizabeth (1282–1316), the teenage daughter of Edward I, was married to the Count of Holland at the King's Hall near St Peter's church. It was a dynastic marriage and the couple had been betrothed as infants.

Elizabeth's trousseau and the curtains for the nuptial bed had taken thirty-five tailors four days and nights to make and were brought up to Ipswich in a couple of carts, rumbling over Cattawade Bridge. The ceremony was marred by a couple of misadventures. Elizabeth's sister disliked the jewels that had been sent from London for her to wear – so much so that she sent them back in disgust. The King lost his temper for some reason and threw Elizabeth's wedding coronet into the fire. Two precious stones were lost and his goldsmith had to find replacements at the last minute. After the wedding, Elizabeth and her new husband set off for Harwich and from there to the Low Countries. (L.J. Redstone, *Ipswich Through the Ages*)

1478: The town authorities ordered all 'Strangers and Dutchemen' who kept inns or shops in Ipswich to pay an annual tax of 20*d*. They wanted to discourage outsiders from trading in Ipswich and to keep an eye on any who did. (Nathaniell Bacon, *Annalls of Ipswich*)

~ January 19th ~

1997: On or about this weekend, a metal detectorist in East Bergholt found a lead figurine, about 2in high, of a man with huge genitalia. Experts thought it probably dated from Roman times. They said it was a simplified representation of Priapus, a fertility god familiar to anyone who has been to modern-day Greece, and an alleged precursor of the garden gnome. (*Archaeological Finds*, Proc. of the Suffolk Institute of Archaeology and History, 1998)

———

2013: On this bitterly cold and windy day, at least fifteen avocets were seen feeding at the mouth of Levington Creek on the Orwell Estuary. These wading birds, with their bold white and black patterning, were sweeping their distinctive long, upturned bills from side to side, searching for food.

It was a sight that would have been impossible to witness even a few decades earlier. Avocets had become extinct as a breeding bird in the UK by the mid-1840s due to the drainage of wetlands for farming. However, flooding on the Suffolk coast in the Second World War and in the 1953 flood provided the perfect habitat of salt water marshes and lagoons for the birds to make a spectacular comeback. By 2014 there were 1,500 breeding pairs on the East Coast in summer and they had even started to over-winter on the Orwell Estuary and thereabouts. (Mick Wright's website: www.mickorwellestuary.co.uk)

~ January 20th ~

1928: St Augustine's church in Felixstowe Road received its licence to conduct marriages, and a month later the first wedding was celebrated there when Herbert George married Evelyn Bridge. The church had been consecrated the previous November and was built to serve the newly built Nacton council estate.

There was a lot of goodwill surrounding the founding of the church. The land had been given by Lady de Saumarez of Shrubland Hall; the architect, H. Munro Cautley, gave his services free of charge; and a local tailor, Charles Bancroft, donated the necessary funds.

Unusually, the church was dedicated to St Augustine of Hippo because he, like Bantoft, had a 'devout and pious mother'.

St Augustine's, with its lighted cross high above the tower, became a local landmark. Unfortunately, its plain concrete rendering made it, for some, 'the ugliest church in Ipswich'. (St Augustine's church: newspaper cuttings and parish registers (SRO))

1970: A spectacular area of coast and heath in Suffolk, stretching from Kessingland in the north to the Shotley Peninsula in the south, was designated an Area of Outstanding Natural Beauty (AONB) on this day or thereabouts. This meant that it was recognised as a precious landscape whose distinctive character and natural beauty was so outstanding that it was in the nation's interest to safeguard them. In the immediate Ipswich area, the ANOB included two bird reserves (Cattawade Marshes and Stour Estuary), two Suffolk Wildlife Trust reserves (Trimley Marshes and Levington Lagoon) and Landguard Point, which is at the furthest point of the Orwell estuary. (Suffolk Coast and Heath website: www.suffolkcoastandheaths.org)

~ January 21st ~

1847: The kindly but reputedly long-winded Rev. John Nottidge died at The Grove, on the corner of Grove Lane and Spring Road. He had been the rector of St Clement's and St Helen's churches for many years.

Nottidge was the son of a wealthy wool merchant. When he realised that Ipswich needed an extra church to serve people living in the new streets that had been thrown up around Fore Hamlet, he had one built at his own expense, costing £2,400. It occupied the site of an old rope factory. Dedicated as Holy Trinity church in 1835, it was the first Anglican parish church to be built in Ipswich since the Reformation, and it was one of Suffolk's few Georgian-style churches.

Above all, in his ministry, Nottidge was an evangelist, wanting to bring all people to Christianity, be they the poor of Ipswich, 'natives' of Africa and India or British Jewry. (M.G. Smith, *Twixt Potteries and California*; Frank Grace, 'Talk on the history of Holy Trinity church')

2003: Jose Camarinha opened O Portugues in Norwich Road. It was the first café in Ipswich to specialise in Portuguese-style coffee and pastries. With the Portuguese community forming the largest group in Ipswich whose mother-tongue was not English, it became an immediate success.

– January 22nd –

1888: Basil Brown, the man who discovered the royal ship burial at Sutton Hoo, was born in Bucklesham, just outside Ipswich. He had no formal education and at first followed his father into farming.

In the 1930s, he was taken on by Ipswich Museum to excavate local archaeological sites. In 1938, he was sent to work for Edith Pretty of Sutton Hoo near Woodbridge, to investigate three mounds on her estate. What he unearthed was incredible: a royal Anglo-Saxon ship burial with magnificent grave goods.

Academics and archaeologists descended on the site as soon as they heard what he had found. Brown found himself sidelined for the rest of the dig and throughout the press hoo-ha which followed. In particular, he had to steer a careful path between Mrs Pretty, various scholars and other authorities who all vied for control of the site and its finds. Eventually, Mrs Pretty gave the treasures to the British Museum.

Despite his discovery, Brown remained a fairly lowly member of staff at the museum until he retired. He died in 1977 in Rickinghall Superior, near Diss. (Tony Copsey, *Suffolk Writers Who Were Born Between 1800–1900*; Sam Newton *Sutton Hoo: Burial: Ground of the Wuffings*)

– January 23rd –

1893: The cabmen's shelter on the Cornhill was opened. It was, according to Robert Malster:

> A timber-framed shelter, intended as a refuge from bad weather for the men from the cab rank. It was alleged, however, that they congregated in the shelter and ignored would-be passengers. The building was therefore removed to Christchurch Park in 1895, on a trolley towed through the street by the corporation steam-roller.

The shelter was restored in 2006 after years of neglect at the Park and moved from the Round Pond to the Westerfield Road entrance. (Robert Malster, *Ipswich: an A to Z of Local History*)

1944: Some Ipswich people were shocked to see the bad feeling between the white and black American servicemen on leave, who were stationed on bases near the town. Occasionally things got so bad between them that their commanding officers had to order that white and black soldiers must come into Ipswich on different nights.

In a town centre pub on this night, one old Ipswich boy said to another: 'What do you think of these Americans then?'

'Well, there're alright, boy,' his mate said: 'But I don't think much of them white fellas they've brought with them!' (Apocryphal, from Roger Freeman, *The Friendly Invasion*)

~ January 24th ~

1903: At Ipswich Assizes, the jury delivered its verdict in the trial of William Gardiner, who was accused of stabbing Rose Harsent to death in Peasenhall. This was the second time Gardiner had been tried for Rose's murder.

The case had shaken the village. Gardiner and Rose were both well-known there. He was a pillar of the Peasenhall Methodist chapel and a family man. Rose was young and single but, it was later revealed, six months pregnant when she was murdered. It also came to light that she had been engaged to a mystery suitor and that she had kept a stash of lewd, unsigned letters in her bedroom.

Rumours of an illicit relationship between Gardiner and Rose had been rife in the village the year before, but nothing had ever been proved. Gardiner was nevertheless arrested a few days after Rose's body was found.

When the case came to the Assizes, the jury could not agree a verdict. Gardiner had to be tried again, and once again no agreement was reached: no conclusive evidence was brought to court. Five days later, Gardiner was released from Ipswich prison. He shaved off his moustache and beard, caught the night train to London and started a new life. Whoever murdered Rose – and fathered her baby – remained a mystery. (Edwin Packer, *The Peasenhall Murder*)

~ JANUARY 25TH ~

1939: The River Gipping burst its banks and much of the Ipswich area was swamped. Homes were abandoned and people took to rowing boats to get around. The *Ipswich Evening Star* reported:

> Damage was estimated at thousands of pounds although the exact figure was never known. Amazingly, only one person was killed.
>
> A lethal combination of melting snow and heavy rain proved too much for the Gipping valley. Within hours it was transformed into a huge lake. Roads, railways and telephone lines were rendered useless as the flood tide rose.
>
> In Ipswich, families were marooned in their homes without food, water or fire. Hundreds of homes were ruined.
>
> The first sign of disaster came at midnight when the river level started to rise. Three hours later the water was pouring from Whitton and settling in the Dales Road area. Properties near Beaconsfield Road and Yarmouth Road were badly affected and at 3.55 p.m. the Gipping burst its banks at the London Road Bridge.

Meanwhile, upriver in Bramford, David Allum, with his shire horse and wagon, braved the torrent of flood water to rescue schoolchildren trapped on the wrong side of the river. (David Kindred, *Ipswich Pocket Images*; *Ipswich Evening Star*, various dates)

‒ January 26th ‒

1963: As the long, hard winter continued, there was a complete breakfast-time power failure throughout Suffolk. The cut was caused by the freak weather conditions. Just a few days before, the temperature was at an all-time low of 80°F (-130°C). Water pipes were already frozen hard and gas was on reduced supply.

After the power went down that Saturday morning, housewives out shopping found the shops lit by hurricane lamps and candles. Hundreds of children were turned away from Saturday morning pictures, and the Cranes factory sent its workers home at 9.15 a.m. as they could not light their furnaces; in fact machinery all over Ipswich came to a standstill. Traffic lights went out, and tropical fish died. Two babies were born at the maternity hospital under emergency lighting. A hairdresser in Princes Street had to look after thirty-five ladies with wet hair. Fortunately, another shopkeeper sent round a 5-gallon urn of coffee so they had something hot to drink as they all sat there in the dark and cold. (*Ipswich Evening Star*, 1963)

— January 27th —

1868: Ipswich's ornate new town hall was officially opened.

A few months before, local people had unsuccessfully petitioned the corporation to ask that the new building should have two clocks: one set at Greenwich Mean Time (GMT), the other at 'Ipswich Time', five minutes later. On the day of the opening, the Council heard a proposal from the Deputy Mayor that the large town hall clock should be set at GMT, which was the time shown at the railway station. This was opposed by Cllr Edward Grimwade. He felt that Ipswich would be better served if the clock were to show local time. He said that many people, including him, were used to having an extra five minutes in hand to get over to the station. The matter was referred to the Estates Committee, which eventually found in favour of GMT. It would be another twelve years before the passing of the Statutes (Definition of Time) Act when Britain finally had a standard time imposed across the country, thereby formally ending 'Ipswich Time'. (*Ipswich Journal*, 1868; www.planetipswich.com)

─ JANUARY 28TH ─

1955: Arthur Benjamin, a young man from the West Indies, was elected to serve as the first chairman of the Ipswich Caribbean Society at a meeting held by 'sixteen West Indians and nine Englishmen' at the Quaker Meeting House.

There were about 250 West Indians in Ipswich at the time, many of them newly arrived from Barbados. Supported by local churches and large firms like Ransomes and Cranes, who employed the men, the Ipswich Caribbean Society was keen to help fellow West Indians settle. Their regular meetings were held at a hall at the Unitarian Meeting House on Saturday afternoons.

Of utmost priority was the lodgings problem. By March the same year, they had set up a welfare office in Berners Street. Apart from a degree of racism which they encountered in Ipswich, there was the added problem that American service families were able to pay higher rents than they could.

For entertainment, the new society founded Palm Branches, a steel band with oil drums provided by Shell-Mex, which played concerts in and around Ipswich. (Anne Porter interviewed about Ipswich's West Indian community (SRO); *East Anglian Daily Times*, 1955)

— January 29th —

1977: Ivan Blatny (1919–90) was admitted to St Clement's Mental Hospital, the latest episode in a sad but interesting life.

Blatny, a well-known poet in his native Czechoslovakia, had fled to England in 1948 after communists took power. When he arrived in England, he found work at the BBC and Radio Free Europe, but the Czech authorities continually pressured him to return, finally making a public announcement in the 1950s that he had died.

Meanwhile, Blatny's mental health was deteriorating. He was eventually diagnosed with paranoid schizophrenia and spent most of the rest of his life in British psychiatric hospitals, including a long stay in St Clement's.

For years, psychiatric staff believed that Blatny was deluded when he said that he was a well-known poet. Eventually – by chance – it was shown to be true. A nurse from St Clement's was on holiday in Czechoslovakia when she met two people who knew Blatny. They told her his story and asked her to take special care of him – which she did. She befriended the poet and he started writing again.

In all, Blatny wrote eight volumes of poetry and his work was translated into English. He was still writing on the day he died in Colchester Hospital in 1990. (Czech Radio website: /www.radio.cz/en/section/books/ivan-blatny-the-strange-story-of-a-czech-poet-in-english-exile)

1805: The *Bury & Norwich Post* reported: 'on Thursday last, a private solder received 400 lashes in the Horse-barrack yard, Ipswich, for uttering seditious expressions in a public house there a short time since. Detachments from all the regiments of the garrison were present at the punishment.' (*Bury & Norwich Post*, 1815)

2008: The dramatic headline 'Scampi Blaze Rescue Drama' appeared in the *Ipswich Evening Star* – there's an episode of the Archers in there somewhere! (*Ipswich Evening Star*, 2008; Flickr)

2009: The final meal in this week's TV competition *Come Dine With Me*, filmed in Ipswich, was shown on Channel 4. Gerard, the butcher from Suffolk Food Hall, was cook and host for the evening. His menu was, appropriately, full of locally sourced meat:

Starter: sautéed chicken liver, black pudding and bacon on toast (which most guests disliked).
Main course: roast pork chops ('too fatty', complained guests) in cider with mashed potatoes and spring greens.
Pudding: strawberries and cream filo tart (which Gerard burned) with a raspberry coulis.

Gerard came third. The prize money went to young grandmother Lisa, who worked as a waitress at Ray's Bistro on the corner of Silent Street. (Channel 4)

1948: Westbourne Library in Sherrington Road opened its doors to the public for the first time.

It had originally been built during the Second World War as an air-raid shelter and gas decontamination centre. The building was designed to be blast-proof, and later gas-proof, and was made of reinforced concrete with a flat concrete roof.

Unusually, the exterior was designed in a Modernist style, rather like neighbouring Broomhill Pool, which was also designed by the borough engineer. As such, the building had rather a boxy shape, which was emphasised by decorative symmetrical grooves that ran along its length. Any embellishment at all was rare on a Second World War functional building.

Inside there was an air lock, an undressing area, showers, an eye douche and a drying room.

It is Britain's only library originally built as a bomb-proof decontamination unit and public shelter. Not many other libraries could say they store books in a Second World War lookout tower! (Ipswich Society; English Heritage; *East Anglian Daily Times*, 2012)

—

2013: The date of the first Holi festival to be held in Ipswich was announced to the public. The Hindu community invited everyone to Holywells Park on Sunday 24 March to welcome the spring with them. At the festival, known as the 'Festival of Colours', people celebrated by covering each other with brightly coloured paints and throwing coloured powder, dye, coconut and popcorn into a bonfire. People planning to attend were advised to wear old clothes! (Ipswich and Suffolk Indian Association)

– February 1st –

1917: Ronald Garnham was born in Ipswich on this Thursday. He served in the Second World War and survived years as a Japanese prison of war.

Early in 1940, Ron enlisted in the army and was sent to the Far East. Captured by the Japanese, he was imprisoned in the notorious Changi POW camp in Singapore. His life there was filled with illness, cruelty, hunger and hard work. After 1943 he was sent to work on the Thailand–Burma Death Railway, and then, finally to Japan to labour in the dockyards.

After the Allied victory in Japan, Ron was liberated by Americans and returned to Ipswich via the USA. Back in Suffolk, Ron eventually married, had children and ran a fish shop in Kirton. After such harrowing wartime experiences, Rob could hardly believe his rotten luck when he found himself being called up again in the 1950s for a fortnight's National Service! (Ron Garnham, *Every Man for Himself*)

1990: Diana, Princess of Wales visited Ipswich to open the Record Office in the redeveloped Bramford Road School building. She also did a walk-about in the Cornhill and visited Crown Pools, where she was photographed crouching down to talk to delighted members of the public who were there having a swim.

Rumours about her troubled marriage to Prince Charles were well known but the princess, who was wearing a tartan coat-frock, looked like she was enjoying every minute of the day – as did the people she met. (Commemorative plaque at Ipswich Record Office; *Ipswich Evening Star*, 1990)

~ February 2nd ~

1644: William Dowsing, a Suffolk-born puritan soldier, arrived in Hadleigh with his men to remove or deface 'idolatrous' and 'popish' images and fittings from churches, such as pictures, crosses, crucifixes, stained glass, monumental brasses and altar rails. In his journal he noted this day:

> Hadleigh: 'We brake down 30 superstitious pictures, and gave order for taking down the rest, which were about 70; and took up an inscription, Quorum animabus propitietur deus [to whose souls may God be propitious]; and gave order for the takeing down of a cross on the steeple; gave 14 days.'
>
> Layham: 'We brake down six superstitious pictures, and takeing down a cross off the steeple.'

The men then went on to the villages of Shelley and Higham, where they found plenty of similar work to do. (Trevor Cooper, ed., *Journal of William Dowsing*)

1933: Ipswich Corporation opened Electric House, a striking art deco building purpose-designed to be their electricity offices and showrooms. The decoration was largely intended to illustrate the use of the new building, so the frontage was covered in motifs such as zigzag lightning, fan-shaped light symbols and pointed stars. The front and sides were embellished with words associated with electricity, such as 'light', 'power', 'heat' and 'cook'. (Ed Broom, *The Seven Wonders of Ipswich*)

– February 3rd –

1776: The *Ipswich Journal* reported that the salt river in the town was frozen over. It had been so cold for so long that people were out skating on the river and had even roasted a sheep on it. Live cod in the wells of fishing smacks had frozen to death and it was quite impossible for ships to move. No one at the time could remember such a harsh spell. (*Ipswich Journal*, 1776)

1984: The *East Anglian Daily Times* reported the unveiling of an 8ft-high 'steyned cloth' or poor-man's tapestry dating back to Elizabethan times. The printed canvas was found behind panels in the Ancient House during restoration works. It depicted Hercules slaying the nine-headed lion – the second of his twelve labours. The cloth was thought to be one of a series of twelve original wall hangings from the late 1570s belonging to George Copping, owner of the Ancient House at the time.

Restoration of the painting involved heat-sealing the canvas to fix the coloured pigments. This prevented total loss of the original artwork, which was described as having been held together for 400 years by 'prayer and hope'. A replica of this hanging was then hung on display above the main staircase in the Ancient House, while the original was taken to Christchurch Mansion. (*East Anglian Daily Times*, 1984; www.planetipswich.com)

~ February 4th ~

1721: This advertisement was published in the *Ipswich Journal*: 'At the Butter and Cheese Warehouse in Ipswich is to be had oranges and lemons directly from Portugal at 5s per hundred or 9d for a dozen, fresh off the trees. And full red-herrings at two shillings per hundred.'

What were red herrings? They were herrings salted for a month and smoked for a week, making them extremely smelly. In fact, they were so foul-smelling that they could even be used to distract a hunting dog from its trail – which is where the expression 'smelling a red herring' came from. (*Ipswich Journal*, 1721; The Smelly Alley Fish Company)

1955: Lilian Redstone, Suffolk archivist and historian, died on this day.

She was born in Woodbridge in 1885 and had a long and distinguished career. She was the first ever Ipswich and East Suffolk Joint Archivist and her work was regarded as the foundation of the Suffolk Record Office. Even the local Boy Scouts knew about her interest in old records. Once, when they were collecting waste paper for recycling, they found a package of old correspondence. They showed it to Miss Redstone, who discovered that it contained secret intelligence about Napoleon's Russian campaign dating from 1811 and 1812.

Miss Redstone was the author of a large number of publications, including the popular *Ipswich through the Ages*. (Ipswich Women's History Trail; *The Times*, 1943)

~ February 5th ~

1941: Bill Bloomfield, born in Ipswich in 1907, spent most of the Second World War in Halewood near Liverpool, in a reserved occupation building military engines. He was a member of the Home Guard up there, and on this cold February morning he reported for a routine training session. He had just come off a twelve-hour night shift, so by the time he got to training he was already shattered. When a fresh-faced young officer told him to run across a frozen field ploughed with rock-hard furrows, Bill retorted, 'Don't be so damn silly.' He was promptly court-martialled for disobeying an order and booted out of the Home Guard.

Bill came back to Ipswich after the war and, in later years, his grandchildren loved hearing the story of how he had had the bare-faced nerve and guts to defy such a pointless order. (Thanks to the Bloomfield family)

1942: Members of Ipswich Home Guard took part in street fighting exercises in the warren of lanes behind Carr Street. Men with blackened faces and armed with Sten guns crept around in carpet slippers (for silence) setting up positions for their heavy machine guns and disturbing unsuspecting courting couples. (David Jones, *Ipswich in the Second World War*)

~ February 6th ~

1771: Sir Thomas Slade (b. 1703/04) was buried in St Clement's churchyard. He was an English naval architect and was most famous for designing Lord Nelson's flagship, HMS *Victory*. (*Oxford Dictionary of National Biography*)

1919: The last patient was discharged from Ipswich's military hospital in Belstead Road. Known as Broadwater Hospital, it had opened at the start of the First World War in a grand house belonging to businessman William Paul.

Ambulances from the Red Cross and St John Ambulance Brigade took arrivals from all over the country from Ipswich railway station up to the hospital. Most of its patients were young men who had been wounded in the trenches of Northern France and Belgium. Volunteers from Ipswich pitched in and made up wound dressings. Towards the end of the war, the Matron – a Miss Hall – was awarded the Royal Red Cross for her work, and William Paul received an OBE for managing the hospital. (Paul Fincham, *Ipswich in Old Picture Postcards*; Neil Wylie, Robert Malster and David Kindred, *Ipswich at War*)

2009: Brewing re-started on the site of the former Tolly Cobbold Brewery in Ipswich. The Cliff Quay Brewery began making beer in the old loading bay there, reviving a tradition dating back to the Cobbold family in the 1700s. A few years later, the firm moved to Debenham to be nearer their sister brewery in Earl Soham, and their beers went from strength to strength. By 2014, their prize-winning brews could regularly be found on draught at eight or so real ale pubs in Ipswich. (Cliff Quay Brewery: www.cliffquay.co.uk)

— February 7th —

1736: The *Ipswich Gazette* had a bit of fun with its readers when it reported the following:

> One Elizabeth Farry of Lanark in Scotland was proclaimed in order to marriage on Sunday, was married on Monday, had a child on Tuesday, her husband stole a horse on Wednesday, for which he was banished on Thursday, the child died on Friday, and was buried on Saturday, all in one week.

(Thanks to Pip Wright)

1826: On this Tuesday, the Ipswich squirearchy met to form an association to protect themselves from theft and civil disorder. Trade Unionist and labour historian Robert Ratcliffe described what happened and why:

> Local employers, squires and magistrates, who, no doubt, fearing a general uprising of the working class and an increase in highway robbery formed the Ipswich Association for Prosecuting Felons and Other Offenders. A meeting of the subscribers to this fund, fifty in number, was held in the Golden Lion, Ipswich, on this Tuesday.

It was decided that anyone giving information leading to the conviction of an offender would be rewarded with £5 (in the case of a felony) or 10s (in the case of theft). The association was generally aimed at combating the menace of highway robbers, but would also be in readiness in case of working-class unrest. (Robert Ratcliffe, *History of Working Class Movement in Ipswich*)

— FEBRUARY 8TH —

1896: About this time, Miss Wiseman played the old church organ in Coddenham for the last time before it was dismantled and taken off in a cart to Needham Market.

Almost eighty years after it had been installed, the parish had completely forgotten that the instrument was originally a 'finger and barrel' organ. It had come to the village in 1817 to replace the small band of village musicians who used to accompany church services. The organ could be played in the normal way, or could be turned by a 'grinder' when there was no organist available. The instrument had two barrels, each set with ten tunes. These were psalms, hymn tunes (such as 'Oh Praise Ye the Lord') and a couple of well-known classical pieces suitable for the beginning and end of services. As it turned out, the parish employed an organist almost straightaway, and so the expensive barrel action was rarely needed. In 1820 it was damaged in a botched repair and had to be removed. The organ itself, though, was perfectly good enough to be played in the usual way for many decades to come. (David Allen, *The Vanished Barrel Organ of Coddenham Church*)

— FEBRUARY 9TH —

2001: The sugar beet factory at Sproughton closed. It had been built during 1924–25 by an Anglo-Dutch company and opened with a government subsidy to help establish what was to become a major industry in East Anglia. Sproughton was chosen as the Ipswich site because of its good rail links.

Jean Soetebier recalled her father's time there as a fitter. He started in about 1926. When he discovered the terrible working conditions there, he said he would only stay for one season – but he said that every year until he retired in 1954 at the age of 65! Jean added:

> From September to February – the production time – machinery was kept in running order without closing the factory. He worked shifts, weekends and Christmas, and always brought that well-known smell home with him. The rest of the year he worked on maintenance.
>
> There were no canteen facilities so the workers took their own food and drink. His first official week's holiday was in August 1937!

Changes in EU quotas during the 1980s and 1990s led to many sugar refineries being shut down. The Ipswich plant closed in 2001, but the large concrete silos for storing granulated sugar remain in place. (Christine Clark and Roger Munting, *Suffolk Enterprise*)

― FEBRUARY 10TH ―

1842: Near Brisbane, Queensland, Australia, an area was proclaimed open for free settlers as the penal colony had been closed.

In convict times this area was called the 'Limestone Hills' or 'Limestone Station', as lime was quarried there, but Sir George Gipps, Governor of New South Wales, changed its name. He visited the site of the new town just before the free settlers arrived and wrote 'to be called IPSWICH' on the surveyor's map.

Why did he choose that name? No one knew for sure, but there were places nearby called Dunwich and Stradbroke Island. These had been named by the son of Viscount Dunwich, Earl of Stradbroke, when he had visited, declaring that the countryside reminded him of Suffolk. Maybe Governor Gipps remembered this and decided to carry on the Suffolk theme. (Ipswich, Queensland, website: www.ipswich.qld.gov.au)

―――

1877: One of the first typewriters to be used in Ipswich went on show at the Ipswich Scientific Society's exhibition in the Public Hall. It was used at Ransomes' Orwell Works by a Mr J. Harper, who had become quite an expert. Visitors at the exhibition were encouraged to have a go on it. (It had been invented in 1875.) (*Ipswich Journal*, 1877)

1643: The Rev. Edmund Boldero, a Suffolk man educated at Ipswich School and Cambridge, was made rector of Westerfield. Unlike many of his Ipswich contemporaries, he was devoted to the Royalist cause in the English Civil War and his fortunes waxed and waned with theirs.

As a staunch Anglican and a Royalist, Boldero was visible and vulnerable in Ipswich, which was largely Parliamentarian in the mid-1640s. When he took over as rector of Westerfield it was almost inevitable that he would not last long – and, indeed, he was imprisoned in London the very next year. His Ipswich land and property were confiscated following an accusation of drunkenness, 'scandalous living and doctrinal misdemeanours' by a powerful committee of Parliamentarians.

In time, Boldero joined the Royalist army and went to Scotland to become chaplain to the Marquis of Montrose. It was said that he had a colourful life there, finding himself captured by Montrose's enemies and narrowly escaping being hanged.

After the Restoration of Charles II in 1660, Boldero's fortunes improved. To recompense him for his loyalty to Crown and Church, he was given the livings of a couple of Suffolk parishes and made Master of Jesus College, Cambridge. He died in 1679. (*Oxford Dictionary of National Biography*)

— February 12th —

1791: The *Ipswich Journal* reported that Thomas Hornby Morland had recently arrived in Ipswich from Newgate Prison in London. He was to be tried at the Suffolk Assizes for bigamy.

Despite the gravity of Morland's situation, he assumed an air of indifference. He had recently been acquitted on a technicality at the Old Bailey, again for bigamy (one wife in London and another in Yorkshire), but as he left the courtroom he was immediately detained again for having yet a third 'wife' – this one in Ipswich. All three of his 'wives' were said to be pregnant by him at the time.

The courts in Suffolk found Morland guilty of bigamy. He was sent to Ipswich Gaol for a year and branded on the thumb, the standard punishment for a bigamist. Several months later, his Ipswich 'wife' lodged a legal claim against him for £500.

Morland was one of the first prisoners in the newly opened Ipswich Gaol. Although he was a 'gentleman', he had to wear a prison uniform of a rough 'linsey-woolsey jacket and trousers, faced with red at the sleeves and collars, and wooden shoes'. He also had to take his turn with prison duties just like the run-of-the-mill inmates. (*Ipswich Journal*, various dates)

~ February 13th ~

1566: Alice Tooley (*née* Purplett) died in Ipswich on or about this day. She was the business partner of her husband, Henry. Henry and Alice Tooley were among the richest Ipswich merchants in the sixteenth century. They traded in cloth, grain and wine and owned a large house and trading-hall on St Mary's Quay. When Henry was away on business, Alice ran the business, supervising shipments, collecting debts, making payments and seeing to correspondence. Unusually for a Tudor woman, Alice took over their company when he died in 1551 and ran it on her own.

Alice and Henry were buried together at St Mary-at-the-Quay church. (Ipswich Women's History Trail)

1977: Ipswich Borough Council designated Anglesea Road and some of the streets running down to Norwich Road as a Conservation Area. These roads had been laid out on the south-facing slopes near Christchurch Park during the nineteenth century and created a leafy middle-class enclave. The area had a special identity, with its handsome houses of local red-and-white brick with Welsh slate roofing, dating from all parts of the Victorian era.

Each of the streets leading off Orford Street preserved its cobbled walkway across the road entrances. These were originally laid down to protect ladies' dresses from getting muddy on the unmade roads. (Ipswich Borough Council; thanks to Dick Glover)

~ February 14th ~

1876: The *Pioneer*, a locomotive built by Ransomes & Rapier in Ipswich, ran its first trials on the new railway line from Shanghai to Woosung: the first railway line in China.

Five men from Ransomes & Rapier had travelled to China with the *Pioneer*. Getting it up and running was no easy task. The extreme climate and long hours caused them terrible health problems. The foreman died and then the general assistant became ill and was sent home with his brother. That left just two engineers and a team of Chinese labourers to get everything operational. Eventually, the line was completed and the service began. But the railway was extremely unpopular. It had been built without Chinese consent and was only ever developed to benefit foreign merchants. By the autumn of 1876, the railway company decided to sell up to the Chinese authorities, who closed the line on the very day that the sale went through. They quickly dismantled the track and disposed of the equipment. (Robert Malster, *Ipswich: An A to Z of Local History*)

— February 15th —

1909: Dame Maurus, a young Roman Catholic nun from St Mary's Abbey in East Bergholt, escaped from the convent. Enlisting the help of the gardener to flee the abbey grounds, she set off for the railway station at Manningtree. Before long, a search party pursued her from the convent in a wagonette. Maurus hid in woodland. She got soaking wet, hopelessly lost and found her slippers weighed down with clods of heavy mud. As Maurus eventually approached Manningtree station, she heard the dreaded wagonette coming up behind her again. Two nuns jumped down and tried to drag her away. Maurus screamed until the station master came out and escorted her to the waiting room to wait for the mail train to London.

Reunited with her mother, Dame Maurus became plain Madge Moult again and, with the support of the delighted Protestant Alliance, she left holy orders. In return, she was happy to give lectures for them on the evils of convent life and Catholicism. She spoke to an appreciative audience in Ipswich in 1910. The Alliance presented the station master with a Bible, Foxe's Book of Martyrs and a watch. Less fortunate was the convent gardener who had helped her escape. He was moved to Canada. (*Nottingham Evening Post*, 1909; Dee Gordon, *Little Book of Essex*)

‒ February 16th ‒

1904: Twenty mess-buildings were constructed at Shotley Gate for a new naval training establishment there. It opened the following year with two ships anchored offshore (HMS *Ganges* and HMS *Caroline*) in addition to the new buildings and training mast onshore. (HMS *Ganges* Museum)

‒ ‒

1956: On this day and throughout February, the *East Anglian* reported on the 'colour bar' which operated at the Rendezvous Restaurant at 28/32 Tacket Street. It had been brought to the public's notice by the Ipswich Trades Council after Mrs Lesley Lewis, one-time mayor of Ipswich, and two West Indian friends had been asked to leave the restaurant at the beginning of the month.

The Polish owner of the restaurant, Jan Sniechowski, claimed that the colour bar was in operation for business reasons. He said that white American servicemen using the restaurant objected to black people being there. But, in a letter to the *Evening Star*, Sniechowski's wife revealed their very real racial prejudice by asking: 'How many people in Ipswich really prefer to eat their meals at the same table as a coloured person?' (*East Anglian Daily Times*, 1956)

— February 17th —

1874: The *Ipswich Journal* bemoaned the fashion for sending Valentine's cards: 'As usual the Post-office was besieged with loungers of both sexes on Friday last, anxious to know who were the senders of the fragile combinations of tinselled paper containing hearts, cupids, etc. subscribed with doubtful rhymes.'

The reporter thought that over 2,000 Valentine's cards had been sent just in Hadleigh, prompting young people to 'stand shivering round the Post-office on a cold February night to watch the post-box.'

The extra work created by Valentine's Day meant 'two deliveries per postman for ten hours', with still yet more to deliver. (*Ipswich Journal*, 1874)

1897: Officials from the English Silk Weaving Union met managers from Brown & Hooper, New Cut East, in Ipswich. They were concerned because the firm had employed skilled English silk weavers from Spitalfields, learned all they could from them, and then promptly sacked them. The English weavers were dismissed on a Saturday and German weavers – cheaper and less troublesome – were brought in on the Monday. The outcome of the dispute is not recorded. (Robert Ratcliffe, *History of Working Class Movement in Ipswich*)

~ February 18th ~

2009: A bronze statue of Russian rugby legend, Prince Alexander Obolensky, was unveiled in Cromwell Square in Ipswich. He was known as 'The Flying Prince', 'The Flying Slav', or simply as 'Obo' by many sports fans. Three plaques on the base of the statue describe his life and connection with Ipswich.

As a baby, Obolensky had fled to England in 1917 from St Petersburg with his family, following the Russian Revolution. In the fullness of time, he took up rugby, was awarded an Oxford University Blue and was selected to play for England – at which point he took British nationality.

Obolensky played on the wing. In his international debut for England against the All Blacks he scored two breathtaking tries, which have gone down in rugby history. Less well-known is the fact that he once played at Portman Road football ground in an international trial.

At the outbreak of the Second World War, Obolensky was in his early twenties. He volunteered as an RAF pilot. His life was cut short when his Hurricane fighter crash-landed at Martlesham Heath during training. He was buried in Ipswich Cemetery.

The statue of Obolensky was paid for by several private backers, including Roman Abramovich, a Russian businessman and owner of Chelsea Football Club at the time of writing. (Rugby History website: www.rugbyfootballhistory.com)

~ February 19th ~

1902: A factory in the village of Brantham caught the attention of the national press on this day all because of a new craze – table tennis. It had originally been set up in Brantham to manufacture xylonite (also known as celluloid) and had moved up from London, bringing much of its workforce with it.

In 1901, celluloid table tennis balls were made for the first time in USA. This led to a huge surge in popularity of the game and so the Brantham factory diversified into ping-pong balls.

The *Sheffield Evening Telegraph* was just one of the papers to report on the phenomenon:

> There is a factory at Brantham ... where work goes on day and night under conditions of secrecy that might well excite curiosity to the highest pitch. The factory is the Xylonite Works, where the balls used in ping-pong are made ... They make all the balls used in the game of the hour, at any rate so far as England is concerned, and some idea may be formed of the extent of the trade that has suddenly been created, by the fact that six tons of balls are turned out every week ... Laid end to end they would stretch from London to Brighton and back.

(*Sheffield Evening Telegraph*, 1902)

~ February 20th ~

1587: Ipswich constables were ordered to search out 'impotent, vagrant newcomers' to the town. They also had to go into 'alehouses, taverns and tippling houses' and arrest people who were 'eating and drinking at unseasonable times' or staying there longer than absolutely necessary. At this time, constables were unpaid members of the better-off classes who were responsible for raising taxes and keeping law and order. (Nathaniell Bacon, Annalls of Ipswich)

1877: The *Ipswich Journal* reported that someone left the churchyard gate open on their way into the Ash Wednesday service at Copdock church. This meant that Mr Marshall's sheep got in. The sheep chomped their way through the yew-wood Christmas decorations which had been cleared out of the church ready for Lent. Poisonous to sheep, the yew clippings killed eight of them, but a veterinary surgeon from Ipswich managed to save the rest. (*Ipswich Journal*, 1877)

2012: Britain's biggest baby girl to date was born at Ipswich Hospital. Her birth weight, at 14lb 4oz, was twice that of an 'average' baby. Her father, Sean O'Halloran, said: 'Everyone in the operating theatre was shocked and surprised. We were told that she was probably the biggest ever baby at the hospital – but now it looks like she is the biggest girl ever born in Britain.' (*Daily Mail*, 2012)

— February 21st —

1943: John Hannah was arrested in Ipswich, the only performer ever to be detained during an engagement at the Hippodrome Theatre in St Nicholas Street.

John had a tragic life. As a very young man he had won a Victoria Cross in 1940, for putting out a fire on a bomber. He was on a flying mission over Antwerp when the plane came under Nazi attack. His hands and face were so badly burned that he needed plastic surgery and was invalided out of the RAF.

His military pension was not enough to support him and his family so he went 'on the halls' for £20 a week. Wearing his RAF uniform with his red Victoria Cross sash, he told audiences how he had won his medal. It was still wartime and audiences were captivated by him and his story. However, the RAF took the view that he was cashing in on his fame. They felt that by appearing in this way 'among seals, acrobats and red-nosed comedians', he was bringing his uniform into contempt.

After the police arrested John at Ipswich Hippodrome he gave up the stage and sadly died of tuberculosis just a few years later. (Terry Davis, and Trevor Morson, *Ipswich Hippodrome: The Place to Go*)

– February 22nd –

1557: The Ipswich authorities ordered that children who begged on the street had to wear a special badge showing that they had the proper authorisation to do so. Otherwise they were committing an offence. (Annals of Ipswich, by Nathaniell Bacon)

1950: Gutted by blaze:

A huge fire destroyed premises in Princes Street, Ipswich, causing an estimated £100,000 worth of damage. The fire started in the premises of Haddock & Baines, paper merchants and printers, and soon spread to the neighbouring Central Cinema, where projectionist Mr Driscoll was in the middle of changing the feature films, *The Dolly Sisters* starring Betty Grable and *Call North Side 777* with James Stewart. The Cinema Manager cleared the audience of 300 as the fire raged through the building.

The fire brigade, who fought the inferno with Second World War tenders and trailer pumps, called in men and equipment from Holbrook, Hadleigh, Needham Market, Woodbridge and Colchester to assist.

The buildings were gutted by the blaze.

(David Kindred, *Ipswich Pocket Images*)

— FEBRUARY 23RD —

1895: Felix Thornley Cobbold presented Christchurch Mansion to Ipswich Corporation. He was a wealthy local businessman with philanthropic ways and he had bought the house and park the previous year from a syndicate of property developers. His ambition was for the corporation to establish a museum and art gallery in the house and to open the grounds to the public. Cobbold had offered the mansion to the corporation as a gift on the condition that they paid for the surrounding parkland. It took him three attempts before they agreed.

The park was finally opened to the public in April 1895. Unfortunately, no celebrations were held. Some people thought it was because the opening clashed with Good Friday and the Easter weekend, while others suspected the Council was just being mean-spirited.

Felix Cobbold had already served a year as mayor of Ipswich, and he was given the honour of a further mayoral appointment for Queen Victoria's Jubilee year in recognition of his generosity to the town. He left considerable sums of money in his will to buy art works for the mansion. (Anthony Cobbold of Cobbold Family History Trust; *Ipswich Journal*, various dates)

FEBRUARY 24TH

1810: William Mason, the first architect ever to live and work in New Zealand, was born in Ipswich on this Saturday.

As a young man, Mason was articled in Ipswich to his father. He worked for a while in the town, designing churches, parsonages and poorhouses, until he emigrated to Australia in 1838, and then on to North Island, New Zealand in 1840. He was a member of the founding party which arrived at the site of the future city of Auckland and became responsible for designing many of its first public buildings.

In the 1850s, Mason and his wife moved to the town of Dunedin on South Island, which was prospering following the discovery of gold there. Again, he set up a successful architect's practice, served as Dunedin's first ever mayor, and retired in 1876, wealthy and respected.

Mason's architectural style was typically early Victorian: his churches were neo-Gothic; his public buildings neo-classical; and his houses were designed in a late Georgian style, but readily adapted to local conditions and the preferences of his clients.

Mason was active in public life, first as president of the Board of Works in Auckland, and then as mayor and chief magistrate in Dunedin. He was also an MP.

William Mason died in Dunedin in his late 80s. (*Dictionary of New Zealand Biography*)

~ February 25th ~

1820: Robert Adams, a shoemaker from Ipswich, was arrested at his central London home in a slum alley aptly named Hole in the Wall Passage.

Adams had been a private in the Horse Guards for five years and then worked as a civilian shoemaker for the British Army in northern France. Here, he had got to know other English men who had been radicalised by the ideals of the French Revolution. After the peace in 1815, Adams returned to England. Like thousands of others, he found himself without work and with only the prospect of the debtors' jail in front of him.

In January 1820, he fell in with a radical ex-soldier he had known in France. They started meeting other activists in pubs and rooms and daring plans were hatched: to burst in on the entire British Cabinet as they dined together one evening, and assassinate them all. Adams was to enter the dining room, raise his sword and shout 'Enter, citizens, and do your duty', at which point the other conspirators would pile in behind him.

However, the plotters were arrested as they gathered in their hiding place in Cato Street. Adams, though, escaped through a window and simply went home. Unfortunately he was captured a couple of days later.

All the conspirators were charged with treason, but Adams turned King's Evidence. All except Adams were either executed or transported. He was not tried for his part in the conspiracy but was imprisoned for debt almost immediately. (Old Bailey records: www.oldbaileyonline.org; E P Thompson, *Making of the English Working Class*; contemporary newspaper accounts; *Dictionary of National Biography*)

- February 26th -

1828: On this day, as on many others, Thomas Hearne, a well-known street hawker, sold watercress in Ipswich. His nickname and street cry was 'Must Go'. He must have shouted exceedingly loudly because Admiral Page of Tower Street paid him to keep quiet whenever he was in the area. Three portraits were published of 'Must Go'. In one he is shown holding an ear trumpet. Being deaf, perhaps he could not hear just how loud his voice was! (Carol Twinch, *Ipswich Street by Street*; John Blatchly, *Eighty Ipswich Portraits*)

1942: Plans for the compulsory evacuation of Ipswich were approved by the Home Defence Committee of the Cabinet. In the event of Nazi invasion, Ipswich was to be completely evacuated within two or three days.

Residents were informed of the plans by a brief official announcement in the *Ipswich Evening Star*: in essence, they had to stay put until the order came to leave. Ipswich was to be emptied of its civilian population, leaving just enough food, water and shelter for 'those whose duty it will be to stand fast in the town'.

Over the next months, parties of evacuees left Ipswich by train, as they had since war had broken out. However, as there was never a German invasion, the mass evacuation plan never had to be put into practice. (*Ipswich Evening Star*, 1942; David Jones, *Ipswich in the Second World War*)

2014: By this day, a major archaeological dig was underway at St Mary-at-the-Quay church. It had started in January and archaeologists were working through wind and rain to get it all finished by April. The focus of the excavation was the old graveyard facing modern-day Key Street, but formerly right on the edge of the waterfront. Many complete skeletons were found, mostly Victorian. However, some of the earliest graves dated back to Saxon times, adding to the evidence that this site had been sacred long before the existing church was built there. Alongside the complete skeletons, a charnel pit was found where numerous bones had been tossed by Victorian gravediggers to make room for family tombs.

In addition to the expected bones and the ubiquitous clay pipes, archaeologists found some trade tokens, minted in Ipswich for spending in the town. The earliest coin was a tiny Roman minim. Pottery fragments also came to light, including pieces of Ipswich ware which was made in the town on a large scale in Anglo-Saxon times.

Norwich Archaeological Unit was brought in to explore the site before Suffolk Mind could give it a new lease of life to create a well-being centre using Heritage Lottery Funds. (Thanks to Paul Field)

— February 28th —

1938: Noel Carrington of *Country Life* magazine had an idea for a major project involving Cowells, the Ipswich printers, so he sat down to discuss it with Allen Lane of Penguin Books at a publishing dinner on this Monday.

It only took Carrington a couple of minutes to convince Lane that a series of well-illustrated paperback books for children would be successful. They were to cost no more than 6*d* and would be called 'Puffins'. Carrington chose Cowells because he knew they could print the sort of brightly coloured books he had in mind.

The world was at war by the time Puffins started to roll off the Ipswich presses. The first title was an illustrated educational book called *War on the Land*, followed by others explaining various aspects of the war to children. The books were often designed and illustrated by artists working directly onto lithographic plates. Some of them, like Kathleen Hale of Orlando the Cat fame, were taught how to do this by Cowells' lithography department.

In 1941, the first Puffin storybook appeared, featuring Worzel Gummidge the scarecrow. Other favourites soon followed, like Noel Streatfeild's *Ballet Shoes*. Despite wartime paper shortages, Cowell's were busy printing more Puffins throughout the war and continued long after. (Ipswich Institute; Puffin Books website: www.puffin.co.uk)

~ February 29th ~

1840: The *Ipswich Journal* reported:

> The quickest passage ever made from Ipswich to London was effected on Thursday 20th inst. by the *Orwell* Steamer, she having performed the journey in six hours and fifty minutes!
>
> We understand that just before the *Orwell* left London on Saturday morning, a large piece of timber was found between one of the paddle-wheels and the box, which some miscreant had placed there evidently with a malicious design. Had the engine been set to work before the discovery was made, the injury which would have ensued must have been very serious. This is a second attempt of the same nature that has been made to impede the progress of the *Orwell*.

(*Ipswich Journal*, 1840)

1840: A selection of advertisements from the *Ipswich Journal*:

Hats: Miss Juby has the latest spring fashions in hats, caps and ribbons for sale at her shop near Mr Steggle's Bazaar, Old Butter Market. Straw Bonnets also cleaned and altered.

Teeth: Mr L J Lyon, Surgeon Dentist, is consulting in Ipswich for a limited period. Specialist in removing 'fangs' and fitting 'artificial teeth'.

Fish: William Townsend, fishmonger, warns customers that imposters are selling stale fish around the town and saying that they work for him. He does, however, have a large quantity of quality cod 'sounds' (swim bladders) for sale – good fried in batter.

(*Ipswich Journal*, 1840)

— MARCH 1ST —

1888: A group of women were invited to meet a representative from the Woolwich Women's Co-operative Guild and George Hines of Ipswich Co-operative Society to hear more about the guild. Eighteen women signed up that night and so the first Ipswich branch of the guild was established.

Nationally and locally, the guild drew its membership from women who 'shop at the Co-op'. It was different from most women's suffrage groups in that most members were married and working class. Their aim was to spread knowledge of Co-operative principles and then extend these principles into social affairs.

In the early days of the guild in Ipswich, they met at the committee room at the Co-op Central Stores on Thursday evenings. Led by Mrs Wigg and Miss Hines, the Ipswich women set to work straightaway to establish a 'coal club' so that they could buy Co-op fuel at preferential prices.

A regular activity was market research. They would delegate a member to visit a number of shops during the week and report back on how the society's groceries and draperies compared with other stores for price and quality. Recipes and ideas about home decorating were often exchanged and several speakers were invited to talk about matters of the day, such as vaccination. For fun, they entertained one another with songs, recitations and 'glees' and once hired a phrenologist to 'examine their heads'. (Guild minute books (SRO))

~ March 2nd ~

1901: Two young men were found drowned in a pond in Witnesham. They were identified as Robert Richer (23) and Edgar Hardwick (18) of Ashbocking. Neither had been seen for several days. Both men were agricultural labourers. Edgar's father knew them to be inseparable, whereas Robert's family were barely aware they were friends. When a William Tricker found the two bodies floating in a pond, he recognised them straightaway. He told the inquest that they were tied together by two belts round their waists, facing the same way, with Robert strapped behind, his face pressed to Edgar's back. There were no signs of a struggle and the inquest returned a verdict of death by drowning. Homosexuality was decriminalised in 1967. (Doreen Smith, *More Sudden Deaths in Suffolk*)

1938: On or about this day, a flu vaccine was tested on boy sailors at HMS *Ganges*. The General Medical Council wrote a report on the experiment and filed it at The National Archives at Kew with instructions that it must not be read by the public. As flu vaccine did not become available for many years, we can only assume that, at best, it did not work – or, at worst, that it was in some way harmful. (The National Archives (closed archive))

— MARCH 3RD —

1764: 'WANTED for a Gentleman that lives most part of the Year in London. A Genteel Person, between 28 and 40 years of age that has had the Small-Pox to be as Companion and Housekeeper.' (*Ipswich Journal*, 1764. Thanks to Pip Wright)

2004: Jack Haste gave an illustrated talk to the Ipswich Maritime Trust about the Gipping Navigation. He traced the development of the waterway, the vessels which used it and its eventual demise. Mr Haste, owner of a local art gallery, was well qualified to give the talk as he owned one of the last remaining Gipping barges and was a long-time waterways enthusiast.

Mr Haste's barge, the *Yare*, was built in Ipswich at St Clement's shipyard by Orvis & Fuller in the 1870s. At 14ft in the beam she was more than twice the width of a traditional narrowboat, and was 65ft long. She joined a fleet of thirty Gipping barges carrying agricultural, commercial and domestic supplies between Ipswich and Stowmarket. Her main cargo was agricultural fertilisers for Packard & Fison.

Mr Haste bought the *Yare* in 1961 at a knock-down price as she was flood-damaged. He spent hundreds of hours renovating her and used her for many years as a houseboat, moored near Pin Mill. (Rightmove website: www.rightmove.co.uk; Ipswich Maritime Trust newsletter, 2004)

– MARCH 4TH –

1848: Major Edward Moor (b. 1771), soldier, orientalist and writer of Great Bealings House, was buried at his parish church.

Moor was fascinated by Hinduism. He had been a soldier with the East India Company and recorded the culture he saw around him. He brought back with him piles of notes and a large collection of statues of Hindu deities and paintings.

In 1810, five years after moving to Great Bealings House, Moor published *The Hindu Pantheon* described by the British Museum as 'the first attempt to present the variety of Indian religious life before an English audience'. He illustrated the text with pictures of his own bronzes and paintings.

Moor built a pyramid in the grounds of Great Bealings House and adorned it with a statue of the fierce Hindu goddess, Kali.

In 1940, Moor's collections were given to the British Museum by his descendants, but three of his paintings were donated to Ipswich Museum and so stayed in Suffolk. (British Museum; Dictionary of National Biography; Village website: www.holmessoft.co.uk/GreatBealings/History.htm)

1995: This was the day that Ipswich Town became Premier League record breakers, but for all the wrong reasons. They suffered a humiliating 9–0 defeat at the hands (or was it the feet?) of Manchester United at Old Trafford. (Pride of Anglia website: www.tmwmtt.com/poa)

~ MARCH 5TH ~

2003: About this time, members of the Ipswich-Beira Health Initiative made their first visit to a teaching hospital in Beira, Mozambique, which they had been supporting at a distance for several years. They were medical staff at Ipswich Hospital who had started a charity to fund training for new doctors in Beira.

Dr John Day, a leading member of the group, explained more. He said that, although Mozambique was peaceful and democratic, people were poor and the average life expectancy was approximately 40 years of age. There were only 350 doctors for a population of 19 million. He said that the Ipswich Initiative would help fund medical posts and training so that Mozambicans would not have to rely on overseas doctors.

Four years after this first visit, the first doctors graduated. One was 28-year-old Kajal Chhaganlal. She was born in Beira, where her father was a shopkeeper, but went to Malawi for her secondary education. At that time educational standards in Beira were low, and living conditions difficult as the civil war had only just ended. Kajal had planned to go university in England but changed her mind when the opportunity of Ipswich-funded medical training in Beira became available. She ended up being awarded the Gold Medal when she graduated and went on to work as a paediatrician at Beira Hospital. (Ipswich-Beira Health Initiative website: www.ipswich-mozambique-health.org.uk)

~ March 6th ~

1538: Richard Argentine became master of Ipswich Grammar School. Later, he was to become a serial religious turncoat.

At first, Argentine was admired in Ipswich. He was a model Protestant clergyman – a well-known preacher and translator of books on Protestant reform. However, when Roman Catholic Mary Tudor succeeded Edward VI in 1553, Argentine enthusiastically embraced the old religion. As John Foxe wrote, there was 'none more hot in papistry and superstition than he, painting the posts of the town with *Vivat Regina Maria*'. He was appointed to bring several Ipswich parishes back to the Catholic faith and helped draw up lists, parish by parish, of 'such as favoured the Gospell'. As a result he was widely disliked and distrusted in the town.

When Queen Mary died, Argentine foresaw that the Protestant religion would be restored. As he was unpopular in Ipswich, he resigned as master of Ipswich Grammar School and left for London. There he soon began to show himself again as the 'perfect Protestant'. Despite this chequered career, Argentine, as an absentee, held on to the living at St Helen's church in Ipswich until his death in 1568. (John Blatchly, *Famous Antient Seed-Plot of Learning*; *Dictionary of National Biography*; Nathaniell Bacon, *Annalls of Ipswich*)

⁓ MARCH 7TH ⁓

1801: On his usual Friday run, drover John Parker from Wickham Market arrived at the Running Buck in St Margaret's Plain, bringing with him cattle, sheep and hogs from villages north of Ipswich. His regular pick-up points were the Crown at Snape, the Coach and Horses at Melton and the Red Lion at Martlesham. After Ipswich, he would call at the Swan at Washbrook and then on to Smithfields meat market in London. Parker would use the drovers' road down to London. It ran separately from the travellers' road because of the damage done by the animals as they passed. In places such as Dedham, the route was marked by elm trees so that drovers could find their way in the mist. (*Ipswich Journal*, 1801; Robert MacFarlane, *The Old Ways*)

⁓

2013: The *Ipswich Star* broke the news that the Borough Council was considering demolishing the prefabs in Inverness Road and Humber Doucy Lane and replacing them with modern houses. Built as emergency post-war housing, these 122 prefabs were among the last in the country to be left standing. Though much loved by many residents, they did not meet modern standards for social housing. Residents were worried and there was a 'who said what' row in the newspapers until eventually the council issued assurances that it had no immediate plans to re-develop the area. (*Ipswich Star*, 2013)

— MARCH 8TH —

1640: Samuel Ward (b. 1577) died. He was the most popular town preacher that Ipswich ever had. A committed Puritan, he was broadly liked in the town.

Ward was elected by Ipswich Corporation to the office of town preacher in 1603 to serve for as long as he lived locally. He received a decent salary and rented accommodation in Lower Brook Street. Ward preached at St-Mary-le-Tower for thirty years – great long, thundering, fire-and-brimstone sermons, with titles like 'Woe to Drunkards' and 'Coal from the Altar to Kindle Holy Fire'. He published a couple of volumes of his sermons and was the founding father of the town library, which eventually found its way to Ipswich School.

When Ward died, the town continued paying his annual stipend to his widow and eldest son as a mark of gratitude and respect. (Carol Twinch, *Ipswich Street by Street*; Neil Ripley, ed., *Parochial Libraries*)

———

1975: The highest attendance ever recorded at Portman Road was just over 38,000 when Ipswich Town played Leeds United in the FA Cup sixth round. (Pride of Anglia; Ipswich Town Football Club supporters' website: www.tmwmtt.com/poa)

———

2014: Inevitable headline: 'Warm Weather Won't Last'! (*East Anglian Daily Times*, 2014)

— March 9th —

1887: On this Wednesday, the noted socialist, atheist and birth-control campaigner, Mrs Annie Besant (1847–1933), addressed a large public meeting in the Cooperative Hall in Carr Street on the topic 'What is Socialism?'

The following year, she played a prominent part in the Bryant & May match workers' strike in London – known to generations of history students as the 'Match-girls' Strike'. (*Ipswich Journal*, 1887)

1909: Poole's Picture Palace opened the previous night in the Mechanics' Institute's Lecture Hall in Tower Street. The programme of silent black-and-white films changed every week and the first to be advertised was a newsreel of Edward VII's recent visit to Berlin. Other short films on the programme were: *A Suffragette's Dream* (a comedy featuring women dressed as men), *The Poacher's Daughter* (a drama of infidelity and grief), and *Women Chauffeurs* (a French comedy) . Sometimes in those very early days there were also lantern shows.

There were two houses each evening, and a 'light soprano' was engaged to sing for both.

Before long, the cinema manager bought a hand-held cine camera and set about making local newsreels which were enjoyed by Ipswich audiences. (*Ipswich Evening Star*, 1909; Robert Malster, *Ipswich: An A to Z of Local History*)

— MARCH 10TH —

1820: Voting was underway in Ipswich in a general election and there were vacancies for two MPs. Four candidates stood: two Whigs (Lennard and Haldimand) versus two Tories (Crickitt and Round). The election was held over six days during which both sides lobbied, caucused and maybe even bribed people to vote for them.

However, after the ballot closed, no winners could be announced for several months, such were the claims of electoral malpractice. It was on July 3rd that Haldimand and Lennard were eventually 'chaired' as Ipswich's new MPs. It was reported that Haldimand paid over £30,000 for his election, Lennard paid £12,000 and Crickitt contributed £4,000 to his committee's funds. (Local and national newspapers, various dates; They Work for You website: www.theyworkforyou.com)

———

2010: Tom and Rebecca Ison, owners of Redeye Records in Ipswich, went to the Custard Factory in Birmingham to be presented with a special award. Their shop had been voted by customers as the best internet drum 'n' bass record store in the country.

Redeye Records had been dance music specialists since 1992, first in Fore Street and then in the Dales area.

Tom said that the award ceremony was held at a drum 'n' bass rave. He reported that he and Rebecca had a great evening but that he had to get up on stage in the middle of the night to receive the award and somehow find the words to make a speech. Rebecca added she had worn completely the wrong outfit on the night: 'I was wearing heels when I should have been getting down and grimy!' (Thanks to Tom and Rebecca Ison)

~ MARCH IITH ~

1663: An official command was written on this day to Captain Lindfield of the local militia warning him that Bramford had become a centre of Quaker activity. In particular, they were holding large unlicensed meetings in the village.

At this time, Quakers were subjected to intense scrutiny and persecution. They were fined for non-attendance at Church of England services, for gathering at unlicensed meetings and for refusing to swear oaths of allegiance or pay tithes. They were seen as subversives and became the most vilified of all the Christian sects.

Captain Lindfield was told to break up the Quaker meetings, arrest the 'ring-leaders' and bring them to justice – the inevitable punishment being prison, with over 4,000 Quakers being incarcerated in England at this time. (G.R. Clarke, *History and description of the town and borough of Ipswich*)

1826: At Ipswich Sessions, John Dalisson got six months' hard labour for defrauding the overseers of Bacton.

Dallison had gone to them to ask for 19*s* to buy a coffin for a local pauper who had just died. It was a scam: the pauper was alive and well and in no need of a coffin! Dallison had just pocketed the money and gone on his way. (*Suffolk Chronicle*, 1826. Thanks to Pip Wright)

— MARCH 12TH —

1898: St Mary-at-the-Quay church was officially closed for the first time. Once the focal point of a parish of wealthy wool merchants, it was by this time one of the smallest and poorest parishes in Ipswich:

> One this day, the Diocesan Surveyor reported that the low level of the church and its close proximity to the river had caused flooding on many occasions in the vaults beneath, resulting not only in dry rot but also deposits of sewage and other unsavoury matter beneath the floor which were producing a 'sickly and disagreeable odour throughout the building, rendering it an insanitary health risk.' Parts of the walls and roof were unsound and liable to fall at any time …

Vigorous fundraising and rebuilding enabled the church to be reopened for several more decades, but on October 18th 1942 the church register recorded 'closed because of enemy action'. It was never to open again for regular worship. (Roy Tricker, *Church of St Mary-at-the-Quay*)

~ MARCH 13TH ~

2012: Ipswich Borough Council decided to make Kiln Meadow a local nature reserve rather than a housing estate.

Wildlife campaigners were delighted and amazed. Jen Jousiffe of Ipswich Wildlife Group explained that the site was of national importance, and particularly known for its toad population. She said that every spring, toads migrated across Kiln Meadow to their breeding grounds beyond Bobbits Lane and that this would no longer be possible if a housing estate was built there. She added that small groups of volunteers had been nurturing the toad colony for several years. They had spent many evenings and early mornings patrolling up and down Bobbits Lane with buckets and torches to catch the little creatures and move them safely across the road to their breeding area. The 'toad patrol' usually moved over 4,000 of the little creatures each spring.

Outlining plans for the future, Jen said, 'Now Kiln Meadow is designated a local nature reserve, it would be a great idea to turn it into a community orchard. This would provide a good home for toads and a little bit of free food for humans.' (Thanks to Jen Jousiffe)

‒ March 14th ‒

1541: A refuse collection service was established in Ipswich. The town authorities ordered every parish to appoint scavengers to collect waste. 'All mucke' had to be deposited in one of the designated places and for each and every week they failed to collect the waste, the scavengers were fined 12*d*. Townspeople at large were made personally responsible for ensuring that their living quarters and land were kept clean and tidy. This had to be done by Saturday afternoon each week. If not, the parish scavengers had the power to fine them 3*d*. (John Webb, ed., *Town Finances of Elizabethan Ipswich*)

—

1781: At this time, Ipswich bookseller John Shave was proud to offer readers of the *Ipswich Journal* the following 'genuine medicines' from his shop in the Buttermarket:

For worms in the human body: 'Sugar Plumbs, sweet and mercury-free, to purge worms and their eggs from the intestines.'

For 'the itch': Bailey's Ointment (to cure scabies in twelve hours 'without danger').

For ladies' problems: Hooper's Female Pills ('it is not necessary to say more').

For wounds and sprains: Fryar's excellent Balsam (and 'internally taken is good for coughs, colds and consumption').

For leprosy and scurvy: Antiscorbutic Concentrated Juices (vegetable juices).

And, as a general pick-me-up: English Coffee (a mixture of plants, herbs and barks), which was even more restorative than 'viper broth' (chicken broth enriched with snake meat). (*Ipswich Journal*, 1781)

~ March 15th ~

1689: Thomas Smith, a former sailor, was getting ready to open his new coffeehouse on the corner of Tavern Street and Tower Street.

Since the first London coffeehouse had opened in 1652, their popularity had spread all over the country as meeting places for men to enjoy the buzz of caffeine and conversation. Coffee – usually imported from Turkey – cost a penny a cup (with unlimited refills) and was served to customers as they sat at long tables to facilitate general conversation.

Thomas Smith's coffeehouse was opened in April and is the first one known in Ipswich. It probably ran along the same lines as others in England at that time. (A.G.E. Jones, 'Early Coffee Houses in Ipswich', *Suffolk Review*, vol. 2)

1907: A stuffed rhino arrived in Ipswich:

A crowd of people gathered in High Street, attracted by the spectacle of an Indian Rhinoceros being unloaded from Fraser's horse drawn pantechnicon van.

Measuring in at nearly 12 feet in length, 12 feet in girth and 6 feet 6 inches high, it took ten men about two hours to ease the rhinoceros into the Central Natural History Gallery. She should have been carried to the rear of the gallery near her present position. It was only because she was so difficult to move that she stood in the entrance of the gallery for over eighty years, welcoming or frightening generations of visitors.

(R.A.D. Markham, *A Rhino in the High Street*)

~ MARCH 16TH ~

1920: St Matthew's parish pump was demolished. It had been in existence since the days of Henry II in the twelfth century. (*The Eastern Counties' Chronology or Book of Dates*)

1987: Frederick Grinke, died at Ipswich Hospital. He was 75, and a British violinist of Canadian birth.

Grinke had trained at the Royal Academy of Music in London. As a professional violinist, he was renowned as a teacher – at the Royal Academy and at the Yehudi Menuhin School – and as a soloist.

In 1945, Grinke performed in front of Winston Churchill, Joseph Stalin and Harry S. Truman at the Potsdam Conference, which marked the end of the Second World War.

Grinke specialised in twentieth-century music. He was admired by Vaughan Williams, who dedicated work to him, and at Williams' request Grinke played in the Bach Double Violin Concerto at the composer's funeral at Westminster Abbey in 1958.

Grinke was buried in Suffolk, at the tiny thatched church at Thornham Parva. His musician friends, David Martin and Florence Hooton, who lived in nearby Stoke Ash, were buried just a few yards away. (Grove Music Dictionary; www. thecanadianencyclopedia.com)

~ MARCH 17TH ~

1860: Frederick Fish, drapers of Ipswich, advertised that they had French flounced silk robes for sale. They were available in mauve and white – and mauve was the colour sensation of the time.

This newly fashionable colour was produced by a dye that had been discovered by accident in 1856. William Perkins, a chemist, was trying to make the drug quinine from coal-tar and realised that he had produced a mauve-coloured chemical dye. The new chemical dye held its colour longer than the old vegetable colorants and produced a much more vibrant hue. When Queen Victoria was seen wearing the new mauve two years later, it became the colour that women had to have. Perkins was soon a millionaire, but mauve took several years before it hit the Ipswich shops – what's new?! (*Ipswich Journal*, 1860)

1900: Cash for gnashers:

> Many ladies and gentlemen have by them old or disused false teeth, which might as well be turned into money. Messrs R D and J B Fraser, of Princes Street, Ipswich (established since 1833), buy old false teeth. If you send your teeth to them they will remit you by return of post the utmost value; or, if preferred, they will make you the best offer, and hold the teeth over for your reply.

(*Bury Free Press*, 1900)

— MARCH 18TH —

1848: The last in a series of six lectures in Ipswich was given by the Astronomer Royal, Sir George Biddell Airy (1801–92). Airy was one of several speakers of national importance who were invited to lecture by Ipswich Museum.

His lectures were held at the Temperance Hall as the Museum rooms were too small to hold the numbers of craftsmen, engineers and mechanics expected to attend. In his autobiography, Airy recalled that there were about 700 people present each evening, 200 more than the capacity of the hall.

Airy's lectures covered many astronomical topics, and were illustrated with mechanical models. The audience enjoyed these and applauded them, 'except that the rollers of the moving piece of sky would squeak'.

Airy addressed a special word of reassurance to the female members of the audience.

> The Lectures will be of what I may call a mathematical kind. But in speaking of this, I beg that the ladies present will not be startled. I do not mean to use algebra or any other science, such as must be commonly of an unintelligible character to a mixed meeting.

This was doubtless reassuring to quite a lot of the men there too! Airy's Ipswich lectures were recorded in shorthand and the transcript was printed under the title 'Lectures on Astronomy by the Astronomer Royal'. (Orwell Astronomical Society, Ipswich)

1830: William Cobbett (1763–1835), farmer and radical journalist, arrived in Ipswich and wrote that from one vantage point he could count at least seventeen windmills on the hills around the town. They looked very fine that morning: white with black sails 'twirling' in the brisk wind, and all set beautifully against the Orwell Estuary beyond. Cobbett wrote that these mills – at Stoke, Constitution Hill, Bishop's Hill and Albion Hill – sent immense quantities of flour to London and, as it was so easy to get it there by barge, Ipswich millers were able to charge more for their flour than their Norwich counterparts.

Mr Cobbett spent two days in Ipswich and addressed crowded meetings on the Friday and Saturday nights. Robert Ratcliffe, the trade unionist and labour movement historian, said:

> He spoke for three hours on the evils of the national debt and church property, and complained bitterly against the government who had spent over £2 million to disband the Hanoverian officers [who had fought within the British Army and had then been stood down at great and unpopular public expense]. At the end of his speeches he was cheered to the echo.

(William Cobbett, *Rural Rides*; Robert Ratcliffe, *History of Working Class Movement in Ipswich*)

~ MARCH 20TH ~

2010: On or about this day, a Suffolk Gypsy woman reminisced about her life:

Right, my name's Ivy Buckley and I live on West Meadows gypsy and traveller park in Ipswich.

Me father was a grinder, brought up round Stowmarket. We used to travel round for our work – pea picking, 'tata picking – all sorts of things. We went down Essex beet picking an' all.

I was born in 1943. Born and brought up in a wagon with three sisters and three brothers and we used to beg for our clothes, beg for our shoes and sell our pegs.

None of us can read or write because we was moving about. You'd probably have a week at school if we was farming. Mother sent us then – but we used to skive from school more than we went. Go an' hide up the hedges all day long.

We was local and the gorgias knew us. They say to me Dad, 'Back again, Moses?' If I talk to old locals now, I say 'Did you know Moses Smith?' and they say 'Yeah, we knew 'em wonderful well, that family.'

What I really miss is moving around – meeting other travellers an' that – and talking and cooking on a camp fire.

(Adapted from interview made for *Atching Tan* radio series, BBC)

~ MARCH 21ST ~

1789: Robert Ransome, an iron founder very recently arrived in Ipswich from Norwich, advertised that he had a large assortment of his own patented cast-iron ploughing equipment for sale at his new premises opposite St Mary-at-the-Quay church.

Quite soon after this advertisement appeared, Ransome moved the works to St Margaret's Ditches (now Old Foundry Road). From here the business expanded and thrived, the breakthrough being when he accidentally discovered how to make a chilled-iron ploughshare which was self-sharpening.

As a Quaker, Ransome endeavoured to run his business on the principles of fair trading and fair-mindedness. He set up a fund for employees unable to work through sickness or injury. He was fully involved in the life of the local Quaker community, and also took a lively interest in politics. Ransome was instrumental in bringing gas street lighting to Ipswich as early as 1821, using gas waste produced at his factory.

Robert Ransome retired in 1825 and his sons took over the business. He died in 1830 and was buried in the Quaker burial ground, which was sadly obliterated when much of the College Street area was demolished in the 1950s. (Robert Malster, *Ipswich: An A to Z of Local History*; *Ipswich Journal*, 1789; Ipswich Society)

~ MARCH 22ND ~

1819: Newspapers reported on a fashionable invention: 'Hobby Horses: – The new machine is already in very general use and the road from Ipswich to Whitton is travelled every evening by several pedestrian hobby horses. At least six are seen at a time and the distance, which is three miles, is performed in 15 minutes.'

The hobby (or dandy) horse was an early bicycle with two wheels (one behind the other) but no pedals. The rider sat on the saddle, held on to the handlebar and ran or walked to propel the machine forward. (*Salisbury & Winchester Journal*, 1819; other newspapers)

———

1939: The Board of the East Suffolk & Ipswich Hospital in Anglesea Road decided to set up a regional radium centre to provide cancer treatment for patients in Suffolk and Colchester. The hospital had held stocks of radium since 1927 but, as time went on, the Board realised they needed to use it under stricter conditions and with more expertise. Accordingly, the hospital appointed its first radiotherapist in August 1939 to advise on setting up the centre and then to run it. He was Dr Charles Woodham, previously of St Bartholomew's Hospital, London. His salary was agreed at £600 p.a. with the possibility of adding to that by seeing private patients. He was described as 'an excellent little fellow'. (Establishment of radiotherapy at Ipswich Hospital 1936–1940, Suffolk Record Office. HD2807)

~ MARCH 23RD ~

1868: Twelve-year-old Emma Smith died on this Monday. She was the domestic servant of a Mrs Steel, who kept a live-in shop in Tacket Street.

The inquest at the Greyhound Inn in Anglesea Road heard what had happened on this terrible day. Mrs Steel was in the shop when she heard panic in the kitchen. She ran in and saw her children screaming. Emma's crinoline dress was on fire. Her immediate impulse was to try to put the fire out with her bare hands. A passer-by and a shop assistant from next door rushed in to help. Emma's dress was on fire for less than five minutes, but she was severely burned on her thighs and lower back because she had been standing with her back to the open fire. As she was wearing a wide crinoline, her dress had caught fire without her noticing.

Emma was quickly taken to Ipswich & East Suffolk Hospital in Anglesea Road but died. The inquest's verdict was 'death by accidental burning'.

Emma's was one of many such deaths reported in newspapers across the country that were related to the fashion for hooped crinoline skirts. The hoops spread the skirts so wide that they caused accidents in the street, took up space in concert halls and created a hazard near any open fire. (*Ipswich Journal*, 1868)

~ MARCH 24TH ~

1831: A year before the Reform Bill was finally passed, which abolished rotten boroughs and extended voting rights, the Vicar of Coddenham wrote in his diary for this day: 'Very cold and snow storms. The second reading of Lord John Russell's Reform Bill carried in the House of Commons by a majority of one. A most dangerous measure. Most ill-timed and pregnant with mischief.' (Diary of John Longe, Vicar of Coddenham)

1874: The Ipswich School Game was played for the last time on or about this day. It was a boisterous ball game played at Ipswich School to its own particular rules. Like many similar games in other schools and in villages, it was a rowdy mixture of handling and kicking the ball. Matches between different schools were a nightmare. Teams needed to play opponents with comparable rules, so chaos was inevitable when Ipswich School played Woodbridge School, whose rules were different.

After 1874, the 'Ipswich School Game' was officially replaced with soccer. A pumpkin-shaped ball thought to have been used in the game was subsequently put on display at Ipswich Museum. (I.E. Gray and W.E. Potter, *Ipswich School 1400–1950*)

— MARCH 25TH —

The Lent Assizes often sat on this day, depending when Easter fell. The following men were taken from Ipswich Gaol to hear their fates:

1780: Jonathan Sawyer (alias Lock) was found guilty of housebreaking in Cretingham and Brundish. He had stolen shoes, buckles and a waistcoat. He was returned to Ipswich and publicly hanged a week later on Rushmere Heath.

At the same Assizes, two other men, also found guilty of housebreaking, escaped the death penalty. They had stolen printed cotton material from a house in Ipswich. Their punishment was conscription into the East India Company, probably as ratings of the lowest rank. Their accomplice was forced to join the West India Service.

1786: Nine men from Ipswich Gaol were found guilty of stealing livestock. Some were hanged, some sentenced to a period on the prison-hulks while others were transported to New South Wales. (Thanks to Pip Wright)

1859: Just as domestic sewing machines were becoming available, the Ipswich & Colchester Times carried this piece of heavy-handed humour:

> The very best sewing machine a man can have is a wife. It is one that requires but a kind word to set it in motion, rarely goes out of repair, makes but little noise, is seldom the cause of dust, and once in motion, will go on uninterruptedly for hours …

(Thanks to Pip Wright)

~ MARCH 26TH ~

1953: A sodden and battered Egyptian coffin came into the Ipswich Museum collections. It had been discovered floating in floodwater in the cellar of a house in Stowmarket. The owner of the house, probably a Miss M. Blomfield, knew nothing about the coffin until the cellar was flooded and things started floating around and bumping into one another down there.

It was found that the wooden coffin was probably made in Thebes for a high-ranking woman. It was painted a golden yellow all over, with the upper part of the body and hair intricately decorated with painted flowers and the lower part covered in devotional scenes. It was over 3,000 years old. Dr Steven Plunkett later said:

> No one knows what caused the flood in the Stowmarket cellar. It may have been a burst pipe, but it is also quite possible that the Great Floods of at the end of January 1953 caused an unusual surge of water as far inland as Stowmarket. We will never know, but without the flood, this beautiful coffin may never have ended up in Ipswich.

(Thanks to Colchester and Ipswich Museum; Steven J. Plunkett, *From the Mummy's Tomb*)

2009: Worrying headline: 'New A14 Missile Attack' (stones thrown). (*Ipswich Evening Star*, 2009)

— MARCH 27TH —

1905: The Hippodrome, a new music hall, opened in St Nicholas Street and townsfolk flocked to see the razzmatazz outside the theatre. A huge number of distinguished guests from Norfolk and Suffolk and many of the townsfolk bought tickets for the opening show. Nearby streets were full of carriages and the occasional motor car. Mademoiselle Florence led a great procession of elephants, horses and artists through Ipswich. She was a famous globe-walker, popular in music hall, and had previously walked on her giant globe from London to Brighton.

The show started after the National Anthem and speeches. It was a variety bill which included singers, comedians and the performing elephants which had processed through the town earlier. The speciality act was a Mademoiselle Alice Lorette who appeared with Ben, her white setter. She was dressed all in white in a man's shooting outfit. Mademoiselle Alice struck poses with the dog and held them for 30 seconds so that together they looked like statues in the stage lighting.

The spectacle closed with Bonnie Goodwin and her Apollo Piccaninnies enacting plantation scenes with songs and dances. The display of little black children singing and dancing brought the house down.

All proceeds went to the Ipswich & East Suffolk Hospital. (Terry Davis and Trevor Morson, *Ipswich Hippodrome: The Place to Go*)

— MARCH 28TH —

1858: Aylmer Maude was born in Ipswich, the son of the long-serving vicar of Holy Trinity church.

As a young man, Maude went to study in Moscow and met Tolstoy, who became a close friend and inspiration. By trade, Maude was a director of the Anglo-Russian Carpet Company but, after meeting Tolstoy, his real life's work was to translate Tolstoy's work into English so that it would reach a wider audience. Between them, Maude and his wife translated most of Tolstoy's writing, including *War and Peace*. For his part, Tolstoy admired the Maudes' translations for their linguistic skill and deep understanding of his philosophy.

In 1897, Maude and his wife retired to England and lived for several years in Tolstoyan communes with people who shared their co-operative and peace-loving ideals. He kept up a regular correspondence with Tolstoy, making occasional trips back to see him on his Yasnaya Polyana estate.

Towards the end of his life, Maude reflected on the time he had spent living in communes. He regretfully concluded: 'the really sad part of the Tolstoy movement was the terrible amount of quarrelling.' (Frank Grace, Talk on the history of Holy Trinity church)

~ MARCH 29TH ~

1845: *Modern Cookery*, written by Ipswich cookery writer Eliza Acton (1799–1859), was reviewed in the *Ipswich Journal*. Many of the recipes had Suffolk connections. For example, there was Westerfield white soup, which she herself used to enjoy at the home of the Edgar family, her friends who lived at Red House on the road to Tuddenham. The soup was a veal knuckle broth flavoured with onion, cream, spices, almonds and vermicelli. Eliza recommended omitting the almonds as they seemed 'unsuited to the preparation and also to the taste of the present day'. She suggested serving the soup in a tureen with a French roll.

Another local recipe was for Suffolk dumplings. Eliza instructed the cook to mix salt with flour and then make it into 'a smooth and rather lithe paste' with water or milk. This paste was then shaped into dumplings to be thrown into boiling water to cook for half an hour. Eliza added: 'in Suffolk farmhouses, they are served with the dripping-pan gravy of roast meat; and they are sometimes made very small indeed, and boiled with stewed shin of beef.' She recommended, though, that much better dumplings could be made by steaming bread dough in well-floured cloths.

Within six months of publication, Eliza Acton had made nearly £68. Her book was already a triumph. (Sheila Hardy, *The Real Mrs Beaton*; *Ipswich Journal*, 1845)

– MARCH 30TH –

1927: On this day, the first metal was poured from Cranes' malleable foundry at their Nacton Road works.

The site had been bought in 1919 by the Crane Company of Chicago, who built a huge factory there to manufacture iron fittings and valves. The company was owned by Richard Teller Crane, whose family originally immigrated to Massachusetts from Ipswich in Suffolk several centuries before.

In 1977, the 50th anniversary of Cranes' foundry was commemorated with a new paved garden next to St Michael's church in Upper Orwell Street. A plaque there marked the close ties between the company and the town. Thousands of Ipswich people worked there over the years.

Sadly, Cranes closed down in the twenty-first century when it switched production to China. A retail park was built on the massive 44-acre site where the factory once stood. (*East Anglian Daily Times* and *Ipswich Evening Star*, various dates)

———

2008: Babergh District Council put two council houses up for sale. They were a pair of cottages in Tattingstone, built in the reign of Henry VIII, and believed to be the oldest houses in council ownership in England. They had been publicly owned for many decades and they sold for £169,000 each. (*East Anglian Daily Times*, 2008)

‒ March 31st ‒

1825: One of the first lectures at the Ipswich Mechanics' Institute was given by a Mr Francis, who spoke about human anatomy to about 150 members. He illustrated his talk with 'numerous large plates, and an infant and adult skeleton'. The Institute had been set up to educate members 'in the various branches of science and useful knowledge'. (*Ipswich Journal*, 1825; Robert Malster, *Ipswich: An A to Z of Local History*)

1888: On this Saturday, the County Coroner held an inquest at Great Wenham to investigate the death of 3-year-old Benjamin Smith.

Benjamin lived in the village with his aunt and uncle. He had come running in from playing outside on the previous Tuesday morning, obviously ill. He was crying and vomiting and said he had drunk 'some stuff out of a bottle'. His Uncle Henry found a bottle of liquid discarded on the roadside and Benjamin agreed that that was what he had drunk. The bottle was labelled 'Fly Wash'. Mr Norman, a surgeon of Hadleigh, was called, but Benjamin died on the Thursday night.

At Saturday's inquest, Robert Dakin, a shepherd from Raydon, confirmed that he had left the bottle in the field the year before when he had finished treating some of his sheep for blowfly. Verdict: accidental death from poisoning. (*Ipswich Journal*, 1888)

‒ April 1st ‒

1967: The Jimi Hendrix Experience supported the Walker Brothers at the Ipswich Gaumont. Also on the bill were Cat Stevens, Engelbert Humperdinck, The Californians and The Quotations. This was just the second gig in their month-long tour across the country. The night before, they had all played the London Astoria, where Hendrix had stolen the spotlight by setting fire to his guitar. In Ipswich, Hendrix also used many of the techniques that made him famous, like playing the guitar behind his back and with his teeth. At that time Hendrix was in the early stages of his career and the band had released two massive singles, 'Hey Joe' and 'Purple Haze'.

William Martin who managed to get a ticket said:

He wore a yellow suit and closed the first half of the show. I think he was on for about twenty minutes. The atmosphere was incredible. Obviously I'd heard of him but at that time he was only really just starting out. He got a great reception and there was a real sense of excitement. I was 22 at the time and I'd never seen anything like it. It was very flamboyant. I think we all knew we were witnessing something very special.

(*East Anglian Daily Times*, 2010)

~ APRIL 2ND ~

1911: About thirty votes-for-women campaigners spent the night in the Old Museum Rooms (Arlington's in Museum Street) to avoid filling in their national census returns. They maintained that if they were considered intelligent enough to fill in a census form, then they could surely put an X on a ballot paper. The women had supper, sang protest songs, played whist and patience and talked about the movement. Suffragists from Hadleigh and Felixstowe joined the Ipswich women. These stalwarts were mentioned in press reports as being there that night:

Constance Andrews from Norwich Road with her sister, Lilla Pratt, who were soon to clash with the law over the non-payment of a dog licence;

Isabel Tippett from Wetherden. She was related to Charlotte Despard, a *grande dame* of the suffrage movement. Isabel had been imprisoned for her part in a suffragette demonstration in Trafalgar Square;

Marie Hossack, who lived in Berners Street and whose husband was a prominent surgeon and Conservative Party councillor for St Margaret's ward;

Margaret Fison, who had a conviction for riding her bike on a footpath when she lived at Allington House in Woodbridge Road.

Police maintained an all-night watch in Museum Street to maintain law and order. (*Ipswich Evening Star*, 1911)

~ APRIL 3RD ~

1722: Daniel Defoe (1660–1731) set off on a tour of East Anglia, travelling through Essex and up to Ipswich via Harwich. He admired Ipswich and wrote:

> I take this town to be one of the most agreeable places in England for families who have lived well, but may have suffered in our late calamities of stocks and bubbles, to retreat to, where they may live within their own compass; and several things indeed recommend it to such …

And then Defoe listed:

> Good houses at easy rents; An airy, clean, and well-governed town; Agreeable and improving company almost of every kind; A wonderful plenty of all manner of provisions, whether flesh or fish, and very good of the kind; Those provisions cheap, so that a family may live cheaper here than in any town in England of its bigness within such a small distance from London; Easy passage to London, either by land or water, the coach going through to London in a day; The best butter and the worst cheese in the country.

(Daniel Defoe, *Tour through the Eastern Counties of England*)

~ APRIL 4TH ~

1821: A lifeboat called *Ipswich* was launched near Stoke Bridge. It was built to a unique design by Jabez Bayley at his St Peter's shipyard. It was 30ft long, light, equipped with six rowing positions and rigged with foul-weather spritsails on two short masts. Fourteen copper tanks and 11ft^3 of cork and along the side provided the buoyancy. It was designed to be launched by about ten men and manned by six oarsmen and a coxswain. 'Our townsman', Admiral Page of Tower Street, raised the funds for it by public subscription. Stationed at Landguard Fort at the mouth of the River Orwell, the *Ipswich* was only called into action once. By 1825 she was condemned as inefficient by the Suffolk Shipwreck Association, converted to a yacht and advertised for sale. For decades after that, there was no official lifeboat at the mouth of the Orwell. (www.planetipswich.com; G.R. Clarke, *History and description of the town and borough of Ipswich*)

1881: This was the day after census night and these surnames were among those recorded commonly in Ipswich but rarely found outside Suffolk: Stannard, first record in Suffolk in 1095, a nickname meaning 'stone hard'; Bloomfield, first record in Suffolk in 1207, from the town of Blonville-sur-Mer in Normandy; Fiske, first record in Suffolk in 1208, an occupational surname meaning 'fish'; and Last, first record in Suffolk in 1385, an occupational surname referring to a shoe-maker's mould of a foot. (Surnames website: www.britishsurnames.co.uk)

~ APRIL 5TH ~

1903: Arthur Welton, a young blacksmith from Benhall, came to Ipswich and started work at Ransomes, Sims & Jefferies. The firm occupied a vast site around the dock at that time. Arthur had a forge of his own in Ransomes' plough shop. His job was making parts and assembling ploughs for home and for export. He reckoned that he had turned out thousands over the years. He said that the noted plough for Suffolk was the YL, good for work on local farms and good in ploughing matches.

At that time, Ransomes used to keep ploughmen and a team of horses at the works to demonstrate the ploughs to customers. Arthur worked closely with the ploughmen and made the alterations they suggested to the machinery.

Arthur worked at Ransomes for nearly sixty years. He started at 6.00 a.m. and worked till 5.30 p.m. Often he would have his breakfast there. A good many times he took a herring and cooked it on his forge. Several of his mates would gather round to cook their breakfast too, and they would eat it together and brew up their own tea. (George Ewart Evans, *The Farm and the Village*)

~ April 6th ~

1782: The *Ipswich Journal* praised a novel local work-scheme for paupers:

> It is with pleasure that we inform the public that at a vestry held Monday last in St Clement's in this town, it was agreed by the officers and principal inhabitants to employ all the able poor in their workhouse in destroying the caterpillars upon the hedges or trees within that parish and we hope every parish in this county will follow the like humane example.

(*Ipswich Journal*, 1782; Thanks to Ray Whitehand)

1846: The men building Ipswich railway tunnel through Stoke Hill were unable to work because of the weather. Thoroughly fed up, they got together at the Cornhill to talk about their dreadful working conditions and low pay. It was feared that violence might break out, so shops closed and the police and Magistrates were called for. 'Navvies' (as they were called) were feared and despised in equal measure by the authorities, but no trouble actually occurred on this day.

Tunnelling was indeed a dirty and dangerous job. A few months later, work was held up again – this time because of a landslip inside the tunnel. The only reason there were no casualties was because the navvies were not back from their breakfast break.
(*Ipswich Journal*, 1846)

~ April 7th ~

2003: Channel 4's *Time Team* arrived in Ipswich ready for a three-day dig in Tranmere Grove, Castle Hill. The experts, familiar faces to regular viewers, were Phill Harding, Carenza Lewis and Roman specialist Guy de la Bedoyere. An enthusiastic Tony Robinson told viewers what drew them there: 'We're here at Castle Hill in Ipswich because the children at the local primary school wanted to know more about the castle that gives this place its name. When we started looking into it, though, we didn't find some medieval stronghold, but something much more exciting.'

Tony went on to explain that Basil Brown, the Sutton Hoo archaeologist, had excavated the area in the 1940s before the housing estate was put up. He believed he had found a Roman villa but he could not complete his dig before the builders moved in.

The *Time Team* archaeologists looked for Brown's original excavation and extended it. After digging up eight back gardens in three days, they confirmed that the castle in Castle Hill was indeed a Roman villa, with the bathhouse where modern-day No. 21 stands, a centrally heated dining room at No. 13 and the main entrance porch at No. 17. (*Time Team*, Channel 4)

~ April 8th ~

1763: A huge crowd gathered at Rushmere St Andrew to witness the execution of two lovers, Margary Beddingfield and Richard Ringe.

Margery had married farmer, John Beddingfield, in 1759, but two years later a young farmhand called Richard Ringe moved into the household and began a steamy affair with her. Soon the lovers were plotting the demise of husband John, and one night Richard strangled him to death in his bedroom.

Astonishingly, the coroner's jury decided that he had died by falling out of bed and no one suspected foul play. But when a former servant told her parents what had really happened, Margery and Richard were arrested. They were tried at the Assizes, Richard for murder and Margery for petty treason – namely, plotting the death of her husband. Both were found guilty. Richard was hanged but Margery was judicially strangled and then burnt at the stake – the accepted, and expected, punishment for petty treason. A final ghoulish detail: boys from Christ's Hospital charity school were given a half-day holiday to go and see them put to death. (Blaxhill village website: www.blaxhall.com; Ipswich Borough Archives, compiled by David Allen)

– APRIL 9TH –

1982: 'A typical gloomy Good Friday with no sun and overcast sky.' (Mrs D.J. Smith's diary, SRO)

—–—

1983: Orwell Astronomical Society Ipswich owned a fireball camera to photograph meteors. On this night, it captured an unusual bright object in the sky. It was comet-like – with a 'companion' – and was a complete mystery to members. The image was sent to the British Meteor Society who also found the sighting 'very peculiar', and then on to the Data Anomaly Centre in Maryland, USA. No explanation was ever forthcoming. (Orwell Astronomical Society Ipswich)

—–—

1987: A gang of water workers repairing a damaged stopcock in Ipswich stumbled across a long-lost tunnel stretching as far as their torches would shine. The tunnel ran parallel with Anglesea Road and was about 8ft high. The well-built structure, still in good condition, was thought to have been a cellar from the old barracks. Ipswich Barracks was on a large site between Barrack Corner and Anglesea Road from the end of the eighteenth century until it closed in 1929. After inspection by borough engineers, the entrance was covered again and sealed. (*East Anglian Daily Times*, 1987)

~ April 10th ~

1963: The *Ipswich Evening Star* carried an excellent review of *Luther*, a new play by John Osborne, starring a young Ian McKellen in the title role. He was 'quite simply superb, brilliantly portraying all his doubts' and spiritual anguish. McKellen was in rep at the Ipswich Arts Theatre. Unlike many other theatres which had a weekly rep, plays at the Arts Theatre were changed every three or four weeks so the cast had time to rehearse properly and also get a decent run of performances. This year, McKellen appeared at the Arts Theatre in a further dozen plays, including *Henry V* as King Henry, and *How Dare We!*, singing, dancing and clowning. (*Ipswich Evening Star*, 1963; Ian McKellen's website: www.mckellen.com)

2013: Ipswich Pagan Council, which promotes the full range of pagan beliefs, from Druidry to Wicca, held a couple of typically diverse and diverting events this week. On April 10, they held what they called a 'moot' at the Margaret Catchpole pub on the subject of the 'archaeology of darkness', exploring the role of dark places as locations for meditation, ritual, burial and art. It was followed a few days later by a ritual to honour Thoth, the ancient Egyptian bird-headed god of knowledge and wisdom. Both events were open to members of the Ipswich Pagan Council and their guests. (Ipswich Pagan Council: www.ipswichpagancouncil.com)

- APRIL 11TH -

1979: The final production of the Ipswich Theatre Company at Tower Street opened on this Wednesday. It was the aptly named musical comedy *Happy End* by Elizabeth Hauptmann, Bertoldt Brecht and Kurt Weill. To create a party atmosphere in the theatre, a working bar was installed on stage and people sitting in the stalls were invited to come up on stage to use it.

The theatre was closing down because it was cramped and old-fashioned, but there were mixed feelings about the impending move to brand-new premises. Ian McKellen, who had appeared many times in rep in Tower Street, had fond memories of the old place. He said:

> I'd rather see this theatre so full every night that they can't squeeze anyone else in. Ipswich only needs a new building when this one is packed out every night. I can't see any point just building a theatre for the sake of it. The play isn't any better because it is in a new building.
>
> Perhaps I'm being romantic about the inadequacies of our theatre because I enjoy the contrast between the dusty confusion backstage and the brightly-lit fun and games onstage.

Later in 1979, the Wolsey Theatre opened in Civic Drive. (Theatre programme April 1979; Ian McKellen's website: www.mckellen.com)

~ APRIL 12TH ~

1957: *Daily Mail* readers were intrigued to see the headline 'Brewers Sack the Nude and the Cardinal' over what could otherwise have been quite a dry story about a corporate merger in Ipswich. Two old family brewing firms, Cobbold and Tollemache, had amicably merged to form 'Tolly Cobbold'. The point of the headline was that the new company had given itself a corporate makeover. Tolly's iconic statue of a naked Bacchante and Cobbold's logo of Cardinal Wolsey were replaced by the words 'Tolly Cobbold' in a modern typeface – red (for dark beer) and blue (for light beer). All brewing was transferred to the Cobbold brewery at Cliff Quay.

Over the years, beers in the range included Cobnut, Tolly Bitter, Tollyshooter (named to mark the visit of TV troubleshooter Sir John Harvey-Jones), Election Ale (1997) and Last Orders – the final brew, in 2002. One of their least successful brews was the appalling Husky Lager which was reportedly described by John Cobbold as 'tasting like dog's piss'.

By the time it closed in September 2002, the Tolly Cobbold beers had a poor reputation and Ridley's Brewery bought out the company. (Suffolk Camra. Thanks to Anthony Cobbold)

~ April 13th ~

1852: A difficult, long-distance courtship ended when Caroline Brown finally married the Rev. Robert Cobbold. She was the daughter of the Rector of Hemingstone. He was a son of the Ipswich brewing family and had been a missionary in China for five years.

The courtship had begun before Robert left Suffolk for China. After two years in his posting – a hotbed of malaria, cholera and piracy – Robert wrote to Caroline proposing marriage. His letter took a year to get a reply from England. Imagine his feelings when he eventually learned that, although she accepted enthusiastically, Caroline's father had refused to give permission. Equally problematically, Robert's employers at the Missionary Society refused him leave to go to Suffolk and also declined to fund Caroline's passage out to China.

After some persuasion, Caroline's father did give his consent to the marriage, but it took pressure from the powerful Cobbold family to get the Missionary Society to consent to Robert returning to Suffolk for his wedding.

Eventually, in 1851, Robert set sail back to England. His ship met terrible weather and more than once he believed he was going to die, but eventually he arrived in Suffolk, gaunt from the ravages of malaria.

Three months after the wedding in Hemingstone, Caroline and Robert set off together for married life together in China. (Cobbold Family History Trust, Anthony Cobbold)

— APRIL 14TH —

1739: The *Ipswich Journal* reassured its readers:

> We have great Hopes that this Town will very soon be entirely free from the Small Pox. We have enquir'd of every Physician, Surgeon and Apothecary that we can think of, in the Town, and can hear only of one Person that has the Distemper, which is a Child in St Hellen's Parish, beyond the Church.

It was common practice to advertise when a town was free of smallpox as it gave a good boost to trade. (Thanks to Pip Wright)

———

1863: The last public execution in Ipswich took place in the archway off St Helen's Street just by the gaol.

John Ducker, a 63-year-old agricultural labourer from Halesworth, was hanged for murder. He had been interrupted during a burglary by PC Ebenezer Tye. Ducker had beaten the PC to death and dumped his body in the river. Ducker confessed to the crime on the gallows in front of over 5,000 onlookers. (David Kindred's website: kindred-spirit.co.uk; Suffolk Constabulary)

———

2013: Birdwatchers spotted that the peregrines nesting high under the Orwell Bridge had produced chicks for the fifth year running. Suffolk Ornithologists' Group had liaised with the Highway Agency to put a nest box under the bridge and there were no records of peregrines breeding in Suffolk for 200 years until 2008. (Mick Wright's website: www.mickorwellestuary.co.uk)

~ April 15th ~

1912: The *Titanic* sank and an Ipswich man was drowned. He was Frank Maybery (1875–1912), born in St Matthew's parish and the son of the minister at Burlington Road Congregational church.

In 1907, Frank immigrated with his wife to Moose Jaw in Canada where he became a land agent specialising in selling farmland. His wife developed a serious eye complaint so the family decided to come back to live in England. The plan was to get up-to-date medical treatment for her, and then Frank would go back to Canada for a short time to wind up their business. So Frank was returning to Moose Jaw to settle his affairs when he boarded the *Titanic* at Southampton, only to drown five days later. His body was never identified.

Responding to the scale of the loss of life, Hope House Orphanage in Foxhall Road offered places to girls who had been orphaned when the ship went down. (M.G. Smith, *'Twixt Potteries and California*; Encyclopaedia Titanica: www.encyclopedia-titanica.org)

———

1945: Bergen-Belsen concentration camp was liberated by British forces on this day. Cecil Warren (1914–2009) from Ipswich was a stretcher-bearer for the 11th British Light Field Ambulance, which went in the following day. In a radio interview, he said: 'We were there for several weeks. One thing I will say is this: I have seen a grave with 10,000 people in.' Warren said that he never really got over what he saw at Belsen, but then it was so shocking that it was not right to forget it either. (BBC Suffolk, Religion and Ethics, interview with Nick Risby: www.bbc.co.uk/suffolk/content/articles/2005/04/21/belsen_interview_feature.shtml)

~ April 16th ~

1876: Joseph Alderton spent this Easter Sunday alone, just like most of the other days of the year. He was the sole occupant and caretaker of the *Jane*, a brigantine moored in the Orwell Estuary near Pond Hall Farm, just downstream from the modern Orwell Bridge.

The ship belonged to the Stowmarket Gun Cotton Company and was used to warehouse their explosives well away from people and houses, following a massive fatal explosion at their factory several years before. Gun cotton was made from cotton soaked in acid and was highly dangerous to store, so Joseph was risking life and limb every day he was out there in the middle of the river.

Joseph lived on the *Jane* for seven years, sometimes with his son coming on board for company or to take a shift so Alderton could go ashore and see his family in St Clement's. Joseph got used to being on his own and liked sleeping afloat in 'a nice cabin' with a cat and a forecastle of pigeons for company. He earned 10*s* per week.

Sometime after 1881, the brigantine was sold and converted into living quarters for farm workers, and Joseph moved ashore. (Thanks to John Alderton)

~ April 17th ~

1876: An indoor roller skating rink opened on the corner of Portman Walk and Portman Road in the newly built Drill Hall. It was thought to be the largest outside London and 300 people turned up to give it a go on the opening day. Bands played for afternoon and evening sessions and a Mr Lilywhite was employed to give lessons to the many women who were keen to learn. (*London Gazette*, 1910; *Ipswich Journal*, 1876)

1880: New sails were being fitted on Shotley Windmill. At lunchtime, the men went for a pint at the Shotley Boot. They were a bit too eager for a drink and did not fasten the vanes properly. A sudden gust of wind caught in the sails and did such damage that the mill was wrecked beyond repair. The miller was ruined and the windmill was never rebuilt. (Brian Flint, *Suffolk Windmills*; A. Woolford, *Windmills with special reference to those in Suffolk*)

1902: The *Cambridge Daily News* reported:

Baptisms are being conducted wholesale in the parish of All Saints', Ipswich. The new vicar, the Rev. Caesar Caine announced to his congregation the other day that in a small portion of the parish he had discovered some hundred unbaptisted children. These are now receiving the rite in batches of 30 or 40 at a time, and the vicar kisses every one.

(*Cambridge Daily News*, 1902)

~ APRIL 18TH ~

1857: On this Saturday, the wife of Sir John Franklin wrote to a senior naval officer, Admiral McClintock, asking him to lead a private expedition to look for her missing husband's remains. McClintock readily agreed and joined the Royal Harwich Yacht Club at Woolverstone to enlist their support.

Sir John had gone missing ten years previously on an expedition to the Canadian Arctic and several attempts had already been made to find out what had happened to him and his men.

Admiral McClintock took command of Lady Franklin's own ship and its twenty-five-man crew, and set sail for Canada, flying the Royal Harwich Yacht Club burgee – a blue flag with the Union Jack in one corner and a yellow lion rampant in another.

After many months in the Canadian Arctic, McClintock discovered what had happened to Franklin and his expedition. They had become stranded in the sea ice north-west of King William Island. After abandoning their ships, most of the crew had gradually perished from exposure and starvation as they attempted to walk across the island looking for safety.

When McClintock's officers and crew returned to England, they shared a £5,000 parliamentary reward, and the admiral was knighted. The burgee from the Royal Harwich Yacht Club was donated to the National Maritime Museum at Greenwich. (Royal Harwich Yacht Club)

— APRIL 19TH —

1953: Television owners in Ipswich were asked on this day to do a good turn on Coronation Day (June 2) by inviting old-age pensioners to come round and watch the ceremony with them. (*Ipswich Evening Star*, 1953)

———

1979: Margaret Thatcher visited Ipswich in the run-up to the general election in which she first became Prime Minister. She arrived by plane and was taken into the town centre amid tight security. She was already a controversial and divisive figure, added to which there was always the danger of IRA bombing.

After a brief walkabout in the Cornhill, Margaret Thatcher took the microphone from the local Conservative candidate and spoke off the cuff from the town hall steps. Her message was: 'We are going to win!' She was greeted by a mixture of support and dissent. There was loud applause from some onlookers and shouts of 'Thatcher out!' from others.

Although the Conservatives won the General Election, Ipswich bucked the trend. Labour MP Ken Weetch retained his seat, and with an increased majority. (East Anglian Film Archive)

~ April 20th ~

1844: The *Ipswich Journal* reported that Rabbi Harris Isaacs' household furniture and effects at 1 Borough Road, Ipswich were up for auction. The Rabbi had decided to emigrate to Jerusalem, but in the end he decided not to go. The same thing had happened a few years earlier, and then happened again a few years later, despite a flattering farewell address from the Ipswich Mayor and Corporation and letters of commendation from national Jewish figures like Moses Montefiore. He kept deciding to stay with his small Ipswich congregation and his school at the Rope Lane synagogue.

Eventually, in the early 1850s, Rabbi Isaacs did leave Ipswich, but for an unlikely destination. He moved to Merthyr Tydfil where he married the daughter of the Rabbi of Penzance. He stayed there for several decades as a rabbi and pawnbroker.

Rabbi Isaac spent the last years of his life in Birmingham, working as a Hebrew teacher, and died there in 1888. The records do not tell us whether he ever managed to get to Jerusalem. (*Ipswich Journal*, various dates; www.ancestry.co.uk; Jewish genealogy website: www.jewishgen.org)

~ APRIL 21ST ~

1767: Thomas Cobbold junior (b. 1708) died in Ipswich. He had run the family brewery which had been founded by his father in Harwich in 1723. It was Thomas Cobbold junior's decision to move the Harwich business to Ipswich. He built the first Cliff Brewery and lived in Cliff House, immediately to its north. When he died, a headstone describing him as a 'common brewer' was placed behind the font in St Clement's church, the last resting place of many Cobbolds to come. (John Blatchly, *Holywells Park: For 75 Years an Ipswich Jewel*)

———

2013: The *Sunday Times* ranked Marcus Evans, owner and chairman of Ipswich Town Football Club, as the 143rd richest man in Britain. This made him the third richest in East Anglia, and the wealthiest person with an Ipswich connection. His fortune was estimated at £625 million, roughly the same as Paul McCartney's.

Evans founded his first company in 1983. His group organised live business, sports and entertainment events around the world, with regional head offices in Dublin, Chicago and Kuala Lumpur. However, Marcus himself was known for maintaining a low public profile.

The other person on the rich list with an Ipswich connection that year was Roy Keane, ex-Ipswich Town manager. (*Sunday Times*, 2013)

~ April 22nd ~

1608: The narrow streets and thatched roofs of old Ipswich made the town vulnerable to fire. On this day, the town authorities decreed that all thatch should be replaced with roof-tiles. The penalty for non-compliance was £5. (Henry Reynolds Eyre, *History of Ipswich Fire Brigade*)

1884: An earthquake centred on Colchester shook the eastern counties. It struck at about 9.15 a.m. and measured 4.6 on the Richter scale. It damaged over a thousand buildings and affected villages all the way to up Ipswich. It was the most destructive earthquake to hit the United Kingdom since the Dover Straits earthquake of 1580. Some sources reported that two or three people were killed. Many people were made homeless, and the large waves triggered by the earthquake engulfed small boats. Overall, it was estimated that the disaster cost about £10,000.

In Ipswich, as elsewhere, builders and masons were in great demand to repair houses and church steeples.

Just two days after the earthquake, the news reached the Australian press by telegraph from London. The *Melbourne Argus* told readers: 'the earthquake was felt with great severity at Ipswich and also at Chelmsford and from thence southwards to London where the shock was felt.' (*Melbourne Argus*, 1884; *Ipswich Journal*, 1884)

— APRIL 23RD —

1891: John Dupuis Cobbold, son of the Ipswich brewing family, married Lady Evelyn Murray in Cairo. A month later, they were back at Holywells for a glamorous party to welcome them home.

But Ipswich life was dull for Lady Evelyn. She had spent part of her childhood in Algiers. She spoke Arabic and was an experienced and adventurous traveller in the Muslim world.

After years of unhappy marriage, Lady Evelyn and her husband went their separate ways. Her wanderlust and eventual conversion to Islam had put ever-increasing strains on the marriage. Now she planned a pilgrimage to Mecca, something no British-born Muslim woman had ever done before. Taking advantage of her social status to ease the journey, she got royal permission to travel across the Saudi desert by car, overtaking other pilgrims on foot or camel as she drove. She was given luxurious lodgings on rooftops where the night air was cool. She was granted special dispensation from the Saudi king to end her pilgrimage early when she became exhausted.

In 1934, the year after the pilgrimage, she published an account of her trip entitled *Pilgrimage to Mecca*. (Cobbold Family History Trust, Anthony Cobbold)

~ April 24th ~

AD 60/61: According to local legend, Boudicca, Queen of the Iceni, and her army camped overnight about this time of year in a large field near Ipswich. It was said to be at the site of the Roman garrison of Combretovium, close to the present-day villages of Baylham and Coddenham.

The Iceni warriors were making their way south from their Norfolk heartlands to protest against Roman rule. Arriving at Combretovium, they must have quickly wiped out the garrison there and, after a short night's rest, been on their way to Colchester, not wanting to lose the element of surprise.

In Colchester, a major Roman settlement, they sacked the town and burned the new temple to Claudius. Further south, they laid waste to London and were not stopped until they were defeated at St Albans by the smaller but better-trained Roman army.

The Roman response to the revolt was quite ruthless. They slaughtered and burnt their way through large areas of East Anglia, giving a clear message that rebellion against Rome would not be tolerated. (Thanks to Doc; Baylham House: www. baylham-house-farm.co.uk)

— April 25th —

1991: The Willis Building in Friars Road became the youngest building to be granted Grade I listed status. It was one of the earliest designed by Norman Foster.

Constructed in the early 1970s, it was a landmark in the development of the 'high-tech' architectural style.

The curved outside wall of the Willis Building is entirely clad in bronze-tinted glass, which reflected the surrounding buildings on sunny days. Inside, Forster created flexible open-plan offices with green floors and glare-free lighting. The central escalators lead up to a rooftop staff restaurant and a garden. There was an Olympic-sized swimming pool for employees to enjoy during their lunch breaks. This was subsequently covered over and the space used for more offices, although the pool can still be seen under the false floor.

Paul Frostick, visiting the building on a Heritage Open Day, said: 'It reminds me of those visions of the future when men would be wearing metallic mini-skirts and go from place to place on moving pavements. It has the feel of the time when people still talked about the "white heat of technology".'

English Heritage, listing the building, described it as 'an exceptional building of its period'. (English Heritage: www. english-heritage.org.uk)

~ APRIL 26TH ~

1700: The Meeting House, in a courtyard off St Nicholas Street, was officially opened. It welcomed a broad range of Protestant dissenters who disagreed with the Church of England's doctrines and forms of worship.

The land had been bought just eight months previously and Joseph Clark, 'house carpenter', undertook to build the prefabricated timber-frame construction. The job, excluding windows, galleries, pews and pulpit, cost just over £254, which included 'four Barrells of good small Beere' for the workmen.

The internal arrangement of the Meeting House was typical of Reform Protestant churches of the time. The high and ornate wooden pulpit dominated the building, emphasising the importance of preaching in this tradition. Boxed pews were set up around the central space to reinforce the idea of the congregation as a 'gathered community'. The window glass was clear, not stained, and there were no images of people, animals or supernatural beings. All reflected the Puritan concern for simplicity.

There was a spyhole in the front door. This lined up accurately with the alleyway into St Nicholas Street so a watch could be kept for attackers or hostile officials; freedom of worship still could not be taken for granted. (Cliff Reed, *A Suffolk Tabernacle: The Ipswich Unitarian Meeting House*)

‒ April 27th ‒

1200: The fair of James the Apostle was first recorded. It was held by the 'lepers of St Mary Magdalen', near the Leper Hospital of St James, which stood opposite St Helen's church and well away from the town centre. (Carol Twinch, *Ipswich Street by Street*)

———

1933: The Royal Hospital School (RHS) in Holbrook opened with a complement of 860 boys. It was originally located in Greenwich, where it had been founded in 1712 for boys from seafaring backgrounds to learn arithmetic and navigation. The school was so successful that larger premises were needed and so it moved to Suffolk in the late spring of 1933. The new RHS campus was built in the Queen Anne style in 200 acres of beautiful countryside on the Shotley Peninsula, with views over the River Stour.

RHS boys went on leave from the Greenwich school at end of March and joined the new school in Holbrook on its official opening day, most of them arriving by special train. (Royal Hospital School)

~ April 28th ~

1779: A boy about 12 years old, son of butcher John Boggis, went with another lad of the same age to look for birds' nests on heath land near Foxhall. Stooping down to explore a rabbit's nest he trod on a viper, which bit him.

Young Boggis collapsed in agony and lost consciousness. His companion was so frightened that he ran back to Ipswich to get help. However, when he tried to guide people to where his friend was, they were unable to find him. Fortunately, Young Boggis had come round enough to drag himself, vomiting and in great pain, to a farmhouse nearby, where he was being cared for.

The viper had bitten him on the back of the hand which was now swollen and greenish. Whitish pimples also appeared all over his body. After some time, his pain decreased and there were hopes of a speedy recovery. (*Ipswich Journal*, 1779)

2006: Work continued on this day to complete the demolition of the Paul's Albion Maltings silo on Ipswich waterfront. Crowds of schoolchildren gathered every afternoon to watch huge chunks of concrete come crashing down to earth. Contractors used the largest grabber in the world to tear into the building. (*East Anglian Daily Times*, 2006)

~ APRIL 29TH ~

1887: The splendidly named Alefounder Bugg, mariner of Fore Hamlet, died aged 70 years. His three brothers also had 'fancy' names: Archer Bugg, Enoch Bugg and Golden Bugg. Their surname derived from the Middle English 'bugg', meaning hobgoblin or bogeyman. (Thanks to Simon Knott)

1915: At about midnight, a Zeppelin flew over Ipswich. The crew dropped four incendiary bombs over the side.

One set fire to the surface of Waterloo Road; another landed near the Presbyterian church at the top of London Road, but luckily did not explode. The third bomb landed on an open field between Bramford and Whitton. The fourth landed on No. 60 Brooks Hall Road, the home of a Mr and Mrs Harry Goodwin. It came crashing through the roof and landed in the bedroom where their 12-year-old niece was sleeping. Her foot was injured but she was rescued from the blazing room. The house was burned out and the fire spread to the neighbouring houses.

The Zeppelin flew on for a further hour and dropped bombs and incendiaries on Bury St Edmunds, where local people responded by attacking the German-owned Griffin Hotel. (Ipswich Museum)

— APRIL 30TH —

1634: About nine local Puritan families set off on the *Elizabeth*, leaving Ipswich for Massachusetts where they could live and worship according to their own brand of Christianity. It was just fourteen years after the Pilgrim Fathers had founded the first European settlement there.

The Elizabeth carried crew, passengers and supplies including farm animals, casks of fresh water and all the food for the crossing. Each family would have cooked their own meals in metal braziers. All washing was done with salt water, as the precious casks of fresh water were only used for drinking. Under the ship's master, William Andrewes, the voyage took over two months and they arrived in Boston in the July.

Many of the newly arrived Suffolk families settled in the township of Watertown, between Boston and Cambridge, Massachusetts.

All the men would have been carefully observed to see if they held correctly Puritan beliefs and lived godly lives. In particular, the colonial leadership wanted to ensure no one was 'tainted' by Anglican, Quaker or Baptist ideas. Once vetted, they were allowed to join a church, become a freeman and vote; and so they were accepted into the community. (Ipswich Museum)

~ MAY 1ST ~

1863: The Brett Drinking Fountain was unveiled just inside the Henley Road entrance to the arboretum. It was given to the town by John Brett – a prosperous shoemaker – after he had seen children playing there and noticed that there was no drinking water for them. It cost £64 and was in the highly ornamental Italian style. Mr Edward Grimwade, Deputy Mayor, declined to attend the opening ceremony, saying: 'cold water is a cold subject to make a speech upon'. (Friends of Christchurch Park newsletter)

1877: Derby Road station was opened on the Ipswich–Felixstowe railway line. The new station was over 6 miles from the main town station by train, but only 1½ miles as the crow flies, because the line went in a long loop around north Ipswich via Westerfield.

At the time, the Suffolk Chronicle described Derby Road station as 'the most inconvenient and out-of-the way spot which could have been selected', and the mayor of Ipswich tried to campaign for an additional and better-located station half a mile to the north, between Spring Road and Woodbridge Road.

Despite this inauspicious start, Derby Road station became particularly popular at weekends for people in east Ipswich wanting to go to Felixstowe for the beach and seaside amusements. (M.G. Smith, *'Twixt Potteries and California*)

- MAY 2ND -

1932: Bailiffs made a surprise visit to Charles Westren's farm early this morning. They had been sent to confiscate corn-stacks and furniture, as Mr Westren had refused to pay his annual tithe tax to the Church of England. The bailiffs were accompanied by lorries from as far away as Cambridge as no local haulier wanted to get involved in the dispute.

Mr Westren's sympathisers rang the Elmsett church bells to alert villagers. The news spread by telephone to neighbouring farmers. A crowd of over 300 people soon gathered at the Westren farm to help block access to the property. They placed wagons across the narrow track leading to the stack-yard, and enlisted a group of men to chop down an elm tree to block the farm drive. They towed a poultry house to the end of the drive and dug a trench across the gateway.

The lorry drivers thought twice about getting more involved. They decided to leave with only a third of a corn-stack – to much cheering from the crowd. Neighbouring farmers' wives rang the church bells in triumph.

Although they were not involved on this occasion, it was common at this time for black-shirted members of Oswald Mosley's British Union of Fascists to visit farms in this part of Suffolk both to support farmers who refused to pay their tithe and to recruit them. (Leaflet found at Elmsett church)

~ MAY 3RD ~

1904: On or about this day, a photograph was taken of the children and nursery-maids at the crèche at William Pretty's factory, one of the largest manufacturers of corsets in the country. At this time the company employed at least 1,200 people, almost half at the Tower Ramparts factory in Ipswich, and many of them were women.

Women had always formed the mainstay of the corset business, but typically working from their own homes, so that childcare was not really a problem. However, when Pretty's built their huge Ipswich factory, they found it hard to recruit enough women workers. One solution they tried was to open small branches near railway stations all over Suffolk, Norfolk and Essex so that garments could be started in Ipswich, finished elsewhere and then sent back to Ipswich for packing and dispatch.

Possibly the factory crèche – very unusual at this time – was another way to solve the shortage of women workers. With a crèche, women could work in the factory without the full expense and worry of finding childcare – a classic case of enlightened self-interest on Mr Pretty's part. (Photograph of crèche, SRO; Robert Malster, *Ipswich: An A to Z of Local History*; Account of a talk on William Pretty by Roger Kennell)

~ MAY 4TH ~

1589: Margaret Coppyn, a poor woman in her late 70s, was given permission to leave the almshouses in Ipswich known as 'Mr Tooley's Foundation'. She had lived there for seven years. Her friends had promised to provide for her for the rest of her life and so she was allowed to go and live with them.

The wardens made one stipulation though – she had to leave behind her best linen gown and her bedding for the next tenant to use. And so it was that Alice Starling, 'a poore, olde and ympotent woman of this towne' took over Margaret Coppyn's gown, bedding, and room, and also received her relief money of 8*d* a week. (John Webb, ed., *Poor Relief in Elizabethan Ipswich*)

1837: The first professional police force was formed to maintain law and order in Ipswich. The entire force consisted of three sergeants and ten constables working from a central office in Norwich Road and serving a population of well over 20,000 people. They wore a blue uniform with white embroidery and buttons. (Police and Constabulary List, 1844, SRO)

~ May 5th ~

1859: Rachel Stebbing died aged 86 at the family home in Orwell Place. She was a trained midwife and had many clients in Ipswich. But also, unusually for the time, she had worked as a surgical assistant to her father, the eminent George Stebbing. (Sally Irvine, *Surgeons and Apothecaries in Suffolk: 1750–1830*)

1910: A large audience consisting mainly of women gathered in the Corn Exchange to hear Christabel Pankhurst speak about votes for women.

The meeting had been arranged by Georgina Roe, a young and enthusiastic suffragette of independent means, who had recently arrived in Ipswich. She was the first East Anglian organiser of the Women's Social and Political Union (WSPU) and had her office at 19 Silent Street. She became one of the Pankhursts' most trusted activists.

At the meeting, a number of women wore scarves with the words 'Votes For Women' on them, probably in the WSPU colours of purple, white and green. At the end of the meeting, £24 3s 6d was collected for the cause. (*Bury & Norwich Post*, 1910)

— MAY 6TH —

1870: The *Diss Express* noted the 'death of a giant, George Page of Newbourne near Ipswich'.

George – who stood at 7ft 4in – and his brother, Meadows Page, used to travel with Whiting's Exhibition (a circus) and were described in the show-bills as the 'Suffolk Giants'. George was 26 years of age when he died. He was buried in Newbourne churchyard close to the church door. The inscription on his headstone read: 'He was exhibited in most towns in England but his best exhibition was with his Blessed Redeemer'. (Thanks to Pip Wright)

—

1882: The foundations of Hope House were laid in Foxhall Road. It would be the new premises for the East Suffolk Girls' Home, which was moving from St Clement's and expanding to take up to fifty girls. The orphanage had been founded in 1875 by Harriet Isham Grimwade (1843–1893) who was known for her work among the poor.

At Hope House, girls were trained for domestic service. They also received elementary education, learned to make and mend clothing and were taught to knit. The training was said to be thorough and girls were always in demand to work in the homes of the better off. The orphanage was closed around the beginning of the Second World War. (M.G. Smith, *'Twixt Potteries and California*, Ipswich Historic Lettering website: ipswich-lettering.org)

~ MAY 7TH ~

1999: Sir Alf Ramsey was cremated at Ipswich Old Cemetery. He had lived with his wife, Vicky, for more than thirty years in a modest three-bedroomed detached house at 41 Valley Road.

Alf had moved to Ipswich in 1955 when he was appointed manager of Ipswich Town Football Club and continued to live there even when he was the England manager.

He had a reputation for being modest, gentlemanly and hard-working. He always wore a shirt and tie, even when popping out for a newspaper. Julian Germain remembered in his book *In Soccer Wonderland* that when he was a schoolboy '[he] put a self-addressed sheet of paper through Ramsey's letterbox, asking for the autographs of the England team. A few days later, the piece of paper, duly signed, was put back through [his] own letterbox, also by hand.'

Sir Alf died in an Ipswich nursing home, aged 79 years. His funeral was at St-Mary-le-Tower church.

The following year, a statue of him was unveiled in Portman Road which became a popular pre-match meeting point for Ipswich Town fans. (Extremegroundhopping, Ralph Morris' blog: http://extremegroundhopping.wordpress.com; thanks to Simon Knott)

~ MAY 8TH ~

1698: On or about this day, Celia Fiennes, traveller and diarist, arrived in Ipswich from Colchester and recorded some of her impressions of the town. She was particularly interested in its commercial life and the apathy of its inhabitants. She wrote:

> So I went to Ipswich nine miles more; this is a very clean town and much bigger than Colchester is now ...
>
> The town looks a little disregarded, and by enquiry I found it to be so through pride and sloth, for though the sea would bear a ship of 300 tons up quite to ye Key, and ye ships of ye first rate can ride within two mile of the town, yet they make no advantage thereof by any sort of manufacture, which they might do as well as Colchester and Norwich. So that ye ships that bring their coals go light away. Neither do they address themselves to victual or provide for ships.
>
> They have a little dock where formerly they built ships of two or three tons, but now little or nothing is minded save a little fishing for ye supply of ye town.

(Celia Fiennes, *Through England on a Side Saddle*)

~ MAY 9TH ~

2005: Humphrey Lyttelton and the Radio 4 *I'm Sorry I Haven't a Clue* teams made their first visit to Ipswich to record two shows. Humph greeted the audience with a selection of well-known local 'facts':

Hello, and welcome to I'm Sorry I Haven't a Clue. You join us this week at the Regent Theatre in Ipswich, the fine county town of Suffolk.

Thanks to sea-trade with Europe, Ipswich flourished during the Middle Ages, and had close ties with Antwerp … later twinned with Dectwerp. In 1903, the world's first ever lawnmower was invented here, and in 1986 it was loaned to the Science Museum. Ipswich still hasn't got it back.

Ipswich houses the court where Mrs Wallis Simpson obtained her divorce before marrying the Duke of Windsor. However, Wallis kept her married surname, preferring not to go back to her maiden name of And-Grommit.

In recent years, the coastline around Ipswich has suffered severe erosion, but this has proved a boon to hunters of fossils that are released by the waves and deposited by the incoming tide, so there's no shortage of washed-up relics here.

Let's meet the teams … Barry Cryer & Graeme Garden, and Tim Brooke-Taylor & Jeremy Hardy.

(Iain Pattinson, *Lyttelton's Britain: a User's Guide to the British Isles*)

– MAY 10TH –

1962: The young South African actor Janet Suzman made her debut on the professional stage at the Tower Theatre, Ipswich, straight from drama college in London. She played the part of Liz in Billy Liar and was paid £13 for eight performances a week.

In the theatre programme for *Billy Liar*, she was billed as Janet Manners because her agent thought she would not get work with a name like Suzman – he thought it sounded too foreign. As her friend Ann Leslie (the journalist) later wrote: 'So Janet Manners she became for short while – a rather limp, who's-for-tennis kind of name – which didn't suit her feisty, exotic, witty personality.'

The Ipswich newspapers gave *Billy Liar* a good review but Janet only received a passing mention: '… other parts are played by Conrad Monk and Janet Manners and the whole cast work hard to make it a rewarding evening.'

The following year, Janet joined the Royal Shakespeare Company in Stratford, met her first husband – the Ipswich-born theatre director, Trevor Nunn – and changed her name back to Suzman. (Arts Theatre Programme, 1962; Ann Leslie, *Killing My Own Snakes*)

~ MAY IITH ~

1926: The Ipswich Trades Council met to discuss the recent General Strike, which had lasted for nine days. What had happened in Ipswich?

The Strike Committee, based at the Labour Institute in Silent Street, had met every afternoon to organise picketing and keep an eye on events. In particular, they negotiated a deal with the local Co-op whereby strikers could have 15s a week credit to buy groceries.

Local passenger transport was nearly brought to a standstill, despite volunteers driving some trains and buses. Corporation employees stopped work.

Meetings were held on the Cornhill, attended by thousands of people. Police from Cambridge were drafted in and made twenty-two arrests in one evening, but there was little real trouble.

Members of the Electrical Trades Union in Ipswich, unsure whether to go out on strike, had been advised against it by the Trades Union Congress, to ensure that the hospital still had power.

Not on the agenda that night was one Lewis Mills, later better known as the actor Sir John Mills, who opposed the strike. He was a clerk with R. & W. Paul and had volunteered to help police escort vehicles through picket lines. (*The Eastern Counties' Chronology or Book of Dates*; The Union Makes Us Strong website: www.unionhistory.info)

1987: The mayor of Ipswich, Mrs Gillian Auton, unveiled a plaque marking the launch the new electrified rail service through Ipswich, running from London Liverpool Street up to Norwich. (Commemorative plaque at Ipswich station)

– MAY 12TH –

1795: An advert appeared in local newspapers on this day and throughout the 1790s and early 1800s offering to provide substitutes for men called up into the Suffolk Militia. For a fee of 5s 6d, a stand-in would take the place of anyone unwilling or unable to serve. As Pip Wright explained:

> Each parish had to provide at least one fit man for the Suffolk Militia at any given time. Volunteers were not often forthcoming, so villagers drew lots. If you could afford to pay a substitute to take your place, you were not too troubled by drawing the short straw. Alternatively, insurance schemes like this existed to offer peace of mind for a relatively small sum. It was the craftsmen and tenant farmers who tended to pay into such a scheme, unable or unwilling to leave their families and businesses for long periods.

(Thanks to Pip Wright)

1937: For the first time, boys from HMS *Ganges* were permitted to march through the streets of Ipswich with bayonets fixed. They were celebrating George VI's coronation with traditional military pageantry. (A.S. Grimmer, *History of RNTE HMS* Ganges)

~ May 13th ~

1867: John Henderson (b. 1823) was buried in Ipswich on or about this day. He had been a horse rider for Pablo Fanque's Fair, a travelling circus, before starting his own show.

Henderson's circus arrived in Ipswich in late April 1867, but a few weeks later he died from pleurisy. Crowds lined the streets as his funeral procession passed on its way to the Old Cemetery where he was buried.

A hundred years later, John Lennon wrote a song, 'Being for the Benefit of Mr Kite', in which he mentioned Henderson several times, inspired by a poster for Pablo Fanques' Fair. Tantalisingly, Henderson's gravestone shows a distinctive riderless horse – could this be the 'Henry the Horse' of the famous Beatles song? (Robert Halliday, *Suffolk Graves*; Thanks to Simon Knott; *Ipswich Journal*, 1867)

2009: On this day (16 Rabi-ul Awwal 1430, in the Islamic calendar) the Ipswich Mosque opened in the old fire station in Bond Street. It had enough space for up to 300 men worshipping together and was open for all of the five daily congregational prayers. As the Mosque leaders were Deobandi scholars and followed a conservative strand of Islam, women were not allowed to attend prayer there but could use the Mosque's community facilities, such as the lunch club. Most of the Mosque and Community Centre users were of Bangladeshi origin, the largest single group of Muslims in Ipswich. (Suffolk Observatory, 2011 census data; Ipswich Mosque website: www.ipswichmosque.org)

~ MAY 14TH ~

1908: 'The Franco', a major world fair, opened at the White City in London to celebrate the new Entente Cordiale between France and Great Britain. On display was the work of Westerfield-born writer Matilda Betham-Edwards (1836–1919). Nine of her books about France were exhibited and she won a gold medal there for her work in fostering Anglo-French understanding.

Miss Betham-Edwards first went to France in 1863 but her first long stay began in 1875 at Nantes. She always stayed *en famille*, never in hotels, and travelled throughout France observing French people from many walks of life at close quarters. She was particularly interested in life in the French countryside, and in education, libraries and museums. Of Huguenot descent, she was a complete Francophile and often totally idealistic in interpreting what she saw. She was the first English woman to be made an Officier de l'Instruction Publique, an award given to people who made significant contributions to French national education and culture.

When she was not travelling in France, Miss Betham-Edwards spent a some of her life in Westerfield, managing the family farm with her sister, and finally settled in Hastings. (Tony Copsey, *Suffolk Writers Who Were Born Between 1800–1900*; Martyn Cornick, *Matilda Betham-Edwards: Franco-British Go-Between*)

— MAY 15TH —

2007: Lukasz, a Polish writer, asked his Ipswich readers to send him photos for a Wikipedia article he was researching about the 'Ipswich underground stations'. Unfortunately, he had been taken in by Simon Knott's April Fool webpage. Simon had written:

The Ipswich Underground Railway opened in 1922, and the Borough quickly set about expanding the system. By 1930, fifteen stations had been completed, built in a lively style that crossed mock-Tudor with Art Deco.

In 1933, the newly-elected Ipswich Borough Council consisted largely of communist sympathisers, and even a few party members. One of its first acts was to send a message of support to Joseph Stalin and his Central Committee. Stalin was so pleased with this kick in the face for the British government that he set about funding the completion of the Ipswich underground. A number of fabulous stations were constructed, among them Gainsborough, Margaret Catchpole and Fore Hamlet, to the designs of the major Soviet architect Vladimir Mayakovsky.

Little survives today of the Ipswich Underground Railway, but once its tunnels and platforms thronged with Ipswich people travelling beneath the streets of their proud town. Today, the tunnels are filled in and the stations have found other uses, but still the memories remain.

(Thanks to Simon Knott)

~ MAY 16TH ~

1840: The first adhesive postage stamps were introduced throughout the country this month and on this Saturday the *Ipswich Journal* gave its readers some useful advice on the new system, namely: 'Stick the stamp on the same side of an envelope as the address. Do not re-use the stamp otherwise you are committing a felony.' (*Ipswich Journal*, 1840)

1990: John Gummer, Agriculture Minister and a Suffolk MP, was famously photographed and filmed tucking into a beefburger with his young daughter, Cordelia. They were visiting the East Coast Boat Show in Ipswich at the height of the 'mad cow disease' (BSE) scare. Gummer was keen to show that British beef was safe to eat. Cordelia refused the burger, but he took a large bite himself, saying it was 'absolutely delicious'. The link between beef and BSE was confirmed six years later. (BBC: http://news.bbc.co.uk/1/hi/uk/369625.stm)

2014: Barry Manilow performed to a packed stadium at Portman Road. The wrinkle-free 70 year old – veteran of a good deal of cosmetic surgery – sang all the old favourites like 'Copacabana' and 'Mandy', and a cheesy good time was had by all. (Thanks to Helena Manning)

─ MAY 17TH ─

1890: The leader of the Liberal Party, William Gladstone, stopped at Ipswich railway station on his way to Norwich by special train. As he sped on his way up to Ipswich, railway workers gathered by the tracks and waved clumps of bright yellow gorse at him, yellow being the Liberals' colour. In Ipswich station, he was greeted by hundreds of well-wishers. After a quick address to the crowd, Gladstone was on his way again, 'the people cheering heartily until their cheers were lost in the distance'.

Gladstone had found favour with many working people the previous year when he had supported the London Dock Strike by contributing to the strike fund and staunchly advocating the rights of 'the labouring man'. (*London Daily News*, 1890)

———

1946: On or about this day, Mary Whitmore (1884–1974) became the first female mayor of Ipswich.

She was born in Sproughton, a farmer's daughter, and as a young suffragette was one of the first members of the Ipswich branch of the Women's Social and Political Union. Mary Whitmore trained as a teacher at Whitelands College near London and had a lifelong interest in education. She was a founder member of the Ipswich Workers Education Association and taught at Nacton Road Mixed School for many years. She joined the Labour Party in 1924 and was elected as a town councillor in 1930. As a local politician she worked hard to improve women's health and education and received an MBE in 1951 for her services to public life. (Ipswich Women's History Trail; www.ancestry.co.uk)

- MAY 18TH -

1823: William Thompson, a baker's son, was born in Ipswich on this day. He became one of the foremost seeds-men in the country.

It all began in a small garden behind his parents' shop in Tavern Street. William worked in the family bakery but, during a bout of ill health, he began to study botany and tended the garden at the back of the shop. William moved from the back garden to a nursery at the edge of Ipswich and then to an even larger site. Eventually there were three Thompson nurseries and he published a magazine called *The English Flower Garden*.

In 1855 William produced his first seed catalogue, the forerunner of an unbroken line stretching through to today.

William specialised in growing rare and unusual plants from seeds sent to him from all over the world. The Royal Horticultural Society invested him with its highest honour, the Victorian Medal of Honour.

William died in 1903 at the age of 80. He lived to see his company become one of the country's greatest seed firms, with a reputation for introducing more species and varieties to the British gardening public than any other. (Thompson and Morgan's website:/www.thompson-morgan.com; Tony Copsey, *Suffolk Writers Who Were Born Between 1800–1900*)

— MAY 19TH —

1536: Anne Boleyn was executed on Tower Green in London. Legend had it that she gave instructions for her heart to be brought to Suffolk and buried at Erwarton church.

Anne had fond memories of Erwarton as she had often stayed at the Hall with relatives when she was a child. Some people said that Henry VIII even visited her there in secret when he was courting her.

In 1838, when the north aisle of the church was being renovated, a small, heart-shaped casket was discovered hidden in an alcove. When it was opened, there was a handful of dust in it – possibly the powdery remains of her heart.

The casket was reburied beneath the organ, and a small plaque says that it is 'recorded that her heart was buried in this church by her uncle, Sir Philip Parker of Erwarton Hall'. (Thanks to Simon Knott)

———

1944: Anthony Ludovici, resident of Henley Road and a convinced fascist, became a member of Ipswich Art Club on or about this day. He was a proficient artist – he had worked for the sculptor Rodin – but he became best known as a leading right-wing author and social critic. He wrote admiringly of Hitler and disparagingly of Jews, 'foreigners' and 'odd people'. He published over forty books and translated more than sixty others.

Ludovici moved to Ipswich in mid-life to escape 'the decadence' of the capital. He opposed the use of all bodily stimulants and so banned his housekeeper from keeping sugar in the house. He died in London in 1971. (*Oxford Dictionary of National Biography*; Greg Johnson, *Remembering Anthony M Ludovici*)

— MAY 20TH —

1628: On or about this day, a procession of parishioners, led by the rector, churchwardens and choirboys, walked the boundaries of St Clement's parish and prayed for its protection, as they did every Whitsun. A local woman, Goody Coulls, fortified the boys with bread and beer, for which the churchwardens paid 9*s*. (Churchwardens' books, St Clement's parish)

1785: The Ipswich to South Town and Bungay Turnpike Trust held its first meeting to discuss improving the road between Yarmouth and Ipswich (the future A12). The idea was to finance the upkeep of the road by charging people to use it.

The first meeting was held in Yoxford as this village was about halfway along the route. Twenty-one trustees were appointed – all members of the gentry who owned land through which the road passed. They were hoping the improved road would bring benefits to their farms and businesses.

The Trust erected seven toll gates at roughly 10-mile intervals along the road. At the Ipswich end, the first gate was at Rushmere and the second was at Kesgrave near the Bell Inn. This was later moved to the 71 milestone (near Kesgrave High School). 'Side gates' were erected near the Rushmere tollgate to prevent people using minor roads to avoid paying – hence 'Sidegate Lane'. (Linda Sexton, *Fifty Four Miles to Yarmouth*)

~ MAY 21ST ~

1825: Rev. John Hartnell, minister of the Salem Baptist Meeting House in Globe Lane, died of cancer after 'a period of suffering from extreme pain'. His wife had also recently died and their four children were left destitute. The oldest was a 14-year-old girl, then a boy of 10, a girl of 7 and the fourth just an infant in arms.

Immediately after their parents' deaths, the children were looked after by members of Hartnell's congregation but − in a laudably ecumenical initiative − a group of prominent Anglian clergymen, Independent ministers and Quakers got together to make an appeal for their long-term support. Sadly, history does not record what became of the Hartnell children. (*Baptist Magazine*, 1825; *Ipswich Journal*, 1825)

1894: 'Professor' Owen of Brooks Hall Road, Ipswich, advertised his fortune-telling services in several northern newspapers. He would describe your future partner to you. All you had to do was send him your birthday, seven stamps and a shilling. (*Yorkshire Evening Post*, 1894)

~ MAY 22ND ~

1659: There is a long-lived popular misconception that 'Major's Corner' was named after some unknown army officer who lived there in times past. In fact, the land was owned by the Major family, who lived in the parish since at least the sixteenth century.

On or about this day in 1659, the area was referred to in a municipal document giving permission for a Joshua Major and his fellow surveyors to divert spring waters flowing from Christchurch Park past 'Maior's Corner'. The diverted water was then to run down 'The Wash' (later known as Orwell Street).

Late in the twentieth century, the misconception about the origin of this corner's name was alluded to by a light-hearted statue called *Major Convenience*, depicting an army officer (a major – geddit?) swatting steel flies crawling over the public loos – hmm, not to everyone's taste! (Carol Twinch, *Ipswich Street by Street*)

– MAY 23RD –

1797: Margaret Catchpole (1762–1819), born in Nacton, stole a horse from John Cobbold and, dressed in men's clothing, rode hard to London. She was quickly arrested, tried and sentenced to death. This was commuted to imprisonment in Ipswich Gaol when the Cobbold family spoke up for her.

After three years in prison, Margaret made a daring escape. Disguised as a sailor in pantaloons, smock, round hat and pigtail, she used a clothes line to scale the prison wall and set off for the coast to be picked up in a smugglers' boat.

However, Margaret was tracked down and recaptured. She was again sentenced to death, but this was reduced to transportation for seven years. This time she was taken to Portsmouth and put on a ship bound for Australia.

Once settled there, Margaret was proud to live a decent and industrious life. She became a midwife and delivered the children of some of the first settlers. Most unusually for a convict and former housemaid, she wrote many letters – some to the Cobbolds back in Ipswich – describing life in the colony. Her writings have added significantly to Australia's early history.

Margaret Catchpole was officially pardoned in 1814 but died five years later from the influenza that she caught from one of her patients. (*Bath Chronicle*, 1800; *Ipswich Journal*, 1800; *Australian Dictionary of Biography*)

– MAY 24TH –

2010: On or about this day, the BBC aired a TV programme about a medieval skeleton which had been excavated in Ipswich during an archaeological dig on the corner of Wolsey Street and Franciscan Way a few decades previously. A burial ground containing the remains of 150 individuals had been discovered, and nine skeletons were thought to be – most unusually – of sub-Saharan African origin.

The show, called *History Cold Case – Ipswich Man*, reported on a scientific and historical investigation by a team from Dundee University into one of the 'African' skeletons.

Scientific analysis suggested that 'Ipswich Man' was a strongly built man in his forties when he died, and of medium height for the time (5 feet 6 inches). The team thought that he lived some time during the thirteenth century and that he had been in a cool climate (probably Ipswich) for at least ten years before his death. He had a large spinal abscess which would have been painful and may have caused his death. Crucially, the scientists thought that he was from the north African coast rather than from sub-Saharan Africa.

So how had he come to be in Ipswich?

Historians found written evidence that in the 1270s crusaders from Suffolk had captured and converted Muslims in Tunis, north Africa, and had brought some of them back to Suffolk. Compellingly, one of these crusaders had founded the Friary in Ipswich, exactly where 'Ipswich Man' was buried. (*History Cold Case – Ipswich Man*, BBC)

~ MAY 25TH ~

1961: Twenty-year-old Toni Gardiner, born on the Shotley peninsula, married the King of Jordan.

Toni had spent her early years at Olive Cottage in Chelmondiston. She met King Hussein – British-educated and a great anglophile – when she was working in Amman for the company which produced the film *Lawrence of Arabia*. They were both at a fancy dress party, and he was dressed as a pirate.

The wedding took place in Amman, capital of Jordan. It was a traditional Muslim ceremony, except that Toni wore an English wedding dress – long and white with a veil held back off her face.

Toni converted to Islam and changed her name to Muna, meaning 'wish' or 'desire'. As she was not of Arab descent she could not be given the title of queen.

A year later, Muna gave birth to her first child, a son and heir for King Hussein. She was then given the title of princess.

Princess Muna and King Hussein were divorced in 1972. She was his second wife, and after Muna, he married twice more. He had twelve children in all, but it was Muna's son who succeeded him as King Abdullah II.

Princess Muna stayed in Jordan and enjoyed a special place over and above Hussein's other wives as she was the king's mother. (*Coventry Evening Telegraph*, 1999)

~ MAY 26TH ~

1940: An armada of 'little ships' set sail for the French coast to rescue Allied troops trapped on the beaches at Dunkirk. Six Thames barges from R. & W. Paul's Ipswich fleet were towed across the English Channel to help, somehow avoiding mines and enemy aircraft.

Under cover of darkness, one of the barges was rowed for the last leg of the journey and the crew shipped their oars whenever German airplanes flew over. It took 273 men off the beach and back to England.

Two of the Ipswich barges had to be abandoned at Dunkirk when they failed to get off the beach before the Germans closed in. Their crews were ordered to abandon ship and they escaped home on a minesweeper.

Another Ipswich barge, the *Ena*, was spotted beached and abandoned by a couple of escaping soldiers. These men made a raft and rowed out to her, using shovels for oars. With about forty men on board, they somehow navigated back to Kent. R. & W. Paul's sent one of their skippers to pick the barge up from Deal and sail her back home to Ipswich. (Association of Dunkirk Little Ships)

— MAY 27TH —

1911: Constance Andrews, music teacher and secretary of the Women's Freedom League, was released from Ipswich Prison. She had been sentenced to a week there because she had a dog but no dog licence. She had refused to get one as an act of civil disobedience: why should she pay tax when she did not have the right to vote?

In prison, Miss Andrews declared herself to be a vegetarian and had her meals brought to her by her sister, Lilia Pratt.

On the morning of Miss Andrews' release, a huge crowd gathered outside the prison. Charlotte Despard, a grand old lady of the women's suffrage movement, was there to greet her and lead the cheering. They were driven together in an open carriage through the streets of Ipswich, accompanied by women walking alongside carrying banners and chanting slogans. The party eventually arrived for breakfast at the Women's Freedom League HQ in Arcade Street. Miss Andrews told her supporters that every woman should withhold the dog tax. If they did not have a dog, then they should go out and buy one so that the prisons would be full. (Carol Twinch, *Ipswich Street by Street*)

– MAY 28TH –

1527: Thomas Bilney, clergyman and admirer of Martin Luther, was arrested when he was preaching in Ipswich. A woodcut in *Foxe's Book of Martyrs* showed him being dragged from a pulpit outside St George's chapel (in St George's Street). In his sermon he criticised pilgrimages to shrines like Our Lady of Ipswich and it was alleged that he said that the miracles seen there 'were done by the devil ... to blind the poor people'.

At the time of the arrest, Bilney was on a preaching tour of East Anglia. Wherever he went he was ridiculed and challenged by priests and friars, but his sermons attracted great crowds.

In the November following his arrest, he was brought before Cardinal Wolsey and the Bishop's Court in Westminster and charged with heresy. Friends tried to persuade him to recant, which he did after two days of intense pressure. He was paraded in humiliation before the Council of Bishops and sent to the Tower.

He was released a year later. But he was determined to preach again so he set off across East Anglia once more, this time preaching in open fields, as he was barred from churches. Bilney was arrested when he got to Norwich and executed in 1531. (L.J. Redstone, *Ipswich through the Ages*; *Foxe's Book of Martyrs*)

~ May 29th ~

1872: The National Agricultural Labourers' Union was formed in Warwickshire and began enrolling members, many of them men from Suffolk and the farms around Ipswich. When their demands for better pay and conditions were refused, pockets of Union members began to go on strike.

Farmers responded by banding together in their own Agricultural Defence Associations. They locked-out Union members from their farms whether they were on strike or not. One notable local exception was the landowner John Tollemache, who told his tenant-farmers at the Great White Horse in Ipswich that he opposed the lock-out and advocated decent homes and working conditions for all labourers.

All over Suffolk, meetings were held in support of the Union members. In Ipswich, one afternoon in the spring of 1874, over 500 factory workers gathered in the Cattle Market in a show of solidarity. But by July that year, the Union had spent over £20,000 on strike pay and could not afford to carry on supporting its members. It then became the sad duty of the Union President, Joseph Arch, to advise men to go back to work and accept lower wages. Many farmers refused to take them back. Conditions were so bad that former agricultural workers were forced to emigrate. In just one week, seventy people left Suffolk for Canada. (Robert Ratcliffe, *History of Working Class Movement in Ipswich*; *Ipswich Journal*, 1872)

— MAY 30TH —

1938: Under the chairmanship of Captain 'Ivan' Cobbold, Ipswich Town Football Club was elected into Division Three of the Football League on this day.

Cobbold got hooked on football when he went to an Arsenal match. He persuaded a team of Ipswich amateur footballers to go professional, with him as chairman.

After Captain Cobbold died, his widow and sons continued to run the club for many years. They would accompany Alf Ramsey and then Bobby Robson on trips to find new players and had a veto on all signings. (Cobbold Family History Trust, Anthony Cobbold)

2000: A memorable day in St Margaret's Plain:

Ipswich Town football team drove past our bedroom window in an open-top double-decker bus. The day before, they had beaten Barnsley 4–2 in the play-off final to win a place back in the Premiership and the whole town was going crazy. The bus was on a celebratory tour, starting from the football ground and ending on the Cornhill. The streets were lined with fans. People were hanging off bridges, out of windows and up lampposts.

As the bus drove past our window, our dog looked out with a big, curly blue-and-white wig on her head. Jim Magilton saw her and was very amused. David Johnson asked us for some beer!

We got some great photos from our vantage point and later were surprised to see us all – including the dog – featured briefly on *Look East*!

(Thanks to Hannah and David Wright)

～ MAY 31 ～

1902: The *Ipswich Journal* reported that a member of the Ipswich Piscatorial Ramblers, fishing off Felixstowe Dock Pier on this Wednesday afternoon, hooked and landed a gigantic lobster weighing 5lb 14oz. (Thanks to Pip Wright)

———

1902: The South African (Boer) War ended on this day, having taken a toll of over 280 Suffolk men's lives. Most of them were from Ipswich and served in the Suffolk Regiment. Their remains were eventually gathered together and buried in the Colesberg Military Cemetery, half way between Johannesburg and Cape Town.

To honour the fallen, a concrete and bronze memorial was erected on the Ipswich Cornhill four years later. It was a life-sized statue of a uniformed soldier standing in mourning, as if by a comrade's grave. The names of the Suffolk soldiers who had died were inscribed around the base. The memorial was later moved to Christchurch Park and placed near the cenotaph. (Robert Malster: *Ipswich: An A to Z of Local History*)

———

1979: On this Thursday, 17 acres of woodland along the riverside cliff at Pin Mill became the property of the National Trust, thereby protecting it for posterity. (*East Anglian Daily Times*, 1979)

1908: Percy Edwards was born in Ipswich, the son of a tailor in Fore Street. He discovered his talent for imitating animals when he was 7. Dozing under a tree, he heard what he thought was a wolf-whistle and discovered that it was actually a greenfinch. For several weeks, Percy kept hearing this bird and found that he could imitate it. He even started eating canary seed before going to bed, hoping that he would wake in the morning singing like a bird!

Percy took to the stage aged 11 and eventually became a 'national treasure'. He was able to produce the sound of more than 600 birds, and some other animals. His repertoire was extraordinary – all 13 calls of the chaffinch, the strangely grinding sound of the amorous capercaille and corgis barking in Welsh accents. He voiced the alien in *Alien*, and provided sheep noises for Kate Bush's song 'The Dreaming'.

He was a stalwart of *The Generation Game* in the 1970s. He worked until the age of 80, giving his very last performance at the London Palladium.

He was awarded an MBE in 1993 for his services to ornithology and entertainment. He died three years later in Hintlesham. (IMDB: www.imdb.com/name/nm0250272/bio; www.ancestry. co.uk)

– JUNE 2ND –

1938: Children's book illustrator, Helen Oxenbury, was born in Ipswich.

As a child she suffered from asthma, which meant she missed a lot of school, and while she was at home she started drawing. Her father encouraged her. He would go to the library to borrow books for her and, when she left school, he decided she should go to Ipswich Art School.

During Art School holidays, Helen worked at the Ipswich Repertory Theatre, mixing paints for the sets. This led her to a course in theatre design, where she was prophetically told by a teacher: 'This is hopeless, you know. You ought to go and do illustrations – you're much more interested in character!'

She married John Burningham and they had their first child. Both inspired her to try children's illustration: John because he was already a children's book illustrator, and her daughter because eczema kept her awake at night and she liked picture books to soothe her. Helen realised there was a shortage of good baby books, so she decided to create her own.

Helen's award-winning illustrations appear in *We're Going on a Bear Hunt*, *Farmer Duck*, *Three Little Wolves and the Big Bad Pig* and *Alice in Wonderland*. (Walker Books website: www.walker.co.uk; Claudia Garza, *Author Study: Helen Oxenbury*)

– JUNE 3RD –

2009: Sir Michael Lord, Conservative MP for Central Suffolk and North Ipswich, was named in the parliamentary expenses scandal. The *Daily Telegraph* investigation revealed that he had claimed approximately £300 a month towards the mortgage on his Suffolk house, nearly £5,000 to refurbish his bathroom, over £8,000 for gardening expenses and over £7,500 for heating oil.

When he was created a Life Peer, he was introduced to the House of Lords as Baron Framlingham of Eye. The alternative would have had him known as Lord Lord! (*Daily Telegraph*, 2009)

———

2011: Nathan Ellington signed a two-year contract for Ipswich Town Football Club. Ellington, a convert to Islam, ran the Association of Muslim Footballers. He had set it up to provide Islamic professional footballers with a support network and to inform others – players, fans and management – about the faith. He said: 'Some of the boys have a joke about me praying five times a day. My nick-name is "Beardo". I can live with that – but, just think, at one club a player was called "The Bomber" because he was a Muslim.' (Sportymuslimah blog: sportymuslimah. wordpress.com)

‒ June 4th ‒

1918: The *London Gazette* announced that Kavas Jamas Badshah had been awarded an OBE in the king's birthday honours list for war services. Badshah was a councillor on Ipswich Borough Council and received the honour for his work on the Ipswich War Savings Committee.

Councillor Badshah was born in Bombay in 1859 to a wealthy Parsi family. Destined for the Indian Civil Service, he had an English public-school-style education in Bombay and continued this classical education when he studied for a year for the competitive Indian Civil Service Examination in London.

Badshah was made the Commissioner for Excise and Salt in Bengal and eventually rose to become the Magistrate and Collector of Bengal, 1st grade.

In 1885 Badshah married Emma Collington Pierson, an English woman whose family had helped govern the Raj for generations. Badshah and his family arrived in Ipswich to settle in 1892. They lived at 11 St Edmunds Road for many years, Badshah eventually joining them permanently in 1904 when he retired from the Indian Civil Service.

In 1913 he was elected as a Liberal town councillor for the Middle Ward of Ipswich, becoming mayor in 1925.

He died in Ipswich in 1931. Badshah Avenue, off Felixstowe Road, was named in his memory. (*London Gazette*, 1918; www.ancestry.co.uk; Ipswich Society)

‒ JUNE 5TH ‒

1784: The *Ipswich Journal* reported that on the previous Tuesday there was a spinning match at the Ostrich Inn near Ipswich. The competitors were two elderly women and a girl. One of the elderly women spun '11 knots within the hour' and that won her the star prize ‒ a kettle, half a pound, ½lb of tea and some blue ribbon. (Thanks to Pip Wright)

1967: Bob Dumper, inspirational English teacher at Ipswich Civic College, arranged a special lunchtime meeting of the Record Society. There was just one item on the agenda ‒ the much-anticipated new Beatles album, *Sergeant Pepper's Lonely Hearts Club Band*. Two of his students, Paul Field and Robin Gilchrist, helped, and Brian Eno from Ipswich Art School came in to do to a light show ‒ coloured oils swirling between the glass plates of a projector.

Years later, Paul said: 'I remember Eno's light show so clearly ‒ but now I'm not so sure he was even still in Ipswich by that time. But, as the saying goes ‒ if you can remember the '60s, you weren't really there!' (Thanks to Paul Field and Bob Dumper)

~ June 6th ~

1839: George Hines was born to an agricultural labouring family in Tattingstone. He was the person who finally succeeded in getting a Co-operative Society off the ground in Ipswich.

He grew up in Ipswich, stepson of a railway labourer, and spent several years in the Navy, including some time in the Crimean War. When he returned to Ipswich in the early 1860s he got married and worked for the Great Eastern Railway as a fireman, which was a heavy, dirty job.

George and a group of like-minded men got a Co-operative Society started in Ipswich in 1867. Earlier attempts had been unsuccessful. A Co-op shop had previously opened at 34 Carr Street in the 1840s (about the same time as the Rochdale Pioneers established the very first Co-op), but it was short-lived.

By March 1868, George and his fellow co-operators had registered the new society as a co-operative and a year later opened their first shop, again at 34 Carr Street.

Eventually, George went to work for the Society full-time, ending up as an accountant and then a director. He was able to move to North Bank, Belstead Road, and employ a domestic servant. He left £2,000 to his young widow when he died in 1914. (East of England Co-operative Society: www.eastofengland. coop/about-us/our-history; www.ancestry.co.uk)

- JUNE 7TH -

1915: Betty Reid (1915–2004) was born in Ipswich on or about this day. As a young woman, she joined the Communist Party (CPGB) and worked at their headquarters in London. A 'tough-minded Stalinist' and a good administrator, she was given overall responsibility for enforcing internal party discipline and making sure the party was not infiltrated by the British security services.

However, in the event, Reid herself was completely compromised. During the Cold War, MI5 followed her everywhere she went, recorded the identity of every person she met, listened to and transcribed every phone call she made, and opened and copied every letter she received. Even the live-in home-help she employed from an advert in the *Soviet Weekly* turned out to be an MI5 plant. (Interview by Andrew Whitehead: www.andrewwhitehead.net; CPGB archives)

2012: A rare prehistoric whistle was discovered in an Iron Age settlement site at Brett Quarry. Coddenham. Suffolk Archaeological Service said that the whistle was an unusual and exciting find. It was a simple one-hole instrument made from a spike of deer antler. It was the first Iron Age whistle discovered in this region, and possibly in England, though a similar bone instrument had been found in Scotland. Archaeologists could not give a precise dating for the new find, but suggested that somewhere between 300 BC and AD 1 was likely. (Brett Aggregates, owners of the quarry)

– JUNE 8TH –

2004: Members of the Orwell Astronomical Society Ipswich observed the transit of Venus using the Tomline Refractor Telescope at their observatory at Orwell Park School. The planet Venus was seen as a small black disc moving across the face of the sun as it passed directly between the Earth and the sun. No one alive at the time had previously seen the phenomenon because the last one had occurred in 1882. Their observations were compiled into a report which was presented to Sir Patrick Moore. (Orwell Astronomical Society Ipswich)

—–—

2012: The second day of the Suffolk Show at Trinity Park was cancelled at the eleventh hour after a night of raging winds. Several marquees had already blown over and force 9 gales were forecast. Suffolk Agricultural Association (SAA) was forced to make the unprecedented decision to cancel the day's events at about 8 a.m. Visitors had to evacuate the showground and stallholders started dismantling their weather-beaten stands. Approximately 30,000 people had been expected that day but the organisers said they had no choice but to call off the event and offer refunds. The cancellation meant that the SAA lost over half a million pounds that day. The previous time that the show had been cancelled was in 2001, when there was a national foot and mouth outbreak. (Coastal Scene online newspaper: www.coastalscene24.co.uk/home; *East Anglian Daily Times*, 2012)

‒ June 9th ‒

2008: A huge sculpture commemorating British computer pioneers was unveiled at Grange Farm, Kesgrave. Bev Price, who worked just round the corner at Autism Suffolk, said:

> We watched them building something next to St Isidore's roundabout for ages. The foundations were so deep we were certain that they were installing some sort of secret underground bunker. We were astonished when we found out that it was a monument to the people who developed electronic computers. Apparently, the beginnings of computing were shrouded in secrecy because it was during the Second World War, so the early pioneers aren't household names.
>
> I was told that the monument is nearly 10m high. It's made up of three enormous curved granite shapes. When they were installing it earlier this year two of the shapes were dropped and had to be re-cut at the factory in Brittany. There are lots of storyboards around the outside of the monument and they tell the story of computing and code-breaking in the early days.
>
> It's very distinctive looking and I'm not sure I like it. Perhaps it will grow on me now I know what it's about.

(Thanks to Bev Price)

– JUNE 10TH –

1892: Margaret Tempest was born on or about this day into a well-known Ipswich family: her father and brother were mayors of Ipswich and her elder brother was Rector of Kersey. Margaret showed an early gift for drawing. She attended the Art School in Ipswich before going on to Westminster School of Art in 1914. Between the wars, Margaret was a member of a successful Chelsea studio and did some freelance teaching. Peter Scott was one of her pupils.

She returned to Ipswich in 1939 and spent the rest of her long life there. By this time, she had already begun the work she was to be remembered for. In 1929, she had accepted a commission to illustrate Alison Uttley's *Little Grey Rabbit* books and continued to do so into the 1960s, by which time thirty-four titles had appeared and the characters of Little Grey Rabbit, Squirrel and Hare were known to generations of girls.

Unfortunately, Alison and Margaret did not get on. Alison often judged other women cruelly. She particularly resented Margaret's claim that it was the drawings, not the writing, that had created the success of the books. Alison wrote in her diary that Margaret 'is a humourless bore, seldom does a smile come, her eyes cold and hard ... she is absolutely awful'. (Manchester University website: www.manchester.ac.uk; thanks to Sheila Hardy)

— June 11th —

1846: The new Colchester to Ipswich railway track was opened, thus extending the London line into Suffolk. Six hundred 'of the fairer portion of creation' waved 'snowy kerchiefs' and greeted the first train. The usual civic celebrations were laid on – bells, bunting, bands and banners – all topped off by a slap-up banquet for the railway Directors and their gentleman guests with iced champagne at the New Assembly Rooms.

The first train left at 10.25 a.m. Ipswich time, bound for Colchester, and it was cheered at all along the way. It arrived back in Ipswich just after 1 p.m.

The original station was in Croft Street in Stoke which was the first convenient point east of Stoke Hill and close to the old quay for the steamboats.

The same year, a continuously curving tunnel was cut through Stoke Hill. The tunnel opened on 26 November 1846 with a trial train running through to Bury St Edmunds.

The railway station moved to its present location in Burrell Road in 1860 and the Croft Street site was used for engine sheds and sidings. (Carol Twinch, *Ipswich Street by Street*; *Ipswich Journal*, 1846)

– June 12th –

1861: St Pancras' Roman Catholic church in Tacket Street was opened and blessed. St Mary's Catholic church in Woodbridge Road was already established but Ipswich Catholics also wanted one in the town centre.

The new building was largely financed by a legacy from the Abbé Simon who had founded St Mary's. Intended originally to be a cathedral, St Pancras' never achieved that status.

The building was austere from the outside but the interior was warm and light, with Venetian-style arches in red-and-white brick, cast-iron pillars and wall tiles.

The Catholic population of Ipswich was only about sixty at the time St Pancras' church opened and there was still generally a good deal of anti-Catholic feeling in the town. Two years after the church was consecrated, St Pancras' was the target of a series of anti-Catholic riots, culminating around the time of Guy Fawkes Night with the curate barricading himself in the presbytery. The riot was only suppressed when the mayor of Ipswich called in 200 special constables. In the longer term, though, the riots were credited with creating some sympathy for the Catholic community among local dignitaries. (St Pancras Catholic church centenary souvenir and guide)

~ June 13th ~

1813: John Dallenger was baptised in Ipswich. He became a rather colourful character who sometimes got caught sailing a bit too close to the wind.

First apprenticed as a clerk, he later became well known in the Woodbridge area as an auctioneer. In 1843 John was appointed to run the workhouse in Wickham Market: he was doing well and living in substantial house in Wickham with his young family. Soon, Dallenger was also elected secretary of the Wickham Market Money Club. But by 1849, problems were coming to light. He was accused of falsifying the Money Club accounts. Although never prosecuted, he left Wickham in disgrace.

Dallenger did not keep his head down for long. He settled in Woodbridge and became an 'inspector of nuisances'. He also helped to run several local charities, played bowls, gave poetry readings, wrote for newspapers and was a keen Freemason. But by 1864, he was in trouble again – this time for embezzling money from the Suffolk Poultry Show. Several court cases followed and he was made bankrupt.

Dallenger and his wife separated in the 1870s. He then lived openly in The Thoroughfare with a straw-bonnet maker half his age, along with their two young sons.

Dallenger came to a sorry end. He died at the lunatic asylum in Melton in 1887. (www.ancestry.co.uk; *Ipswich Journal*, various dates; Tony Copsey, *Suffolk Writers Who Were Born Between 1800–1900*)

– JUNE 14TH –

1905: John Glyde died in Ipswich on this day. He was an energetic social historian and a well-known reformer of his day.

Glyde was born in Ipswich in 1823. He lived much of his early life in Eagle Street. The son of an Ipswich hairdresser, he worked in his father's shop after leaving school, but from an early age was interested in politics, religion and current affairs, and so he joined the Mechanics' Institute at 15.

Glyde's first major work was *The Moral, Social and Religious Condition of Ipswich*, which was published in 1850. He drew on published reports and surveys about Ipswich, to which he added his own observations, so compiling a vivid picture of contemporary Ipswich – warts and all.

Glyde took an active interest in a wide range of social topics. He wrote to the newspapers, went to meetings and campaigned tirelessly. His causes included the abolition of slavery and capital punishment, and the improvement of conditions for the poor. He had a wide circle of eminent correspondents and set up a free library in the town. Gradually, Glyde moved away from hairdressing. He eventually ran a business as a bookseller and stationer and was also Registrar of Marriages for Ipswich for forty years. (Hilary Platts, *John Glyde*)

— JUNE 15TH —

1528: The Bishop of Lincoln laid the foundation stone for St Mary Cardinal College of Ipswich – Thomas Wolsey's grand project for his hometown.

The new college was to be built near modern-day College Street, and the powerful Wolsey financed it by summarily closing down the Priory of Saints Peter and Paul and several local parish churches.

The college, with its dean, secular canons, clerks and choristers, was opened with a pageant later in 1528, but it was only a matter of months before Cardinal Wolsey fell from grace. He died shortly afterwards and the college in Ipswich was closed. The Crown took possession of the college buildings and, over the years, the only part left standing was Wolsey's Gate. This was built as a small brick gateway for people arriving at the college by water, the quayside being then where College Street and Key Street were later built, some 50m from the modern waterfront. (Carol Twinch, *Ipswich Street by Street*; Robert Malster, *Ipswich: An A to Z of Local History*)

~ June 16th ~

1381: Ipswich was taken over by rebels who had gathered under two local leaders of what became known as the Peasants Revolt. They were John Battisford, parson of Bucklesham, and Thomas Sampson of Harkstead, a wealthy tenant farmer – so neither of them peasants! In Suffolk, as in the rest of the country, the new Poll Tax had united an impoverished and dissatisfied population, and open rebellion against the Crown broke out.

Several thousand men entered Ipswich unopposed on this day. They looted the Archdeacon of Suffolk's house, and damaged property belonging to tax officers. Wealthy men fled and one was murdered. Rebels spread out over east Suffolk and attracted two more leaders – James Bedingfield and Richard Talmache of Bentley, both young men training to be knights. Insurgents burned court records and destroyed property. They were searching in particular for Edmund Lakenheath, a wealthy magistrate, who had escaped them in Ipswich. He finally got away from Suffolk in a boat, only to be captured by a French pirate.

On 23rd June, 500 lancers under the Earl of Suffolk arrived in Ipswich from London. There was no battle – the rebel bands just melted away without resistance. (Charles Omam, *Great Revolt of 1381*; Alistair Dunn, *Great Rising of 1381: the court records*; Edgar Powell, *Rising of 1381 in East Anglia*)

– June 17th –

1564: Emme, widow of wealthy merchant Thomas Pownder, died in Ipswich. The Pownders' ships sailed far and wide, with cargoes marked with a capital T and two crosses. Thomas had even sailed to Iceland in 1506 with a mixed cargo to barter with the islanders for dried cod and blubber. When he died in 1525, Emme was allowed to continue the business as a freewoman of Ipswich.

After Thomas' death, a beautiful brass depicting him with Emme and their eight children was installed at St Mary-at-the-Quay parish church. A gap was left in the text for her name to be filled in when she died. But Emme was not buried there and the gap left for her name never filled in.

But why was the brass never completed? The answer lay in the religious changes of the Reformation which occurred between Thomas' death in 1525 and Emme's in 1564. Emme adhered to the new religion, which was not even known to Thomas. She stopped going to St Mary-at-the-Quay church and started worshipping with her daughter at St Clement's, where many fellow Protestants gathered. And that is where she was buried and why the family brass was never completed. (John Blatchly and Peter Northeast, *The Pownder Memorial*)

— JUNE 18TH —

1958: Benjamin Britten's children's opera, *Noyes Fludde*, received its world premiere at Orford church, starring young people from Ipswich and east Suffolk schools. It was Britten's most extended and elaborate work for children, with the music often tailored to take account of the abilities of the less accomplished players.

With the exceptions of Noye himself, Noye's wife and the Voice of God, most of the main vocal parts were written for children, many whom wore lifelike animal masks. The orchestral forces comprised strings, recorders, bugles, handbells and a large assortment of percussion including such home-made instruments as sandpaper blocks and slung mugs.

The congregation (not to be called an audience, at Britten's insistence) was no doubt packed with proud parents as well as the usual Aldeburgh Festival crowd. They all got the opportunity to sing three hymns, 'Lord Jesus, Think on Me', 'Eternal Father, Strong to Save' and 'The Spacious Firmament'.

A young Tom Peters of Ipswich played double bass in the performance. He said: 'We learned our parts from a demo recording which Britten gave to our music teachers. He played the piano and recorder parts. I loved doing it and I'm so proud I was in it.' (Introduction to *Noyes Fludde*: www.brittenpears.org/index.php; Thanks to Tom Peters)

– JUNE 19TH –

1918: The last person in Britain to die of a naturally occurring outbreak of plague was Mrs Gertrude Garrod of Erwarton. Gertrude lived in an isolated cottage in Warren Lane. Her neighbour, Annie, fell ill early in June and Gertrude called in one day to help. What a shock when Annie died the following day and Gertrude also took ill.

Gertrude's GP suspected the plague when he saw that she was breathing rapidly and coughing up blood. Plague was confirmed, and Gertrude died three days later. Everyone who had been in contact with Gertrude and Annie's families was sent into isolation at Tattingstone Workhouse. All their clothing and bedding was burnt.

How did plague reach this remote part of Suffolk? It was thought that infected rats had been brought ashore in grain sacks from ships moored in the Orwell and Stour. Between 1906 and 1918 a total of twenty-two people died of plague on the Shotley peninsula and along the Nacton shore. (John and Dorothy Black, *Plague in East Suffolk 1906–1918*; www.ancestry.co.uk)

— June 20th —

1774: Wheelwright and carpenter John Day, from Ipswich, built a watertight compartment into the hull of a small wooden ship. He had tested it in Norfolk but, in order to win a wager that would provide funding to develop this prototype submarine, he had to climb on board and sink it for twelve hours in the rocky depths of Plymouth Sound.

So, on this day, the ship was towed into Plymouth Sound. John took a candle, water and biscuits on board with him, the boat was locked, weighted down and sank beneath the waves. Shortly afterwards, a great bubble of air burst to the surface as the vessel imploded. John Day and his craft were never seen again.

John holds the sad distinction of being the first person to die in a submarine accident. (BBC *Making History* programme, broadcast on Radio 4 on December 31st 2013)

1938: A passenger service from Ipswich airport to Clacton came into operation. It was run by the Straight Corporation using a five-seater Short Scion. The fare was 9s 6d return or 6s 6d single, and the flight lasted 15 minutes each way. The service was short-lived. When war broke out in 1939, the RAF moved in and Ipswich airport became a satellite of RAF Wattisham. Blenheim bombers bound for German targets replaced the daily Clacton passenger shuttle. (Philip Langford, *Ipswich Airport*, Robert Malster, *Ipswich, an A to Z of Local History*)

– JUNE 21ST –

1959: Maggie Parsons said:

The Caravan Mission to Village Children came to our village on this day, which was my 10th birthday. The evangelist was a Mr Price, who arrived in his caravan and set up the mission tent for a few days at Giddings Farm, which was right in the middle of the village.

Some of the kids went every morning on the way to school, and most of us went on the way home too. We loved it. We sang choruses and learned bits of the Bible. Mr Price played the harmonium and we sung our hearts out as if we were at the Saturday morning pictures. It was something different to do and I'm afraid the Christianity bit didn't really go in.

I remember the text we learned for the day of my birthday was 'The heart is deceitful above all things, and desperately wicked – Jeremiah 17: 9'. You had to say the whole lot.

I got a prize for good attendance. It was a book called *The Secret of Woodside Cottage*, but the secret was Jesus. I was disappointed because I thought it would be about smugglers or burglars!

Mr Price travelled all round Suffolk and Cambridgeshire and we were jolly glad to see him again when he came back the following year.

(Thanks to Maggie Parsons)

‒ June 22nd ‒

1340: Edward III set sail from Ipswich at the head of a great fleet of 200 warships. The expedition to fight the French completely filled the port. Preparations had occupied all of Ipswich and the surrounding countryside, and men were recruited from every quarter – including the prisons.

The battle was fought two days later off Sluys (now in Belgium) and was a decisive victory for the English. Most of the French fleet was destroyed, ensuring that England was not invaded for the rest of the Hundred Years' War.

On his return to Ipswich in the July, Edward was welcomed back with a victory celebration which included a procession of local friars who were given 1 groat each for taking part. (L J Redstone, *Ipswich Through the Ages*)

2007: Work began on a prestigious £70 million regeneration project on the site of Cranfield's Flour Mill at Ipswich Docks. It was the tallest building in Suffolk: a twenty-three-storey block intended to house over 300 apartments, a hotel, restaurants, shops, bars and a state-of-the-art dance house. However, with the Irish banking crisis, the developers went into administration and work stopped. The dance house opened but there were no hotels, shops or restaurants. Construction of two-thirds of the flats was still incomplete several years later. (*Ipswich Evening Star*, 2007)

~ JUNE 23RD ~

2006: A security guard was airlifted to Ipswich Hospital when fire broke out on Sealand, the former military platform off Felixstowe, owned and 'ruled' by the self-styled Prince Roy. A helicopter from Wattisham airfield rescued the injured man from the 'kingdom' and the Harwich lifeboat was in attendance. It was thought that a generator had caught fire and set light to the top of the structure.

Sealand was badly damaged but, fortunately, Prince Roy was not in residence at the time. The founder of the micro-state had already abdicated and retired with his wife to Spain. He had originally taken over the windswept outpost in 1967 and declared it an independent nation with its own passports, coinage and stamps. Its territorial waters included most of the Orwell Estuary, extending nearly as far up as the A14 bridge.

Considering the extensive damage done by the fire, repairs to Sealand were completed quickly. According to reports, in addition to the usual living accommodation, Sealand soon boasted a new roof with helicopter pads, a royal palace, an employees' suite, a chapel, a parliament room, and an office for the Bureau of Domestic and International Affairs. (BBC News: http://news.bbc.co.uk/1/hi/5110244.stm)

~ June 24th ~

1897: As part of the town's Diamond Jubilee Celebrations marking Queen Victoria's sixty years on the throne, upwards of 12,000 children were given a treat in Christchurch Park by the mayor of Ipswich. The catering was provided by Messrs Kitton, bakers and confectioners of Norwich Road. (*The Eastern Counties' Chronology or Book of Dates*, 1906)

1898: The Eastern Counties Coal Boring and Development Association met at Ipswich town hall to wind up their operation. Encouraged by the work of Dr John Ellor Taylor of Ipswich Museum, they had been looking for mineable coal deposits near Ipswich but had failed to find any. Their first trial-boring was at Crepping Hall, Stutton. The bore had drilled down to 1,525ft without discovering any coal. Soon after this, a similarly unsuccessful bore was sunk in Weeley in north east Essex. Following these fruitless attempts, the association ran out of money and could fund no further explorations, much to the relief of many villagers and subsequent generations. (*Ipswich Journal*, 1898)

2010: This mindboggling headline appeared in the *Evening Star*: 'Ipswich "Jesus" in my Garden'. (*Ipswich Evening Star*, 2010)

~ June 25th ~

1887: Work to erect Holly Lodge Mission Hall in Bramford Lane began, encouraged by the four Peddar sisters, who owned the land. It was a cheap-and-cheerful iron pre-fab. Some 100 years later, Simon Knott was enthusiastic about the building:

> There is something very jolly about corrugated-iron churches, especially when they are brightly painted and clearly loved by the community that uses them. They were very popular as a means of providing new churches for expanding populations in the last years of the nineteenth century and the early years of the next. Relatively cheap and easy to assemble (typically costing about £100), they were churned out in large numbers by many firms, including Boulton & Paul in Norwich.
>
> Popularly known as tin tabernacles, about half a dozen survive in East Anglia. Easy to assemble, they were easy to demolish as well …
>
> Holly Lodge Baptist church sits in the narrow terraces of Bramford Lane, and you wouldn't even know it was there unless you looked for it. Less ambitious than some, it has no bell turret or spire, but the frontage is pleasingly gothic, and that bright red paint makes the church an adornment to the street.

The building was demolished in 2008 and replaced by a bricks-and-mortar church in the following year. (Thanks to Simon Knott)

~ June 26th ~

1853: On or about this date, Mary Ann Adams and her brother Thomas, from Copdock, started their one and only summer season at the Cremorne Pleasure Gardens in London. At 3 years of age, Mary already weighed 6 stone, while Thomas was 5 and weighed 8 stone. The pair were billed as the 'Suffolk Prodigies, the most wonderful examples of colossal infantile development'.

Mary and Thomas had been put on show by Frederick de Grey, rector of Copdock, to raise funds for their upkeep as their parents were too poor to support them.

The children topped the bill and drew the crowds in. Other performers included Hungarian musicians, comic turns, acrobats, and fireworks, all topped off with a balloon ascent.

Such was their success that the siblings were immediately booked to appear on a variety bill in Hoxton, but they went back to Suffolk instead. Sadly, Thomas had become ill, and by the Christmas that year he had died. (www.ancestry.co.uk; theatre poster; London newspapers, various dates and titles)

2009: The unappealing headline: 'Swimmers Reassured Over Brown Sea Foam' appeared in the *Ipswich Evening Star*. (*Ipswich Evening Star*, 2009)

– JUNE 27TH –

1857: An advertisement appeared in the Ipswich press on this day, and it was one of the first to advertise that babies' perambulators were on sale in the town. Prams started to become popular among the upper and middle classes in the 1840s. Before then, small children had to be carried by their mothers or nursemaids if they went out. According to the advert, prams were available in Ipswich from E.W. Bishops' Brush Manufactory in the Post Office Buildings. They sold 'fancy wicker perambulators', which were, in essence, large wicker baskets on wheels. (*Ipswich Journal*, 1857)

2003: A fly-on-the-wall documentary was aired on BBC Two depicting a year in the life of Jimmy Doherty and his girlfriend, Michaela Furney. The TV series *Jimmy's Farm* told the story of how Jimmy and his partner set up the Essex Pig Company, a rare breeds piggery, on the outskirts of Ipswich.

Twenty-eight-year-old Jimmy knew nothing about pig farming and the series followed his efforts to produce high quality meat from the endangered Essex pig, as well as from other rare breeds of pig, sheep and cattle. The show was so successful that Jimmy's career as a TV presenter was assured and his farm became a local attraction. (*Jimmy's Farm*, BBC)

~ June 28th ~

1838: Queen Victoria was crowned at Westminster Abbey. Two days later, the *Ipswich Journal* struck an indignant tone, complaining that all our town got in the way of civic celebrations was 'a dinner for children'. It was all very well that 450 children from charity schools were treated to a meal in the grounds of Christchurch Park. And it was all very well that the mayor and a few of his friends spent the afternoon in the Suffolk Hotel drinking Her Majesty's health in 'flowing bumpers'. But compared with surrounding towns and villages, Ipswich's festivities were sadly lacking. Where, the *Journal* thundered, were the 'cakes and ale' for the poorer classes? Why was there no quaffing of the Queen's health in 'nut-brown October beer'?

Elsewhere in Suffolk, towns and villages were decorated with shrubs, flowers and flags. There were gun salutes, music in the streets, rustic sports and people tucking into 'excellent dinners of roast beef and plum pudding'.

Why were celebrations so stinted in Ipswich? The *Journal* explained that although the mayor had declared the day a holiday, he had not offered any funds for the townsfolk to celebrate in the proper manner. (*Ipswich Journal*, 1838)

– JUNE 29TH –

1200: Ipswich people gathered in the churchyard of St-Mary-le-Tower to elect two bailiffs and four coroners for the first time. The town had recently received a charter from King John allowing them to run their own affairs.

'With one voice', John fitz Norman and William de Beaumes were chosen as bailiffs and were also elected to be two of the coroners. They were brothers of Norman descent, and their family were to become borough leaders for the next few generations. Philip de Porta and Roger Lew became the other two coroners. All four men swore to behave well and faithfully to both poor and rich.

On the same day, it was decided 'by common counsel of the town' that they should choose a council of twelve sworn men (portmen) to help govern and maintain the borough, and so it was agreed that the whole town should return to the churchyard on the following Sunday to elect them.

Over the course of the next months, town meetings continued to be held in St-Mary-le-Tower churchyard to choose more officials and to decide the nuts and bolts of how the town was to be run. (Medieval towns website: users.trytel.com/~tristan/towns/towns.html)

~ June 30th ~

1795: Race Week, the highlight of the Ipswich social calendar, began this Tuesday. The town filled to overflowing with county families, their guests and their servants. Hardy race goers made their way to the 2-mile loop on Nacton Heath where the racecourse was set out. 'The better sort' would have breakfasted well, and the races started in the middle of the day to accommodate this early feasting.

Gentlemen and officers from the cavalry barracks made their way to watch the racing from the covered Gentlemen's Stand, while the hoi polloi stood next to the course, unprotected from the elements.

The main event this Tuesday was His Majesty's Plate race, run for 100 guineas. It was actually poorly attended – it rained all afternoon so most racegoers stayed undercover in town. There was plenty for them to do. Every Race Week hosted an entertaining sideshow of some kind, and this year it was a menagerie, complete with an elephant. Admission was a shilling; servants paid half price. The evening was taken up with dining, public balls and trips to the theatre for those who could afford such diversions. (Robert Malster, *Ipswich: An A to Z of Local History*; Sheila Hardy, *Frances, Lady Nelson*; *Ipswich Journal*, 1795)

~ July 1st ~

1971: Nobel Prize winner Sir Lawrence Bragg (b. 1890) died in Ipswich Hospital.

Born in Australia, Bragg came to England to study mathematics and physics at Trinity College, Cambridge. At the age of just 25, he and his father were jointly awarded the 1915 Nobel Prize for Physics for their work on X-rays and crystals. Even into the twenty-first century, they remained the only father and son team to receive the prize and Bragg junior was still the youngest winner to date.

For a period of Bragg's professional life, he was the director of the Cavendish Laboratory in Cambridge where Crick and Watson discovered the structure of DNA in 1953. James Watson wrote that, even though Bragg played no direct part in their work: 'the X-ray method he had developed 40 years before was at the heart of this profound insight into the nature of life itself.' As their head of department, it was Bragg who announced Crick and Watson's epoch-making discovery to the world. He also successfully lobbied for them to be awarded Nobel Prizes in 1962.

Bragg spent his retirement at Quietways in Waldringfield where he enjoyed painting and gardening. He died of cancer and was cremated in Ipswich after a funeral in Waldringfield. (Tony Copsey, *Suffolk Writers Who Were Born Between 1800–1900*; *Dictionary of National Biography*)

– JULY 2ND –

1937: On or about this day, Chloe Vulliamy, a solicitor's daughter from Ipswich, opened a colony at Wherstead Hall for children who had been evacuated from Spain.

When the Spanish Civil War broke out in 1936, Miss Vulliamy was living on the Costa Brava. She returned to Britain and became involved with caring for children escaping the fighting. These children, mostly from Republican families in the Basque region of northern Spain and travelling without their parents, left for Britain on the steamship *Habana* in May 1937. They arrived in Southampton and stayed at a large camp there before being dispersed to smaller colonies around the country, including Wherstead Park.

Many of the *niños vascos* had fond memories of their time at Wherstead. They were comfortable in the large house and grounds and admired Miss Vulliamy. A feature in the Basque Children's newsletter remembered her affectionately:

> She was striking-looking, quite Spanish in her polka dot dresses, her hair parted in the middle, pulled back behind the ears and twisted into a bun. She was rarely seen without a cigarette and the *niños* thought her daring. She organised parties for the older girls in the colony, inviting pupils from nearby schools, allowing them to stay until midnight and playing the piano for them to dance to.

(Basque Children of '37 Association: www.basquechildren.org)

~ July 3rd ~

1811: The *Bury & Norwich Post* carried the news that the Rotunda, a market house on the east side of the Cornhill, was being pulled down after being condemned as a public nuisance. The circular building looked attractive but was never popular because, even though it housed a series of butchers' stalls, it did not have adequate ventilation. It stank! (*Bury & Norwich Post*, 1811)

1851: During the visit of Prince Albert to lay the foundation stone at Ipswich School:

> … an incident occurred which resulted in the town being banned from seeing members of the royal family visit the borough for seventy-five years …
>
> Somewhere along the route, six words shouted out in broad Suffolk by someone in the crowd, were to have a disastrous consequence. 'Goo hoom, yer rotten ole Jarman.' Albert probably did not understand but courtiers reported this to the Queen on return to Buckingham Palace and Victoria banned visits to the town. No member of the royal family came to Ipswich for the next three-quarters of a century.

(David Kindred's website: kindred-spirit.co.uk)

– JULY 4TH –

1904: The *Dundee Evening Telegraph* reported that the entire body of inhabitants of the village of Harkstead were indicted at the Ipswich Quarter Sessions for permitting the highway to be out of repair. Two residents, John Smith and Robert Wrinch, went to court to represent all the villagers. Verdict: not guilty. (*Dundee Evening Telegraph*, 1904)

———

1937: The Cobbold Stand at Ipswich Town's football stadium at Portman Road was refurbished with 650 tip-up wooden seats bought second-hand from Arsenal Football Club. Previously, the club's groundsman had kept sheep, goats and poultry in the stand – which had become known as the 'chicken run'.

Four decades later, the whole seating stand was moved to Foxhall Road where it stood for many years overlooking the track at the Ipswich Witches Speedway circuit. (Extremegroundhopping Ralph Morris' blog: http://extremegroundhopping.wordpress.com)

———

1940: A Second World War naval base was commissioned at Ipswich Docks on or about this date. It was at Cliff Quay and acted as a base for Allied patrol trawlers and naval launches operating in the North Sea. They were armed with anti-aircraft guns made at the nearby Cocksedge engineering works. The base was named HMS *Bunting* after its master ship. (Robert Malster, *Ipswich: An A to Z of Local History*)

– July 5th –

1902: The first ever case to be bought under the new Public Bodies Corrupt Practices Act was reported on this day. It had been heard at Ipswich Quarter Sessions.

Charles Freeman, a butcher of Claydon, was convicted of attempts to bribe the master of Ipswich workhouse, the allegation being that he offered him a forequarter of lamb if he would overlook a default in the meat contract. Fine: £10.
(*Northamptonshire Evening Telegraph*, 1902)

2012: The Olympic torch relay arrived in Ipswich by boat, coming up the Orwell from Fox's Marina.

Ken Feltwell, who had to be dragged down to the docks by a friend to see it, said:

> I thought it was going to be all hype and PR, but it was exciting. We stood by the lock into the wet dock and had a grandstand view. Hardly anyone else was there – all the crowds were down on the Waterfront. So we saw the press helicopter, then the boat carrying the torch bearers coming up the river. The flame was handed over to another boat in the lock and then taken into the wet dock to be greeted by the thousands of people gathered there.
>
> There were hardly any of the press or commercial razzamatazz where we were, although we did see some of the *Look East* TV team rushing about looking hassled. We had a great view. I'm glad I went.

(Thanks to Ken Feltwell)

~ July 6th ~

1911: On this day, as on many other schooldays, the 13-year-old Percy Burrows sold rosebud buttonholes outside Ipswich railway station.

He had applied to the council for an official street trader's badge and was given a permit when he showed that he could do simple sums in his head. On days when there were excursions leaving from Ipswich station, he would make his way there from his home in Cavendish Street with his basket of flowers on one arm and his trader's badge on the other.

He sold each buttonhole for a penny, including a pin, and paid 3*d* in the shilling for the pitch.

Trade was always brisk, and all his buttonholes were sold in half an hour. Then it was back home via Boasts' Coffee Shop in Duke Street for a penny cup of coffee and a dough bun, then off came his badge, and it was time to go to school. (*Ipswich Evening Star*, 1982, letter from Percy Burrows)

1919: Peace Day was celebrated to mark the signing of the Treaty of Versailles – the official end of the First World War.

At Warren Heath, a twenty-one-gun salute was fired at midday, followed by the National Anthem and *Speed the Plough*, the official march of the Suffolk Regiment.

In the town, huge crowds gathered in the Cornhill and they followed a military pipe band up Northgate Street to Christchurch Park, where there was a spectacular swimming display in the Round Pond, which had been cleared with an oyster dredge to get rid of the old rubbish. (Neil Wylie, Robert Malster, and David Kindred, *Ipswich at War*)

~ July 7th ~

1657: On or about this date, Cave Beck, master of Ipswich Grammar School, resigned his teaching post and published a book explaining the universal written language he had devised. The Universal Character described how the letters of the alphabet and the numbers 1 to 9 could be combined to encode words so that readers of every language could read and understand what was written. As an example, 'Honour thy father and mother' became 'leb2314 p2477 pf2477'.

The system may have been logical but it was far from easy to use. The book itself was so full of printing errors that the printer had to add a list of corrections (which actually did not cover half the errors made) with a polite note: 'Reader, be pleased to correct these mistakes with thy pen.'

Beck hoped that his work would promote trade and make the work of converting the world's peoples to Christianity easier. The engraved frontispiece of the book shows a European (thought to be Beck himself) handing down a scroll to a turbaned Indian, an African and a Native American.

Not surprisingly, Beck's system did not catch on. (Robert Malster, *Ipswich: An A to Z of Local History*; linguistics website: fiatlingua.org)

– July 8th –

1939: Havelock Ellis (b. 1859) died at his house, Cherry Ground, in Hintlesham. He was a medical doctor and a prolific writer about sexuality.

In 1897, he wrote the first ever study in which homosexuality was not characterised as a disease, a crime or immoral. The book was banned as 'lewd, wicked, bawdy, and scandalous' and one bookseller was convicted of obscene libel for stocking it.

Ellis published works on a variety of other sexual practices and inclinations, often from a psychoanalytical point of view.

Ellis' personal life was unusual, to say the least. He got married in 1891 to Edith Lees, a women's rights activist and a lesbian. At the end of the honeymoon, Ellis went back alone to his bachelor rooms in Paddington and Edith continued to live at her previous home.

After his wife died in 1916, Ellis had several fervent though chaste relationships with women. According to Ellis' autobiography, his close friends were amused that he was nevertheless considered to be an expert on sex. They knew that he suffered from impotence until the age of 60, when he discovered that he could after all become aroused, but only by the sight of a woman urinating. (Tony Copsey, *Suffolk Writers Who Were Born Between 1800–1900*; *Australian Dictionary of Biography*; Spartacus Educational website: www.spartacus.schoolnet.co.uk)

‑ JULY 9TH ‑

1656: John Evelyn – royalist, Anglican and diarist – travelled from Dedham to Ipswich. He recorded: 'at Ipswich I had the curiosity to visit some Quakers there in prison – a new fanatical sect of dangerous principles. They show no respect to any man, magistrate or other, and seem a melancholy, proud sort of people – and exceedingly ignorant.' (John Evelyn's diary)

2010: On this Friday evening, the internationally renowned Suffolk artist, Maggi Hambling, opened the old Ipswich Art School as an art gallery. She was a appropriate choice as she had trained at the art school, attended Amberfield School near Ipswich, and was born in Sudbury. The opening exhibition displayed works from Charles Saatchi's gallery in London, including a giant sculpture of a bed. Work by former Ipswich Art School artists, such as intricate botanical drawings by Guy Eves, was also exhibited. The Greyhound, just round the corner, was packed with former students, art teachers and visitors meeting up for a couple of drinks before the grand opening. (Thanks to Paul Field)

– JULY 10TH –

1803: A local farmer bemoaned the changes he saw in Ipswich:

> Barracks for soldiers are building everywhere at a most shamefaced
> and enormous waste of public money. 1800 men are employed at
> Ipswich and as many at Woodbridge. They are paid from 3/6 to 5/6
> each per day and are paid double wages on Sundays, when carting,
> sawing, building, drinking, swearing and debauchery go on in a
> greater degree for being the Lord's Day. Thousands of this mob meet
> a few sober folks going to church. What an excellent example this, set
> by a pious Government?

(Mrs Rothery, ed., *Diaries of William Goodwin of Street Farm, Earl Soham*)

1940: RAF Martlesham Heath was attacked by Nazi aircraft
on this Wednesday. Fortunately, little damage was sustained, as
most of the British planes were airborne at the time. The base
was the most northerly of the 11 Group airfields during the Battle
of Britain.

During the early part of the Second World War, Blenheims,
Hurricanes, Spitfires and Typhoons all operated from
Martlesham Heath. Among the famous airmen based there
were Douglas Bader, Peter Townsend (later famously coupled
with Princess Margaret), Ian Smith (the last Rhodesian prime
minister) and flying ace Robert Stanford Tuck.

The airbase was handed over to the United States Air Force in
1943. (Martlesham Heath History leaflet)

~ July 11th ~

1910: Ipswich-born Edith Cook, balloonist, parachutist and pilot, took part in a display over Coventry and fell to her death.

Originally from Fore Street in Ipswich, Edith had left Suffolk in her early 20s to learn to fly at the Bleriot School in France where she was the first woman to qualify.

Edith returned to England – the first female pilot in the country – and had a successful career performing in air shows.

However, in Coventry, where she was billed as Viola Spence, her display went badly wrong. She made a routine parachute jump from a hot air balloon, watched by a crowd of over 3,000 people. But a gust of wind blew her on to a factory roof, the parachute turned over and she fell 40ft on to the roadway, injuring herself severely. Edith was rushed to hospital where the switchboard was jammed with calls from well-wishers.

She died a few days later and was buried in Coventry in an unmarked grave. She was just 31 years old.

The sad fact was that Edith was never meant to be parachuting that day. A fellow aviatrix had been due to make the jump but Edith had taken her place.

Her name faded into obscurity until 2013, when Suffolk Aviation Heritage Group began a campaign to create a memorial to her in Fore Street. (Ipswich Society; Ipswich Women's History Trail; Martlesham Heath History leaflet)

‒ July 12th ‒

1872: By this day, work had started in St-Mary-le-Tower churchyard on a memorial to Bishop Patteson, the first Bishop of Melanesia. He had been killed by Solomon Islanders the previous year. Patteson had Ipswich connections: he was related to the Cobbold family and had spent many holidays with them as a boy.

He became a Church of England missionary and worked in the South Seas. Whenever he visited an island for the first time, he would swim ashore wearing a top hat filled with presents for the islanders. He was quick at making friends and at learning enough of the local language to be able to use it when he visited again.

However, in September 1871, he arrived on one of the Solomon Islands and was mistaken for a slave trader. He was promptly killed and his body placed in a canoe, covered with palm-fibre matting, with a palm branch in his hand, and sent to float on the ocean. His death became a *cause célèbre* all over England.

The Ipswich memorial, a crucifixion scene, was finished in September 1872. (*Ipswich Journal*, various dates; *The Encyclopaedia of New Zealand*)

―――

1929: The annual Poor Children's outing saw 2,400 Ipswich children taken from Alderman Road Recreation Ground to Glemham Hall, home of the Cobbold family. They travelled in a procession of hundreds of cars decked with bunting, flags and balloons. As they went along, the children sang music hall songs at the tops of their voices. Each child was given a packed lunch and a van went with them from Ipswich carrying enough lemonade to give every child two full glasses. At Glemham Hall, they ran three-legged races, played tug of war, and balanced eggs on spoons. A great day was had by all. (East Anglian Film Archive)

– July 13th –

1855: The *Stamford Mercury* reported on the trial in Ipswich of George Whimper Hughes, formerly a surgeon at East Suffolk Hospital. 'Every nook and corner of the court was filled to suffocation' to hear him answering eight charges of embezzling a total of approximately 12 guineas from the hospital. The court had to decide whether he was just careless or a criminal.

Hughes was found not guilty on one charge; the others were dismissed on technicalities – to gasps in the courtroom – and the Recorder warned him to be more careful in future.

In the same week and at the same court, a lowly Charles Fielding was sentenced to one month's imprisonment with hard labour for the theft of 3s. (*Stamford Mercury*, 1855; *Bury & Norwich Post*, 1855)

1985: Nik Kershaw, who spent his boyhood in Ipswich, was one of the stars of Live Aid and performed at Wembley in front of 72,000 people to raise money for famine relief. He played for nearly 15 minutes, preceded by Elvis Costello and followed by Sade.

Nik went to Morland Road Primary School and then to Northgate Grammar, where art teacher Michael Lumb remembered the impressively complicated string sculpture he constructed as part of his A-level project. Halfway through the sixth form, though, Nik left school to concentrate on making it in the music business.

In the 1980s, Nik hit the big time with his breakthrough song 'Wouldn't It Be Good', which was issued with a video of him as an angst-ridden alien wearing a shiny suit. He became a teen idol, with his albums going platinum and invitations to sing with the cream of showbiz. (Thanks to Michael Lumb; Nik Kershaw's website: www.nikkershaw.net)

‑ JULY 14TH ‑

1866: Miss Leonora Biscoe, a Nightingale-trained nurse, reported to the Ipswich District Nursing Society on her first two months as Ipswich's first district nurse. Her job was to nurse the sick poor in their own homes in the parishes of St Matthew, St Peter and St Mary-at-the-Elms and to teach women there about hygiene and health care.

Miss Biscoe had been appointed by a committee of philanthropic businessmen, doctors and clergymen. Their original plan was to employ three trained nurses, but funds never stretched that far, so only Miss Biscoe was ever appointed. She was helped in her work by two volunteers: Mrs Harriet Grimwade (wife of Edward Grimwade, mayor and chemist) and Miss Bidwell, a teacher.

Unfortunately, Miss Biscoe resigned early in 1867. The scheme was never fully funded and lacked support from the medical staff at the hospital. When it was wound up, there was only £2 left in the kitty, which was donated to the hospital. The linen and utensils which had been bought were left 'in use among the poor'.

Miss Biscoe went back to hospital nursing and in time became matron of Chelmsford Hospital. (*Ipswich Journal*, 1866–67; www. ancestry.co.uk)

‒ July 15th ‒

2003: Andy's Records, formerly in Dog's Head Street and then in the Buttermarket Shopping Centre, closed after ten years' trading in Ipswich. Rather like the Purple Shop, it had been part of growing up for many local people.

Andy Gray started his business selling old records on Felixstowe pier in 1969 and slowly expanded into market stalls and shops across East Anglia, so that by the early 1980s he had twelve retail outlets.

He was well known for undercutting competitors by importing records from Europe at a bargain price and then passing the savings on to customers. He did come a cropper though with the *Evita* album, when he bought a load in cheap and did not realise they were sung in Italian until customers brought them back demanding refunds!

Andy's advertising was often slightly humorous, as was the company's motto: 'Purveyors of fine music at cheapo prices'. By the mid 1990s, the company had climbed into the Top 500 of UK companies, owning more than thirty shops nationwide.

But it all started to unravel in the early 2000s as a result of competition from supermarkets, online stores and larger companies. Andy's shops began to close and the company went into administration in May 2003. Andy, by then a multimillionaire, was unwilling to fund his company after three years of letting it rack up substantial losses. (Thanks to Sri Dvae)

~ JULY 16TH ~

1937: Arthur Ransome's adventure story, *We Didn't Mean To Go To Sea*, was published, the seventh in his *Swallows and Amazons* series of children's books. In the story, the Swallows were paying guests of a Miss Powell of Alma Cottage, Pin Mill.

Miss Powell was, in fact, a real person. She was born in Alma Cottage when it was still the Alma Inn, one of two pubs in the picturesque hamlet. Arthur Ransome would have known her well, because he and his wife lived at Pin Mill for several years. The Powell family had been licensees at the inn since the 1860s.

After the success of the book, the real Miss Powell found young Arthur Ransome fans turning up in Pin Mill to see her. She learned to make omelettes after they started asking for the pea soup and mushroom omelettes that her character had cooked in the book. (*We Didn't Mean To Go To Sea*, by Arthur Ransome; Pub history website: deadpubs.co.uk; Arthur Ransome wiki: arthur-ransome.wikia.com/wiki)

- JULY 17TH -

1888: William Churchman announced in the *Ipswich Journal* that he was taking over his late father's tobacco company. The firm had been founded in Ipswich by the original William Churchman in 1790 and began as a small pipe tobacco manufacturer and owned a shop in the town centre. By 1890, the company had started making 'white cigarettes' and six years later they installed one of the first industrial cigarette-making machines, which could produce 20,000 cigarettes an hour. In 1891 Churchman's opened a new factory in Portman Road, which became one of the largest cigarette factories in the country, and a major Ipswich employer.

Churchman's were famous for the quality of their cigarette cards, which are widely collected and sought-after to this day. Later they become a part of the Imperial Tobacco Company, and produced the famous John Player Special brand for many years, before closing in the 1990s. (*Ipswich Journal*, 1888; Ipswich Historic Lettering website: ipswich-lettering.org/index.html)

1994: A 'Gatka' was held in Christchurch Park by the Maharaja Duleep Singh Centenary Trust. Gatka was a form of Sikh martial arts where fighters sparred with 6ft-long bamboo sticks. The aim of the day was to commemorate the life and achievements of the first Sikh to settle in England, Maharaja Duleep Singh. He was the last prince of Punjab and lived in exile in Suffolk at his magnificent palace at Elveden. (*East Anglian Daily Times*, 1994)

– JULY 18TH –

1818: An advertisement appeared in the *Ipswich Journal* for Madame Marie Tussaud's travelling exhibition which was due to open at Mr Sparrow's Upper Ware Rooms, Old Buttermarket (also known as the Ancient House).

Some of Madame Tussaud's very earliest work was displayed, including the death masks she had been forced to make during the French Revolution. By the time of the Ipswich exhibition she had sculpted models of George III, Napoleon and his wife Joséphine, Voltaire and Robespierre – all from life. Visitors may also have been able to marvel at one of the earliest examples of animatronics. This was Sleeping Beauty, a 'breathing' likeness of Louis XV's sleeping mistress, sculpted by Tussaud's former employer and mentor. In total, waxworks of ninety famous characters went on display.

After Ipswich, where it had been met with 'unbounded appreciation', the exhibition then travelled to Bury and beyond. (*Bury & Norwich Post*, 1818; *Ipswich Journal*, 1818; Carol Twinch, *Ipswich Street by Street*)

2013: The 'autumn wader passage' was well under way at this time with a wide variety of species spotted along the Orwell Estuary. Birds which had bred in the Arctic earlier in the year were already on their way to winter in Africa. At Trimley marshes these waders were noted: a spoonbill, little egrets, black-tailed and bar-tailed godwits, ruffs, green and common sandpipers, a greenshank and a hen harrier. (Mick Wright's website: www.mickorwellestuary.co.uk)

~ July 19th ~

1957: Ken Lightfoot became a railwayman at Ipswich railway station when he was demobbed from the army. His first job was as a porter, which meant he did everything.

On this Friday, a couple of specialised pigeon-racing wagons came in which he had to load up with hampers of birds going to Calais to be released on the Sunday to race back to Suffolk. Ken put buckets of maize and water in the wagons for the journey (Ipswich, Liverpool Street, Dover then ferry to Calais). Off they went – job done. Or so he thought …

At the end of his shift, Ken went back to the parcel office to get his bike, only to find another hamper there, containing two pigeons he had missed. They belonged to a pigeon racer in Elmswell. He decided to hide them over the weekend and release them on the Sunday so they would look like they had raced home with the others. He stowed the hamper behind some parcels and came in secretly on the Saturday to feed them. On the Sunday, he released them and went home feeling pleased with himself, having checked with a pigeon fancier friend how long it would take the other birds to fly in from France.

On Monday morning, Ken reported for work only to be called in to the stationmaster's office. 'How come', the angry stationmaster demanded, 'two pigeons got home on Sunday afternoon when the race had been called off in Calais due to fog over the Channel?' (Thanks to Ken Lightfoot, railwayman and raconteur)

– July 20th –

1907: The legendary musical hall artist Marie Lloyd made her first visit to the Ipswich Hippodrome in St Nicholas Street. Over the years, she appeared several more times, including at three performances during the First World War when she took wounded soldiers off for a treat at her own expense. At the end of her wartime shows she would always finish by wishing her soldier boys 'good luck and a safe return'.

Always well-dressed in a smart blue and white outfit or a little French number, she was famous for putting over a song with a wink and a cheeky pause. No wonder the Ipswich audiences loved her saucy songs like 'Oh Mr Porter' and 'A Little Bit of What you Fancy'.

She used to have bottles of stout and fish and chips smuggled into her dressing room – forbidden by the Hippodrome management! (Terry Davis and Trevor Morson, *Ipswich Hippodrome: The Place to Go*)

—·—

1925: Harry Walters was a well-known photographer in the town. He died at home in St Margaret's Plain, on or about this day, in his 70s. He was renowned for his trick photographs, such as the one he took of himself posing as all three musicians in a concert party band. (Robert Malster, *Ipswich: An A to Z of Local History*)

— July 21st —

1962: Pete Barham, a Junior at HMS *Ganges* naval training establishment in Shotley, celebrated his 16th birthday in Ipswich. Pete said:

I remember it so well. I was 16 on a Saturday so I was allowed to go into Ipswich in the afternoon anyway. We got the bus from Shotley in our full naval uniforms – no civvies allowed – got off at the Old Cattle Market and wandered round the town a bit.

We stuck out like sore thumbs. Some of the Ipswich lads were up for a scrap with us, as usual, but we were hoping to meet girls! We weren't old enough to go into pubs so we went and had that frothy coffee they did in the 1960s.

Then we went to the Odeon and saw a cowboy film. The place was packed with rows of us boys. We always liked going there – it was a break from the discipline of *Ganges*. It was harsh at *Ganges*, even by naval standards, but I was a Barnado's boy so I wasn't used to home life anyway.

Then we caught the last bus back to Shotley. It went before 9 o'clock, so you couldn't stay in town late. You daren't miss it. It was always heaving with us boys, boasting about what we'd got up to.'

(Thanks to Peter Barham)

~ July 22nd ~

1352: Edward III gave the 'homines de Gippeswico' the freedom to strengthen their town walls and to make battlements along them if they wanted to. The town authorities were allowed to raise a tax (murage) to pay for the work.

The town walls ran to the north and west of Ipswich, with the river providing a natural defence to the south. The 'walls' – earthen ramparts for the most part – had existed since at least 1204, but how much of them were ever built of stone is still unknown. (*Philip Davis, Gatehouse: Gazetteer of Medieval Castles and Fortifications*)

1861: A train from Woolwich arrived at Harwich bringing twenty-eight men and two officers to mount army canons on the Martello Tower (code named L) at the tip of the Shotley peninsula. These sixty-eight-pounders were used widely elsewhere for coastal defence and the army wanted to test whether this tower, strategically sited overlooking the Stour Estuary, was strong enough to carry them. The experiment was successful. A couple of years later, a battery with fourteen guns was established there.

In later years, this squat brick tower – and its nearby twin (M), which overlooked the Orwell – became part of HMS *Ganges*, the naval training base. Tower L was then used as a signals station and Tower M formed the base of a large water tank. (R.M. Telling, *English Martello Towers: A Concise Guide*)

~ July 23rd ~

1825: The *Ipswich Journal* reported that 'a spring or fountain of extremely fine water has lately been discovered at Melton near Woodbridge' and found to be beneficial for 'bilious and other complaints'.

'The spring issues from a bed of crag or fossil and, if not disturbed for a short time, a thick sulphurous skim floats at the top. Nearly 500 persons partook of it Sunday last, and are daily using it.' (*Ipswich Journal*, 1825)

1831: David Elisha Davy was an antiquary travelling through Suffolk to collect information about every church he visited. After breakfast on this Saturday, he went to St Clement's churchyard to record what he found there: 'The churchyard is kept in very bad state; numerous footpaths cross it; boys are constantly playing, and it is made the drying ground for all the neighbouring inhabitants.' The tombstones were broken and defaced.

While he was there, Davy witnessed a sexton digging a grave, from which 'he turned up a body in such a state as to render the disturbing of it – in my eyes – a great indecency'. He saw the gravedigger shovelling out the bones with disturbing indifference, along with parts of the coffin which had not even started to disintegrate. (David Elisha Davy, *Journal of Excursions*)

~ July 24th ~

1890: The foundation stone of the new Lyceum Theatre in Carr Street was laid by Edward Terry, actor and member of the famous theatrical Terry family.

The Lyceum was moving from its old premises in Tacket Street where David Garrick had made his debut over a century before, playing the part of a blacked-up slave.

The new theatre opened the following year. Edward Terry and his London Company were back again to do the first matinee. Also on the bill was Mrs Keeley, an 85-year-old actress and singer from Ipswich who had worked under the name of Mary Ann Goward. She was said to have a sweet but very quiet voice.

The new theatre was designed in an Italian style and could seat a thousand people. The interior was decorated in a terracotta and biscuit colour scheme, picked out in yellow and gold. The boxes had curtains in old gold plush with fringes and tassels. Quotations from Shakespeare decorated the walls.

The Lyceum Theatre's life in Carr Street was rather short, as it was eclipsed by the Hippodrome in St Nicholas Street at the beginning of the twentieth century. (*Ipswich Journal*, various dates; Robert Malster: *Ipswich: An A to Z of Local History*)

‒ July 25th ‒

1767: Shipbuilder John Barnard announced in the *Ipswich Journal* that, on the following Tuesday, he would be opening tidal saltwater baths to the public at his St Clement's shipyard. It was near what later became Coprolite Street. He declared that the baths were 'lately captivated and completed in an elegant manner', being suitable for both ladies and gentlemen. This was the earliest mention of spa baths in Ipswich, but it never took off as a spa town. (Ipswich Corporation, *Ipswich Information 1965*; *Ipswich Journal*, 1767)

―――

1991: Crop circles appeared in a field of wheat in Akenham. A row of five evenly spaced circles appeared, each about 25–30ft across. They were similar to other crop circles that had been found dotted about all over southern England in the previous couple of decades – the wheat was flattened, not broken, and there were no signs of machinery having been brought into the field.

Two months later, retired artists Doug Bower and Dave Chorley admitted that they were responsible for the crop circle phenomenon – although they did not specifically mention the Suffolk appearances. They described how they made them, but despite this, some people thought their confession was itself a hoax. (*East Anglian Daily Times*, 1991)

~ July 26th ~

1848: The *South Australian Register* of Adelaide carried a report of a 'clerical error' at a wedding near Hadleigh. Their report went something like this:

In a small Suffolk town, not far from Hadleigh, a wedding party repaired to their parish church. The bride and bridegroom, as is the custom, were accompanied by a bridesmaid, a best man and others.

The party, on the arrival of the officiating clergyman, proceeded to the altar to have the marriage ceremony commenced, gone through and concluded. This having been done, the parties retired to the vestry to record their names on the register; but on the bride and bridegroom being asked to attach their names thereto, some of the party whispered and stared at each other, and commenced laughing outright. The clergyman inquired the reason of such strange conduct, and it became clear that the person who had officiated as the best man had been married by mistake to the bridesmaid. The rector was sent for, to whom was represented what had taken place, and the wedding party left the vestry, and went to the altar for the second time. (*South Australian Register*, 1848)

~ July 27th ~

1839: On this Saturday, the *Ipswich Journal* carried the news that the Copdock Cricket Club had played a team of officers and men of the Royal Lancers garrisoned at Ipswich and had beaten them by 92 runs. It was this newspaper report that lay behind the modern-day claim that Copdock is the oldest cricket club in East Suffolk.

In the beginning, the Gentlemen of Copdock played most of their matches against troops who were quartered locally. The military teams used to bring their bands with them, helping to make the matches quite an occasion.

In the 1840s, Copdock engaged the famous cricketer John Lillywhite Junior as a practice bowler, and he also played for them for a time.

The Cricket Club merged with the Old Ipswichians in 1997, becoming one of the largest and most successful clubs in the area. (*Ipswich Journal*, 1839; Copdock 150 years souvenir programme, SRO)

1881: Joseph Chamberlain, President of the Board of Trade and a close friend of the sitting Ipswich MP, arrived in the town for a great day of municipal celebrations and civic pride. Chamberlain had three public duties to perform: he opened the new lock gates at the wet dock, the new post office on the Cornhill and Ipswich Museum's grand new premises in High Street.

– July 28th –

1841: Foster Barham Zincke (1817–93) became the curate of Wherstead, which was to be his parish for over fifty years. He was a remarkable man: a clergyman, writer, teacher, historian and traveller, he explored Switzerland, Ireland, France, the USA and Egypt – usually on foot, and often publishing his experiences.

As a teacher, Zincke wanted to improve the lives of the 'labouring classes' through education. He became Principal of Ipswich Men's College, and published many works on education, land ownership and history. (*Ipswich Journal*, various dates; *Oxford Dictionary of National Biography*)

1885: The diarist, Ann Watkins, died in Ipswich and was buried in the Quaker section of Ipswich Cemetery. Her simple headstone was identical to all the others there, with the month of her death given as 'seventh month', in traditional Quaker style.
She had been born in 1813 in Ipswich into a Quaker family. She started writing her diary in her early 30s and kept it up for the rest of her life. She described her experiences travelling in Belgium, Normandy and Brittany with her husband, who ran a successful dairy business in Birmingham. On his travels to track down new sources of butter and cheese she would give ministry as a preaching and prophesying Quaker.

When her husband died in 1876, Ann moved back to Ipswich. Her diary was published posthumously in 1888. (Tony Copsey, *Suffolk Writers Who Were Born Between 1800–1900*; www.ancestry. co.uk)

~ JULY 29TH ~

1939: The discovery of Anglo Saxon treasures at Sutton Hoo gave the *East Anglian Daily Times (AEDT)* one of its biggest scoops:

Because of fears over the security of the site, Ralph Wilson, the managing editor of the *EADT* and the *Evening Star*, had agreed to a news blackout on the story until such time as all the priceless treasure had been made safe.

That was fine, until word inevitably started leaking out, mainly at the London end. The curator of Ipswich Museum then had a conversation with Mr Wilson, during which he voiced his fears about two things: firstly, that Fleet Street would break the story first, and secondly that the big London museums would take all the glory, and the real hero, Basil Brown, would be forgotten.

Spurred into action, Mr Wilson briefed his chief reporter, Herbert Bowden, about the story of a lifetime. He then supposedly locked the startled journalist in the old boardroom at the *EADT*'s Victorian premises in Carr Street, Ipswich, while he wrote the story.

Bowden worked long into the night to produce his epic, before being 'released' and allowed to go home – where he found his wife had given birth to a baby. So, a world exclusive and a baby in one night!

(*East Anglian Daily Times*, 2009)

~ July 30th ~

1538: On this day, Thomas Cromwell's steward sent him a letter to let him know that the image of Our Lady of Ipswich was now safe in London. It had been smuggled out of the town and taken in secret to Cromwell's mansion in London. The steward added: 'There is nothing about her but two half shoes of silver and four stones of crystal set in silver.'

It was reported a few months later that Thomas Cromwell had burned the statue in a great conflagration of religious images from all over England and Wales. The following January, his accounts recorded over £21 received for 'stuff of Our Lady Chapel in Gypwich'. Cromwell was particularly keen to get rid of the Ipswich shrine as it was one of the most popular sites of Marian devotion in pre-Reformation England.

From the evidence, it seemed clear that Our Lady of Ipswich was well and truly destroyed. However, the legend grew that the statue was, in fact, saved from Cromwell's fire by English sailors and taken to Nettuno in Italy where, in modern times, an old wooden statue of the Madonna and Child was found, closely matching descriptions of the Ipswich statue. (John Blatchly and Diarmaid MacCulloch, *Miracles in Lady Lane*)

‒ July 31st ‒

1776: On this day and into the August of this year, Simon Hyam, Jewish silversmith of Ipswich, placed a series of notices in the *Ipswich Journal* asking if anyone knew the whereabouts of his friend Benjamin Isaac. Isaac, also Jewish, was a pedlar of gold and silver trinkets whose usual route took him from Yoxford to Aldeburgh, and then on to Dunwich and Southwold. Isaac was described as about 46 years old and wearing a cinnamon-coloured greatcoat and a red plush waistcoat. He had left Ipswich over a month before and not returned. A reward was offered for any information.

Hyam's anxiety was understandable. Benjamin Isaac was not just his friend and, possibly, his employee. He was also needed back at the new synagogue in Rope Lane (now Rope Walk) where, in such a small Jewish community, they needed every adult male Jew they could muster to make up the quota of ten (minyan) required for religious observation.

Sadly, the remains of Isaac's body were eventually found some thirteen years later in a roadside bank between Leiston and Theberton. He was identified by his clothes and beard. All his trinkets had long gone. (Malcolm Brown, *Jews of Norfolk and Suffolk Before 1840*; R. Halliday and B. Susser, *Ipswich Jewish Community in C18th and C19th*; *Ipswich Journal*, various dates)

~ AUGUST 1ST ~

1085: Noblemen, including some holding lands in the Ipswich area, swore allegiance to William I at a convocation in Salisbury, marking the transfer of land from Anglo-Saxons to Normans and, in some cases, from women to men. Before the Conquest, Queen Edith and Edeva the Fair, two wealthy Anglo-Saxon noblewomen, held much of the Ipswich area in their own right and were themselves the overlords of rich and powerful men. After the conquest, their lands around Ipswich were mainly given as rewards to Roger Bigod and Alan of Brittany who had come over with William in 1066. (L.J. Redstone, *Ipswich Through the Ages*; Domesday online: domesdaymap.co.uk)

1964: The final episode of the *Doctor Who* story *The Sensorites* was aired. Ipswich actor Giles Phibbs took the part of Second Human, with William Hartnell as the Doctor and Peter Glaze (of Crackerjack fame) as Third Sensorite. Decades later Giles said: 'I only had one line in the show, but of all the roles I've played, *Doctor Who* is what I'm remembered for now. We had no idea we'd find ourselves part of a cult. I'm still contacted by *Doctor Who* fans. Last year *The Sensorites* was made into DVD. All of us who were still alive got together to reminisce and that conversation went out as an extra on the DVD.' (Thanks to Giles Phibbs)

– AUGUST 2ND –

1794: The *Ipswich Journal* reported that workmen had begun to demolish North Gate because it was in such a state of disrepair. This was the last remaining town gate and stood at the top of what became Northgate Street. (Robert Malster, *Ipswich, an A to Z of Local History*)

———

1870: Ipswich Corporation Asylum was opened in Foxhall Road. At full capacity, it catered for 200 patients with mental illness. Many came from the town, but to recoup costs, patients were also drawn from other towns and counties.

The sorts of psychiatric conditions suffered by patients at that time would be recognised on many admission wards today, but, unlike now, over 10 per cent of all inmates were suffering from 'general paralysis of the insane' – now known to be the result of syphilis.

There were no voluntary patients. Patients were certified by two doctors and a magistrate and admitted for an indeterminate length of time.

Right from the beginning the asylum had a farm which provided food for the institution. Male patients worked there, looking after pigs and growing crops. They also had a laundry, sewing room, cobblers, butchery – all the services they needed – plus a cricket pitch and a croquet lawn. It was an island community, railed off and isolated from the town and surrounding countryside. (Peter Watkins, *St Clement's and the Victorian Asylums*)

~ August 3rd ~

1867: An Ipswich woman named Suttle, living in Lower Orwell Street, gave birth to three children, Frederick, Henry and Lydia. She received a bounty of £3, given at Queen Victoria's discretion to women who had multiple births within wedlock. Sadly, none of the triplets survived their first month. (*Cambridge Independent Press*, 1867)

2007: A crowd of people turned up to Ipswich docks on this day to see a replica of the ship *Discovery*, which had carried adventurers to America in 1607. The original ship was one of three vessels commanded by Vice-Admiral Gosnold of Otley who had been granted an exclusive charter by James I of England to colonise Virginia. The emigrants, many from Suffolk, founded a settlement they called Jamestown, which became the first permanent English-speaking township in the New World.

The replica ship arrived in Ipswich by road. It had set off from Bristol the previous night and arrived on a flat-bed lorry. It was then lowered into the water. Visitors were welcomed on board and were amazed at how tiny the ship was, and how brave, ambitious or desperate the adventurers must have been when they crossed the unknown Atlantic in it. (Extremegroundhopping, Ralph Morris' blog: http://extremegroundhopping.wordpress. com; *Ipswich Evening Star*, 2007)

~ August 4th ~

1964: Controversial artist and teacher Roy Ascott became a senior lecturer at Ipswich Art School on or about this day. He had come from Ealing School of Arts, where he had run the radical Groundcourse, based on a philosophy that, broadly speaking, emphasised the importance of ideas and originality rather than traditional craft and manual skills.

Ascott's short time in Ipswich was exhilarating or egregious, depending on your point of view. He set students group activities rather than individual work. He notoriously introduced 'behaviourial projects', such as locking a student group in the courtyard for over an hour (the 'Quadrangle Incident'). The weaving looms were sold and antique plaster casts were smashed and used as hard core in the car park. The cast of Venus was 'liberated', though, and stored on a farm at Darsham. Some students like Brian Eno thrived. Others were just baffled. Some staff who had formed the backbone of the school for years found themselves sidelined.

Years later, former student Maggi Hayward laughed as she recalled one of Ascott's more conceptual projects. Her task was to dispense portions of jelly from a bath on the Cornhill to bewildered passengers as they queued for the buses. (Paul Bruce and Richard Scott, *High Street Heyday*; *Frieze* magazine, 2006)

~ August 5th ~

1634: The Massachusetts coastal township of Agawam changed its name on this day to Ipswich, after Ipswich in Suffolk. John Winthrop junior, a member of one of the Massachusetts 'first families' and of Suffolk heritage himself, explained that the name was chosen in 'acknowledgment of the great honor and kindness done to our people which took shipping there'. (Journal of John Winthrop, 1630–49)

1907: Baffling headline: 'Ghost Scare in Alexandra Park (Donkey)' (*The Eastern Counties' Chronology or Book of Dates*)

1916: Allan Denny was 16 and a First Boy rating at HMS *Ganges* when there was a German Zeppelin raid over Shotley. Zeppelins were rigid cylindrical airships which the German military used for reconnaissance over the North Sea and for bombing. Allan was killed in the raid – the only fatality this day. He was buried at the Royal Navy plot at Shotley churchyard and was also remembered on the war memorial at Hales in Norfolk. Over 500 people were killed in Zeppelin raids over Britain in the First World War. (Commonwealth War Graves Commission website: www.roll-of-honour.com)

~ August 6th ~

1825: Eliza Mee, 'an interesting and well-known personality', was born in Bramford, where she worked for many years as a professional musician.

Eliza, a thatcher's daughter, was blind from birth. As a child, she joined the villagers who sang for services at Bramford church. They all sat up in the West Gallery, gathered round a few violins to help them keep to their parts, as described in Thomas Hardy's *Under the Greenwood Tree*. As a young woman, Eliza became the choir leader, which gave her a small income.

Few occupations were available to blind women at the time. Traditional 'blind trades' included basket weaving, brush making, rug weaving and piano tuning. Fortunately, as Eliza was musical, she was taught to play the piano by one of the well-to-do ladies of the village. This meant that when Bramford church was looking for its very first organist in the mid 1850s, she was the natural choice. She was paid £10 a year, with a pay rise to over £13 in the 1880s. Her duties also included training the new choir which replaced the old rough-and-ready West Gallery singers.

Eliza remained the church organist for thirty-five years and retired in 1890. Inside the church there is a tablet commemorating her life. (Author's own family history research)

~ August 7th ~

1590: When one John Cumberland of Ipswich died, appraisers made an official list of his belongings. His workshop contained some quite unusual and distinctive items, including:

> various types of waters
> ointments and oils
> weighing scales and weights
> mortars and pestles
> powdered whale horn, and
> herbal and mineral concoctions for making poultices.

Martyn Burnside, a modern-day Tudor re-enactor at Kentwell Hall near Sudbury, examined the inventory and concluded:

> From what I can see, John Cumberland ran a still-room where he made cosmetics and medications. The oils and scented waters, for example, could be used in soap and cosmetics, or could equally have a medicinal use. For example, rose oil was used both for its perfume and for its anti-inflammatory properties.
>
> We've got a still-room at Kentwell Hall where we go if we feel ill on the reentactment days. They give us herbal infusions for headaches and wrap healing plants round cuts and scratches.

(Ipswich Probate Inventories, by Michael Reed. Thanks to Martyn Burnside)

‑ August 8th ‑

1651: At a court held on this day, Nathaniell Bacon (1593–1660) was elected town clerk and clerk of the peace for Ipswich. Born just outside Ipswich and a strong supporter of the Puritan cause, he became a key figure in the town's political life in the mid-seventeenth century. He also compiled the *Annalls of Ipswich*, an invaluable transcription of the early customs and proceedings of the borough. (Ipswich Society)

1902: A summer camp was held near Ipswich to train members of the newly formed cyclist battalion of the Volunteer Corps.

The bikes were designed to enable the rider to travel as a completely self-contained one-man fighting unit. Everything he needed could be stowed away on the machine, from his rifle to his cape and groundsheet. A small kitbag carried behind the seat held rations and personal items, and an emergency toolkit hung from the crossbar.

With the brisk east-coast wind up their jackets, recruits were trained to patrol the area between the Deben and the Waveney in the event of war. (Neil Wylie, Robert Malster, and David Kindred, *Ipswich at War*)

1986: Sally Read became Ipswich's first female locoman and worked as a second-person on diesel locomotives, so ending nearly 140 years of men-only on the footplate. She eventually became a driver at the London Bridge Railway Depot. (Jill Freestone and Richard Smith, *Ipswich Engines and Ipswich Men*)

– AUGUST 9TH –

1561: Queen Elizabeth I visited Ipswich on her progress through East Anglia. She was so outraged at seeing wives, widows and children diverting her clergy from their duties that she issued an order from Ipswich banning women from college and cathedral lodgings throughout the country. (John Nichols, *Progresses and Public Processions of Queen Elizabeth*)

1881: Surveyors had been in Suffolk for several years, compiling data for a large-scale Ordnance Survey map of the whole county and, on this day, they were working in Brettenham to the north west of Ipswich. Ipswich had already been surveyed and the maps which were published in 1883–84 showed incredible detail. At a scale of 6in to the mile, even lamp posts, letter boxes and man-hole covers were marked. (Frank Grace, *Rags and Bones*; *Bury & Norwich Post*, 1881)

1992: Three members of Ipswich Ladies' Hockey Club were part of the British team that won the bronze medal for hockey at the Barcelona Olympics. They were Sandie Lister, Vickey Dixon and Joanne Thompson.

Their Club was part of Ipswich Sports Club in Henley Road. (Ipswich Hockey Club website: www.ipswichhockeyclub.co.uk)

2011: The *Ipswich Evening Star* carried this mind-boggling headline: 'Raiders Snatch Invisible Creature' (*Ipswich Evening Star*, 2011)

~ AUGUST 10TH ~

1910: The Lattice Barn pub in Woodbridge Road was opened on the site of the old Britannia Inn. Its unusual name came from an ancient barn in Goring Road, which had been a local landmark. (Suffolk Camra)

1924: East Suffolk County Council made an offer to the Ipswich Guardians of the Poor on this day. They wanted a cheap workforce to clean out the River Deben and so offered to give the work to some of the 3,000 Ipswich people registered as unemployed at this time. In return, the Ipswich Guardians would have to pay £1,000 to the County Council and the men would be paid 30s a week. (The average rate for a labourer at this time was more like 40s weekly.) It was considered a humiliating offer and 'at the weekly meeting of the unemployed held in the Corn Exchange, some very strong language was used'. The Guardians turned down the scheme and the men were sent instead to rebuild Cattawade Bridge on more satisfactory terms and conditions. (Robert Ratcliffe, *History of Working Class Movement in Ipswich*; *Hansard*, 1924)

— AUGUST 11TH —

1787: Desperate middle-class women in Ipswich were offered a confidential service in the small ads in the local newspaper:

> PREGNANT LADIES whose situation requires a temporary retirement, may be accommodated with genteel separate apartments to lie-in … and depend on being treated with the utmost care, attention, and secrecy; their infant put out to nurse and humanely taken care of. Apply to Mr White, surgeon and man-midwife, or Mrs White, midwife of London.

(*Ipswich Journal*, 1787)

1986: On or about this day, two RAF helicopters were filmed flying under the Orwell Bridge for an exciting scene in the Cold War motion picture, *The Fourth Protocol*. Author Frederick Forsyth had set his original book in Ipswich and at RAF Bentwaters (then a USAF base), which he called Baywaters.

In the story, a Russian undercover agent (Pierce Brosnan) arrived in England and set up home at 12 Cherryhayes Close, Ipswich, a fictitious address in the Hayes cluster of roads off Belstead Road. An MI5 agent (Michael Caine) and his SAS team raided the house.

The two film stars were never required to come to Ipswich. In the strange world of cinema, this part of the action was actually shot in Milton Keynes. (www.planetipswich.com)

— August 12th —

1925: Ex-Inspector John Syme of the London Police Force, co-founder of what was to become the Police Federation of England and Wales, addressed a meeting of the Ipswich Trades Council. He gave a detailed description of his many battles with the police authorities.

The dispute had started in 1910. He had been disciplined for 'undue familiarity' with his men when he spoke up on behalf of two of his officers. When he protested about *his* treatment by senior officers, he was summarily dismissed.

Over the next few years, he tried to pursue a legal case against the police. He was imprisoned several times and, at length, admitted to Broadmoor criminal lunatic asylum. When he was discharged, he went to Suffolk to recuperate.

The feeling of the Ipswich Trades Council meeting after hearing him speak this night was that he was 'in no way a lunatic and it was evident that his detention in prison, especially that relating to Broadmoor, had been nothing but a case of vindictiveness.' (Robert Ratcliffe, *History of Working Class Movement in Ipswich*)

~ August 13th ~

1636: Sir Robert Hitcham died in Ipswich on or about this date.

He was originally from the village of Levington on the banks of the Orwell and came from quite humble origins. Educated in Ipswich and later at Cambridge, he became a lawyer and an MP and was knighted in 1604 by King James I.

In 1635 he bought Framlingham Castle from the Earl of Suffolk for the sum of £14,000. He also had a house in Ipswich where he spent the last part of his life.

Sir Robert was buried in Framlingham church. In accordance with his will, the castle was demolished and the stone used to build a poorhouse with a school. Only the outer castle walls were left standing. (*Oxford Dictionary of National Biography*)

2007: Joe Petrollese, American creator of a collectable gothic doll called Evangeline Ghastly, explained why he had set her backstory in Ipswich: 'I read that Ipswich was one of the oldest places in England and that made it seem interesting. I pictured it with large manor houses and imagined that the town could possibly be haunted. It made it very easy to give Evangeline a very old family history.'

The doll was 19in tall and came with many gothic outfits, including white high-heeled boots called 'Ipswich Lace-ups'. Petrollese added: 'Myself and Evangeline feel honoured to be part of Ipswich.' (www.planetispwich.com)

~ AUGUST 14TH ~

1941: World-famous Lancashire singer Gracie Fields gave a morale-boosting concert to war workers at Ransomes Sims & Jeffries. (Neil Wylie, Robert Malster and David Kindred, *Ipswich at War*)

———

1969: Mike Read MBE, lately of Sproughton near Ipswich, swam the English Channel for the first time.

At school, polio and asthma had prevented him from taking part in sports but, as a teenager, he discovered he was an excellent swimmer. He was selected for the 1960 Rome Olympics but could not take part because of injury. Overcoming his disappointment, Mike decided to train for long-distance swimming instead.

After his first Channel swim, Mike worked towards winning the King of the Channel title given to the swimmer making the highest number of crossings. He took the crown in 1979 and retained it for over twenty years. That year he also held the record for the most crossings in a single year (six) and for the latest crossing in the year – at the end of October, when there was frost on Dover beach as he walked into the sea. By the time of Mike's last Channel swim in 2004, he had clocked up thirty-three crossings.

Only eight swimmers have ever been King of the Channel – amazingly, fewer than the number of astronauts who have walked on the moon! (Thanks to Mike Read)

~ AUGUST 15TH ~

1972: Ipswich Town Football Club started the new season in a new football kit. The fresh design came about because the club's badge had been revamped by John Gammage. John was treasurer of the Supporters' Club and had won a competition to come up with a new take on the old design.

Explaining his thinking, John Gammage said:

> I regard the Suffolk Punch as a noble animal, well suited to dominate our design and to represent the club. And to complete the badge, I thought of the town of Ipswich which contains many historical buildings, including the Wolsey Gate, and is close to the sea with a large dock area. The turreting indicates the ancient buildings, the wavy lines represent the sea and as a final touch I decided to place a football under the horse's foot. When I added the name of the club on a sharp-looking shield, the design was complete.

Sadly, the team's first match in their new strip was won by Norwich 2–1! (thebeautifulhistory.wordpress.com/clubs/ipswich-town)

~ AUGUST 16TH ~

1775: George Stebbing, surgeon of Ipswich, wrote up one of his recent cases for the journal of the Society of the Recovery of Persons Apparently Drowned.

John Sage, aged 7, went into a malting shed with his father. When the father went outside to check some machinery, John decided to explore but fell down a chute, setting off an avalanche of barley. So much grain fell on top on him that he was buried to a depth of 5ft.

When John was discovered, he looked dead. His face was red and his mouth and nose were clogged with barley. George Stebbing was sent for, but his locum attended instead. He opened a vein, but blood did not flow. Then the locum remembered what he had read in one of the Society's pamphlets and ordered the boy's chest and arms to be rubbed with warm flannels. This got the blood flowing and the boy started to breath. When Stebbing arrived, the boy was put in a warm bed and poultices were prescribed for his arms and legs. Within three weeks, the young John Sage was fully recovered. (*The Annual Register: A View Of The History, Politics, And Literature For The Year Of 1775*)

~ August 17th ~

1853: William Flack was executed by the common hangman at Ipswich Gaol on this Wednesday for the murder of 85-year-old Maria Steggles.

Maria was the housekeeper at Bacton Rectory where Flack also worked. One Sunday she sent him a note saying that she was giving him the sack. Maria then stayed at home to cook the Sunday meal while the rector and a girl servant went to church.

Flack was at church, ringing the bells. When matins started, he left for the rectory and battered Maria to death there in the kitchen. He also stole some small items from upstairs.

Returning home at lunchtime, the rector found Maria's body slumped on the kitchen floor. His servant girl worked out that Maria must have been murdered about 11 a.m. because of how far she had got in preparing the Sunday meal.

Flack completely failed to conceal what he had done. Muddy footprints were found at the scene of the crime and on the path between the church and the rectory. Flack had asked his neighbours that afternoon for a clean shirt and pair of boots. He tried to sell some of the items he had stolen and was later heard saying malicious things about Maria. Finally, a knife belonging to Maria was found in his privy.

The jury took just 15 minutes to find him guilty. (*Bury & Norwich Post*, 1853)

~ August 18th ~

1807: The following report appeared in the *Ipswich Journal*:

> A poor woman of this town, the mother of two children, having a quantity of linen to wash, procured a poppy head, the juice of which she gave to one of her children, a little girl of about ten months old to make her sleep while she pursued her employment.
>
> On the husband's return, he enquired for his little favourite, and was much alarmed at her altered appearance. On taking the child in his arms, she went into convulsive fits, and almost immediately expired.

(*Ipswich Journal*, 1807)

1971: Celebrity TV chef Robert Carrier bought Hintlesham Hall after seeing it advertised in *Country Life*. He did not view the building beforehand so it was quite a shock when he saw it was more or less derelict, with rotten floors and ceilings. In the fullness of time, Carrier opened the hall as a hotel and cookery school. His trademark recipes were excessive – full of double cream, liqueurs and exotic ingredients. His food was as camp and flamboyant as he was. (*Country Life* magazine, 1971)

~ August 19th ~

1882: Agnes Grimwood, a young unmarried woman, gave birth alone and in secret on this Saturday night. She lived with her widowed mother, brothers and sisters in a meagre cottage in Harkstead.

Other villagers had seen her gleaning in the fields after harvest and rumours had spread that Agnes was heavily pregnant. But after that, no one ever saw her with a baby.

Agnes was questioned by the police and at first she denied she had ever been pregnant. Eventually, though, she admitted that she *had* given birth. She said the baby's father was her brother-in-law, Thomas Sharman, who lived next-door. The baby was stillborn, she said, and she took the police to Freston Brook to show them where she had hidden her dead child in a drain.

An inquest was opened and Agnes was accused of concealing the birth of a baby. The inquest returned an open verdict as there was no evidence that the baby had ever sustained life once it was born.

Agnes got married in 1888 to one George Briggs and bore several children. They lived all their lives on the Shotley Peninsula, never far away from Thomas Sharman and his wife. We can only speculate how the two couples managed to get on with each other. (*Ipswich Journal*, 1882; www.ancestry.co.uk)

~ AUGUST 20TH ~

1869: Mildred Ransome, daughter of Robert and Elizabeth Ransome of the Ipswich firm Ransomes Sims & Jefferies, was born on or about this day. She became the first woman doctor to practise in Ipswich.

Mildred was born at Orwell Lodge, the family home in Belstead Road. She was a pupil at Ipswich High School and went on to study medicine at Glasgow University, qualifying as a doctor in 1896. This was only two years after Glasgow's very first women medical students graduated. She then studied midwifery in Dublin and started work in Glasgow.

When Mildred married her father's colleague, John Dillwyn Sims, in 1898 she moved back to Ipswich and lived at 26 Fonnereau Road. Mildred had her medical practice in Queen Street.

Mildred was well known for treating patients too poor to pay. She served on several committees and took particular interest in the medical welfare of children in institutional homes in Ipswich. She helped host the Annual Congress of the British Medical Association in Ipswich in 1900, which welcomed hundreds of delegates to the town from all over the world.

Sadly Mildred's husband died after only seven years of marriage. She moved to London and died there in 1915, aged just 45, leaving two children. (Ipswich Women's History Trail; *Ipswich Journal*, 1869)

– AUGUST 21ST –

1847: The *Ipswich Journal* reported rather sourly on the farewell soirée held for Henry Vincent, the radical Chartist who had stood twice for election as MP for Ipswich.

Over the years, Vincent had addressed packed meetings on the Cornhill, in warehouses and at the Lyceum Theatre. His themes were always those of the People's Charter, namely, extending the vote and reforming Parliament so as to improve the lives of the labouring classes.

Vincent was popular in Ipswich. He stood in the 1842 and 1847 by-elections, coming fourth both times, but with a fair percentage of the vote. After the second defeat, he decided to call it a day in Ipswich.

On the evening of the farewell do, a marquee was erected in the grounds of the old Grammar School. Over a thousand people were expected to attend. Teas were provided (but anyone wanting alcohol had to bring it themselves). A sneering *Ipswich Journal* reported: 'there was a good muster of Dissent there, in all its phases, as the most thorough Church-hater could desire.' Vincent was presented with a gold watch by admirers – or, as the newspaper put it, he 'quietly pocketed the gold'.

Crowds of supporters who could not afford the 1*s* entrance fee gathered at the gates to say a fond farewell. (Robert Ratcliffe, *History of Working Class Movement in Ipswich*; *Ipswich Journal*, 1847)

~ AUGUST 22ND ~

1940: The decision was taken in Ipswich to ban pets from public air-raid shelters following reports of cat and dog fights and chaotic scenes of all sorts of animals running wild. (David Jones, *Ipswich in the Second World War*)

2000: Michael Bates, also known as Prince Michael of Sealand, bought a dormant British company and renamed it HavenCo Ltd. It operated from Sealand, his self-declared sovereign principality, located on an old military platform approximately 6 miles off the Suffolk coast.

The company was a 'data haven' – a self-contained, ultra-secure data fortress. They prohibited child pornography, spamming and malicious hacking, but all other computer data was acceptable, with no questions asked. When they set up, they envisaged a client list that ranged from the exiled Tibetan government to pyramid selling schemes, and from online gambling to companies sending porn into Saudi Arabia.

Probably inevitably, the company failed. There were personal disputes between the 'IT geeks' and the 'Royal Family'; it was costly to bring in every single piece of equipment to Sealand by boat or helicopter; and the organisation was said by insiders to be chaotic. Visitors were kept away from the South Tower, where the servers were said to be housed, because actually there was nothing there!

HavenCo stopped trading in 2008 … but, equally inevitably, reappeared in 2013. (Welcome to Sealand. Now Bugger Off: http://archive.wired.com/wired/archive/8.07/haven.html; HavenCo facebook page: www.facebook.com/eCryptoLibertas)

~ AUGUST 23RD ~

1878: Shortly before 5 p.m., Father Drury, the Anglican Rector of Claydon, set off along the bridleway towards Akenham church to bury Joseph Ramsey, the 2-year-old son of a village farmhand.

Father Drury already knew that young Joseph had not been baptised because his parents, as Baptists, did not believe in baptising infants. There were no nearby graveyards for Nonconformists so Joseph was to be buried at the parish church. Father Drury was not allowed by law to hold a burial service for Joseph, but he still expected to be able to accompany the coffin into the churchyard. The grave would be on the north side – 'like a dog', as Joseph's poor parents were told.

The situation was fraught with difficulty. The tiny coffin arrived, accompanied by family, villagers and a minister from one of the Nonconformist chapels in Ipswich. The minister was conducting a service in the field across the track from the churchyard when Drury approached. There was a heated argument, with Drury storming off and locking the churchyard gate behind him, and so the funeral party had to carry the little coffin into the churchyard through the hedge and bury it themselves.

When this nasty scene was reported in the *East Anglian*, Father Drury sued the newspaper for libel.

As a result of this case, the law was changed so that burials could take place in parish churchyards, with or without Church of England liturgy. (Thanks to Simon Knott)

1852: At the age of 20, John Lawrence Toole, an amateur actor from London, made his debut on the Ipswich stage. He was received with such applause and laughter that he decided to go professional a few months later.

Over the next four decades, Toole became one of Britain's most famous performers. He was particularly known for tragi-comic roles, where he had to 'provoke tears and laughter in equal measure', and so Dickensian parts became a speciality.

Toole was the first actor to have a West End theatre named after him. He bought the Folly Theatre in Charing Cross, renamed it Toole's Theatre and put on music hall and burlesque shows.

By the time of his death in 1906, Toole was hailed as Britain's leading comedian, famous for his catch phrases 'Still, I'm not happy' and 'It does make me so wild'. (*Leeds Times*, 1895; Roy Hudd Music Hall Archive)

1871: Day trips left Ipswich railway station every half hour bound for Stowmarket, bringing thousands of sightseers to view the after-effects of the recent explosion at the gun cotton factory. Twenty-eight people had been killed and over 100 maimed. The pubs were open all day and drunkenness was rampant. During the evening, 'the melancholy procession of some ten bodies passed through the town to the cemetery, surrounded by a drunken mob'. (*North Devon Journal*, 1871)

~ August 25th ~

1794: The *Ipswich Journal* reported:

> A very extraordinary instance of recovery from the dropsy [water retention or oedema], by one tapping, has occurred in this town in the person of a widow lady, near 70 years of age, who had 63 pints of water drawn off on 25 February 1782 and is now in perfect health.

(*Ipswich Journal*, 1794)

1915: An official report was published about the annual mortality rates in British towns. The average was 11.4 deaths per 1,000 people. In Ipswich it was 13 per 1,000 (the same as Hull, Newcastle-upon-Tyne and Salford). The highest death rate was in Gateshead (22 per 1,000) and the lowest was Halifax (6 per 1,000). (*Western Daily Press*, 1915)

2010: This small-town headline appeared in a local newspaper: 'Cat Last Seen At Sausage Shop'. (*Ipswich Evening Star*, 2010)

~ AUGUST 26TH ~

1786: An advertisement appeared in the *Ipswich Journal* calling for subscriptions to help establish the Orwell Estuary as a base for whale fishing. New whaling companies were formed and, the following year, two ships, the *Ipswich* and the *Orwell*, with crews of forty to fifty men each, returned from their first season in northern waters.

The *Orwell* had taken seven whales, providing 150 butts of blubber and several hundredweight of whalebone. The ship could not get beyond Wherstead Strand because of the poor state of the river, so the blubber was taken in lighters to Nova Scotia on the west bank, just below the town. Boilers had been erected there for rendering it down. The stink of boiling blubber did not seem to have caused a nuisance – the newspaper reported: 'the stench did not reach any part of the town, neither was it scarcely to be smelled within 100 yards of the place'.

The *Ipswich* caught no whales that season but did slaughter fifty-four seals.

The following few seasons were poor and by 1793 whaling was abandoned. The rendering plant at Nova Scotia, the whaleboats, harpoons and lances were all put up for sale. (Robert Malster, *Ipswich: An A to Z of Local History*)

~ AUGUST 27TH ~

1909: This day saw the first motorised taxi cabs up for hire in Ipswich. (*The Eastern Counties' Chronology or Book of Dates*)

1920: Today saw the final gathering of the pupils, teachers and manager of Blue Coat School before it closed. It had been in existence for over 200 years.

The school had opened in 1710 in Curriers Lane and was founded by the Church of England. It was one the earliest of the charity schools in Ipswich and aimed to give Christian instruction to poor girls. It clothed and educated them at little or no cost. Pupils usually left to go into domestic service and so the girls' writing classes were withdrawn in 1737 as the expense seemed to be unwarranted. (Robert Malster, *Ipswich: An A to Z of Local History*)

1924: Robert Stanmore died in Ipswich aged 98. He was born in Chatham in Kent and joined the Royal Navy as a boy. During the Crimean War he served on board HMS *Trafalgar,* and took part in the bombardment of Sebastopol in the 1850s. When he retired from the navy, he married and settled in Ipswich, where he worked as a Customs Officer. Robert was the last survivor of the fifty-seven Ipswich Crimean veterans. (*The Eastern Counties' Chronology or Book of Dates*; www.ancestry.co.uk)

‑ August 28th ‑

1834: The Ipswich annual Lamb Fair was held, as usual, just west of Handford Bridge, and was widely reported in the national press. Farmers (and pickpockets) attended from all parts of the country. Ipswich taverns were full to overflowing, and surrounding roads were crowded with livestock being driven to and from market. At the show, Mr Ransome demonstrated a new turnip slicing cart which would slice a load of turnips and spread them over a field for sheep to eat as the horse walked forward. (*Devizes & Wiltshire Gazette*; Thomas Greene Fessenden, *New England Farmer*, Vol. 13)

1914: In the first few weeks of the First World War, William Whitehead, who lived in Dovercourt and was a naturalised Englishman from Poland, was charged with conveying British state secrets to the Germans by carrier pigeon. He was remanded for several days in Ipswich Gaol. When the naval authorities from Shotley failed to turn up for his trial to present their evidence, he was released. In a statement, Mr Whitehead denied even keeping pigeons. (*Daily Herald*, 1914)

~ August 29th ~

1813: This sad story of a young woman came to light:

A discovery of rather a curious nature took place a few days ago at Ipswich. Mr Embleton, mate of the *Edmund and Mary*, collier, having reason to suspect one of his apprentices was a female, took an opportunity of making some inquiry on the subject. A confession was immediately made. This was on the passage from Blyth to Ipswich.

Mrs Embleton happened to be on board at the time, and to her the young adventurer related the particulars of her case.

She was the daughter of a widow, near Blyth in Northumberland, and becoming pregnant, she determined after her delivery to quit her home, never more to return. She accordingly procured male attire and made a coasting voyage; after which she applied to the owners of the *Edmund and Mary*, to whom she was indentured. It was during her second voyage that the discovery was made. She refused to discover her name, and declared that nothing should induce her to return home.

(*The Times*, 1813)

~ AUGUST 30TH ~

1884: A great scare was caused in the town by several cases of hydrophobia, which was one of the best-known signs of rabies. Constables were appointed to walk the streets and secure all stray dogs, which were killed the next day if no one came forward to collect them. A resolution was passed in St-Mary-at-the-Elms parish that no poor relief should be given to anyone keeping a dog. (Thanks to Pip Wright)

1905: On this Wednesday, a total eclipse of the sun across Western Europe, was expected to be visible in Ipswich, turning midday into twilight.

Street vendors were planning to do a good trade in smoked glass but, in the event, they were not needed. A strong northerly wind prevailed in Ipswich, blowing dense masses of cloud before it.

Then it rained and there was nothing much to be seen, except at 1.00 p.m. when the moon could just about be seen in front of the sun. It never got appreciably darker and some people in Ipswich were heard to say that it should have been postponed until the weather was better! (*The Eastern Counties' Chronology or Book of Dates*, 1906; *Suffolk Chronicle*, 1905)

‐ AUGUST 3IST ‐

2011: On or about this day, the Iceni Project drugs rehabilitation charity was given a £25,000 donation, collected from audiences of a play about the murders of five Ipswich women. Collections were made at performances of *London Road* at the National Theatre. Brian Tobin, director of the Iceni Project in Ipswich, said it was an 'absolutely staggering' amount of money to receive.

The bodies of Gemma Adams, Tania Nicol, Anneli Alderton, Paula Clennell and Annette Nicholls were found over a ten-day period near Ipswich in 2006. They were all drug addicts who worked as prostitutes. Steve Wright, who lived in London Road in the red-light district of Ipswich, was jailed for life for their murders two years later.

Mr Tobin had met some of the murdered women during his work with Iceni. He said: 'We're going to spend this money on the most vulnerable people in Ipswich and that's going to include preventing young women from becoming tomorrow's prostitutes and drug addicts.' (BBC: http://www.bbc.co.uk/news/uk-england-suffolk-14731117)

— September 1st —

1645: On this day during the English Civil War, Mary Lakeland, a barber's wife from St Stephen's parish, was sentenced to death for witchcraft.

She had been found guilty at the Ipswich Assizes of murdering several people (including her husband), making people ill and causing a shipwreck. Mother Lakeland, as she was also known, confessed to having been a witch for twenty years and said that the Devil had given her three imps – two dogs and a mole – which she had sent to bewitch and torture her victims.

Charges had been brought against her as part of Matthew Hopkins' crusade against witches. Hopkins and his team recruited local searchers to help them root out devilry in Suffolk and they identified at least twenty-six people (mostly older women) as witches in and around Ipswich. The town authorities paid Hopkins about £20 for these diabolical services.

Nine days after sentencing, Mother Lakeland was burned in a barrel of pitch in the south-east corner of the Cornhill. A bellman summoned the townspeople to witness the gruesome event and a drummer struck up a solemn beat. She was the only woman to be burned for witchcraft in East Anglia. (Malcolm Gaskill, *Witchcraft*)

– September 2nd –

1923: This Sunday saw the start of the Ipswich Corporation trolleybus service. It was introduced with an experimental route between the Cornhill and the railway station. There were just three vehicles, each manned by a driver who also acted as a conductor. They were powered by overhead cables but, unlike the old trams, ran on ordinary road wheels rather than on tracks. The experiment was a success and a fourth trolleybus, made in Ipswich by Ransomes Sims & Jefferies, was brought into service the following year. In time, the service expanded to run all over the borough and Ipswich became the first town in the country to switch entirely to trolleybuses. (Brian Cobb, *Ipswich and its Trolleybuses*; Robert Malster, *Ipswich: An A to Z of Local History*)

2007: Coinciding with a memorial service for Princess Diana, ITV gave the film *The Queen* its TV premiere. Starring Helen Mirren, the film depicted what happened immediately after Diana died, and how the British establishment dealt with her death.

What was the Ipswich angle? Helen Mirren's co-starring corgis – Anna, Poppy, and Poppy's puppies – all belonged to Liz Smith of Little Blakenham. The five corgis went on to win at the inaugural Fido Film Awards. (Suffolk Tourist Guide website: www.suffolktouristguide.com)

~ September 3rd ~

1637: Robert Leman (one-time Lord Mayor of London) and Mary, his wife, died on the same day as each other and were buried at St Stephen's church. Their memorial, made of coloured marble, shows them facing each other across a prayer desk above carved images of their mourning son and daughters. Robert Leman was a fish merchant and the nephew of Sir John Leman, who founded the school which bears his name in Beccles. (Carol Twinch, *Ipswich Street by Street*)

1924: Suffolk County Library opened new premises in Northgate Street. The stained-glass windows in the upstairs room represented many aspects of Suffolk public life – literary, political, ecclesiastical and industrial.

Taking pride of place was the fourteenth-century writer, Geoffrey Chaucer. Although he was a Londoner, his family were from Ipswich. His great-grandfather, Andrew Chaucer, had a hostelry on the corner of Tower Street and Tavern Street, marked later by a brass plaque showing a pilgrim on horseback. Geoffrey Chaucer's father, John, was a London vintner, but he also exported wheat from Ipswich.

The other large figure, at the other end of the room, was of Sir Francis Bacon, who was MP for Ipswich in Tudor and Stuart times. Unfortunately, his passing resemblance (in some twenty-first-century eyes) to Blackadder diminishes his gravitas somewhat! (Ipswich Society; Thanks to Paul Field)

‒ September 4th ‒

1993: Watched by Giles from his wheelchair, the actor Warren Mitchell unveiled a statue of 'Grandma' in Ipswich town centre.

Carl Giles was born in Islington in London in 1916. He moved to Witnesham in 1943. A motorcycle accident had left him blind in one eye and deaf in one ear so he was rejected for war service, but he was able to continue his pre-war work as a cartoonist. He started working for the *Sunday Express* at about the same time as he moved to Suffolk. A few years later his popular 'Giles family' first made an appearance in the paper, featuring the distinctive matriarch of the family, known simply as 'Grandma'.

Giles never worked at the *Express*'s office in London – he always sent his drawings in from home. Lynn Barber, who joined the *Sunday Express* in 1982, recalled:

> Picture editors quailed before him and silently endured the thrice-weekly nightmare of getting his work from Ipswich … When the trains were delayed they sent a taxi; when Giles was snowed in, they sent a helicopter. His rare trips to London for lunch with the editor were as meticulously planned as a royal visit.

Giles died in hospital in Ipswich in 1995. (Ipswich Historic Lettering website: ipswich-lettering.org/index)

‒ September 5th ‒

1758: Joseph Priestley (1733–1804), the discoverer of oxygen, left Needham Market on or about this day after a rocky three years there as a Presbyterian minister.

It was Priestley's first position as a minister and he was wholeheartedly disliked by his 100-strong congregation. They did not understand his sermons, which he delivered with a stammer and a strong Yorkshire accent. They disapproved of his theological beliefs, and they refused to support the school he planned for the town.

When Priestley left Needham, he took a position in Nantwich. This, and subsequent positions, were more successful and he came into his own as a scientist, theologian, educator and philosopher. For example, he invented soda water, discovered oxygen, experimented with electricity and helped lay the foundations of Unitarianism.

Priestley spent his last days in the backwoods of Pennsylvania, USA. By this time, he had been made a member of every major scientific society in the western world. His old church in Needham Market had closed down long before. (Robert E. Schofield, *The Enlightenment of Joseph Priestley*)

‒ September 6th ‒

1588: Thomas Cavendish (1560–92), explorer, pirate and local boy from Trimley St Martin, returned to England after circumnavigating the world. He was showered with gifts. For their part, the Ipswich authorities presented him with a selection of expensive foodstuffs, imported from all corners of the known world. He received: two gallons of hippocras, wine heavy with sugar and cinnamon, and two marchepanes – made with sugar, almonds, and rosewater. A marchepane would be moulded, baked and lavishly adorned with gold leaf, sugar confits and little coloured decorations. They would have depicted Cavendish's exploits at sea. Further to this, he received a good quantity of sturgeon. These 'royal fish' were for prestigious banquets, and often cooked with parsley and vinegar, and sprinkled with powdered ginger. (John Webb, ed., *Town Finances of Elizabethan Ipswich*)

1916: The young Enid Blyton (1897–1968) arrived in Ipswich on or about this date to train as a teacher at Ipswich High School for Girls, which was then housed in Constable Road. She lodged with friends at 73 Christchurch Street. By the end of 1918, she had completed her course with first-class passes and left Ipswich to start teaching in Kent. She went on to become a well-known children's writer, publishing more than 700 books worldwide. (Enid Blyton Society: www.enidblytonsociety.co.uk/index; Wikipedia)

~ September 7th ~

1577: Christopher Long, aged 19, was taken into Christ's Hospital in Ipswich to be dealt with under the new Poor Law system introduced in Elizabeth I's reign. Originally from Cornwall, he had been apprenticed to a man in London but had run away to Ipswich where he was detained as an 'undeserving' wandering beggar. For some reason, Christopher escaped a whipping this day. Instead, he was discharged almost immediately and sent back to London on a vagrant's passport. This passport gave his details and required parish officers to give him Poor Relief as necessary as he passed on his way back to his master in London. It also stipulated the number of days within which he should make the journey, yet again on pain of a whipping. As young Christopher left Ipswich, he disappeared from history. (John Webb, ed., *Poor Relief in Elizabethan Ipswich*, J.L. Redstone, *Ipswich Through the Ages*)

1839: The *Ipswich Journal* reported that a remarkable discovery had been made near Woodbridge: 'The jaw of a monkey and that of an opossum – completely fossilised – have been obtained from a pit by the side of the Deben, where the clay is dug for the purpose of making bricks.' This was the first time monkey and opossum remains had been found in England. (*Ipswich Journal*, 1839)

~ September 8th ~

1528: Cardinal Wolsey's plan for a magnificent procession through Ipswich failed to materialise. Wolsey had wanted to mark the opening of his new Ipswich school with a grand pageant.

The school, St Mary Cardinal College, was on the site of St Peter's Priory, alongside St Peter's church. Wolsey's aim was to produce scholars in Ipswich to feed into the Oxford college he had recently established (later known as Christchurch).

The day before the opening pageant, Wolsey and his guests observed the Eve of the Nativity of Our Lady at the chapel in Lady Lane. Powerful men including Thomas Cromwell, Stephen Gardiner and 'neighbouring magnates' were there, accompanied by the dean, fellows, choir men and choristers of the new school. But the next day, it poured with rain. None of the grandees wanted to expose their finery to the wet weather and so the procession through the town was called off. They confined themselves to the school instead, while townsfolk looked in on them from the churchyard.

Two years later, when Wolsey had fallen out of royal favour, Henry VIII ordered the school to be closed. The reusable building materials were shipped to London, destined for the King's new palace at Whitehall. All that remained of the school was a plain brick water-gate. (J.L. Redstone, *Ipswich Through the Ages*)

— September 9th —

2009: The world's oldest ring of five bells rang out once again over Ipswich town centre after a pause of almost a quarter of a century. A BBC News reporter wrote:

> The restoration of the church, its tower and the five bells, which date back to the fifteenth century, has cost more than £100,000.
>
> The oldest were cast in the 1440s. For hundreds of years they rang out from the church's distinctive tower in the heart of Ipswich town centre. But when the parish at St Lawrence dwindled away, the building fell into disuse, then disrepair. The tower was declared too unstable for the bells to be rung, and they have been quiet since 1985.
>
> Henry VIII's most influential adviser, Cardinal Wolsey, grew up in the area and would have heard them as a boy.
>
> Neil Thomas, of the Whitechapel Bell Foundry, helped to install the bells in the newly reinforced tower. He said they sounded exactly the same now as they would have done in Wolsey's childhood. 'They are completely intact,' he said. 'They have never cracked and nothing's been done to them during the restoration except for some cleaning inside. The clappers are the originals, so they sound exactly the same as hundreds of years ago.

(BBC: http://news.bbc.co.uk/1/hi/uk/8247631.stm. Thanks to Hilda Jones, who heard the bells ring on this day)

~ September 10th ~

1840: Mr Stanton, an American abolitionist, gave a first-hand account of the evils of American slavery at a meeting held in the Temperance Hall in Ipswich. He was in England on honeymoon with his young wife, Elizabeth Cady Stanton, an anti-slavery campaigner in her own right. On this trip, Mrs Cady Stanton was outraged by the way that, as a woman, she was habitually excluded from debates. Radicalised by this experience, she later became a leading figure in the women's rights movement in the USA. (Robert Ratcliffe, *History of Working Class Movement in Ipswich*; *Ipswich Journal*, 1840)

1928: Harry Becker (1865–1928) died of pneumonia in Ipswich Hospital. He was a little known artist who had barely scratched a living. Becker worked with a complete disregard for his health and comfort. He was out in all weathers, sketching landscapes, labourers and farm animals. His pictures showed a raw and honest view of rural life, without a hint of sentimentality. They were quickly and vigorously drawn.

A few years before Becker died, his work was collected by the Loftus family, who exhibited it in Southwold in 1925 and championed him whenever they could.

In the late 1990s, the art historian David Thompson stumbled on a large number of Becker's pictures in a dealer's storeroom in Woodbridge. From this chance discovery, he wrote a definitive book about Becker and brought him to a wide and appreciative audience. (The Becker Society, *Harry Becker – Truth and Light*)

~ September 11th ~

1909: The first Trades Union Congress to be held in Ipswich ended on this day.

Over 400 delegates had made their way through 'disadvantages and inconveniences' to get to such a distant town. Halls, lodgings and hotels were booked up for the week. Public interest in the congress was high, and the gallery of the Public Hall in Westgate Street was packed with spectators.

Philanthropist and local Liberal MP Felix Thornley Cobbold welcomed the congress and urged the labour movement to 'Go Forward!' Keir Hardie, the first ever Labour MP, attended as a fraternal delegate and the leading women trade unionists Gertrude Tuckwell and Mary McArthur were there. For the first time in several years, the Eastern Counties Agricultural Union sent delegates. Many speakers made the point that working conditions in Ipswich and area were particularly bad because the trade union organisation was so weak locally. The Congress passed resolutions on many topics, including retirement pensions, safer working conditions and the expansion of state education. (TUC Report 1909. Thanks to Cathy Hunt; Robert Ratcliffe, *History of Working Class Movement in Ipswich*)

2011: Gary Avis returned to his home town to perform at the Regent Theatre. He was the principal character artist with the Royal Ballet and he had been the award-winning partner of the great British prima ballerina, Darcey Bussell. (Gary Avis' website: www.garyavis.com)

‑ September 12th ‑

1868: Kathleen Nibloe was born in Ipswich on or about this day. She was one of the class of forty-three girls who started at Ipswich High School for Girls on the day it opened in 1878. She won a scholarship to read classics at Cambridge. As one of the few female students there who had ever been to school, Kathleen was able to study at degree level, pass her exams, and start a teaching job in Wimbledon. Sadly, she died in her early 20s. (Ipswich Women's History Trail)

1915: On or about this day, 'Australian Alberto', who was lodging at No. 2 Edgar Street, Ipswich, added his name to his landlady's daughter's autograph book. He wrote: 'Here's to love – the only fire against which there is no insurance.'

Young Lily Fielding asked all her mother's lodgers to put something in her book. Some just wrote their signatures, others penned a verse or did a little line drawing. Many of the lodgers were artists performing at the Ipswich Hippodrome, and 'Australian Alberto', whose act combined 'a neat mingling of magic and humour', was just one of them.

Over the years, Miss Fielding collected many autographs of music hall performers and she took good care of her book. It eventually became part of Roy Hudd's archive, which aimed to record just how important music hall entertainment had been in the lives of ordinary people. (Roy Hudd Music Hall Archive, *Melbourne Argus*, 1920)

― September 13th ―

2003: Joseph Phibbs' composition, 'Lumina', received its world premier at the 2003 BBC Last Night of the Proms concert. It was performed by the BBC Symphony Orchestra, conducted by Leonard Slatkin.

Joseph had moved to Ipswich as a child with his actor parents, Giles Phibbs and Mary Gillingham. Starting with the cello at St Margaret's Primary School, he took up the piano and, by the time he was at Northgate, Joseph had such an obvious talent that his teachers recommended him for a County Council scholarship to the Purcell School. A career as a composer followed.

Talking about his commission for the Proms, Phibbs said that 'Lumina' was inspired by the 'light on landscape' in New York State. He scored the piece for percussionists, timpani, harp, piano and strings.

'Lumina' was well received. The *Musical Review*'s critic reported that Phibbs had been 'saddled with the task of writing something interesting while appealing to a Last-Night audience and overcame these disadvantages with genuine aplomb. Lumina… was excellently crafted; displayed a subtle use of the orchestra … and kept a boisterous audience quiet for more than ten minutes. No mean feat.' (Thanks to Mary Gillingham; Joseph Phibbs' website: www.josephphibbs.com)

―――

2009: Forty years after the Stonewall riots in New York, Suffolk's gay, lesbian, bisexual and transgender community celebrated with its first Pride event. (BBC: http://www.bbc.co.uk/suffolk/content/articles/2009/08/24/suffolk_pride_2009_lw_feature.shtml)

‒ September 14th ‒

1844: Ipswich's annual Holy Rood Fair – also known as St Margaret's Fair or Holy Cross Fair – was held on St Margaret's Green just outside the town centre.

Previously, it was famous as a great cheese and butter market with a pleasure fair held alongside. Theatrical shows were mounted, and gingerbread stalls put up. Nearby taverns would have done a roaring trade. However, from the earliest days, the fair was associated with rowdiness and trouble, not least because there were continuing disputes about who was in charge of it. Over the centuries, control passed from the nearby priory, to the Crown, to the Withipoll family, and then to Ipswich Corporation.

By the first half of the nineteenth century, butter and cheese sales at the fair were poor. In 1844, *White's Directory* recorded that it was now 'only noted for sausages and sweetmeats'. Two decades later, only the sausages remained. By then, it was known as 'a feast of fried sausages; and there was a general understanding in the town that the sausage season came in with St Margaret's Fair'. It is not known when the fair was last held. (R.L. Cross, *Ipswich Markets and Fairs*)

— September 15th —

2012: When the final curtain came down on Peter Shaffer's play *Five Finger Exercise*, it marked the end of Maurice Rubens' twenty-first year as production designer for the Jill Freud Theatre Company.

Maurice, an Ipswich resident for many years, was a teacher for much of his working life, but when he retired he jumped at the chance to be the regular designer for Jill Freud's summer rep.

Maurice worked on his intricate sets during the winter at home in Anglesea Road, filling his study with scale-model mock-ups. In the summer he would move up to Reydon to be on hand for the productions in Southwold and Aldeburgh. Each season he had five plays to design, and had to make sure that each set would fit the theatres in both towns.

Maurice excelled in designing glimpsed hallways and off-stage rooms which gave audiences the illusion they were looking at a complete house on stage rather than an isolated box-shaped room.

Thinking about how long he had been with the company, Maurice said:

> There are times when we do plays that we've done before. I don't like repeating myself but I do find myself thinking: 'Here I am, faced with an empty space. Can I fill it one more time?' But however much I would like to try and persuade them to reuse my old set, I usually end up doing something new.

(*East Anglian Daily Times*, 2013. Thanks to Maurice and Ursula Rubens)

— September 16th —

1790: A Quaker boarding school opened in Ipswich in late summer this year with William Candler appointed as Master. One of the first pupils was Bernard Barton who became well-known in his time as the 'Quaker Poet'.

Within ten years the school ran out of money. By this time, the premises were in the 'so-called parish of St Matthew' (as contemporary Quakers styled it). When the school closed in 1800, its premises and equipment, including twenty bedsteads and three beer casks, were sold. (Leslie Johnston, 'The Friends School in Ipswich', *Suffolk Review*, 1957)

—

1963: A new sculpture was installed high on a wall of the small shopping centre on the corner of Berners Street and Norwich Road. Created by former Ipswich Art School student, Mervyn Crawford, it was made of long spikes and curved aluminium sheets. It was part of the new St Matthew's Street roundabout development.

Unfortunately, the public did not take to it and there was correspondence complaining about it in the local newspapers. One of these letters contained a couple of typographical errors, so 'We don't want this sort of thing in Ipswich' became 'We don't want this sor of hing in Ipswich'. The name stuck, and the sculpture became forever known as 'Sor of hing'! (Ipswich Borough Council)

~ September 17th ~

1840: A ploughing match between fifteen men was held at the Royal Buckinghamshire Agricultural Show in Aylesbury. As he handed out the prizes, the chairman announced that nearly all the successful ploughs that day were made by Messrs Ransome of Ipswich. Ransomes' ploughs and ploughmen continued to win prizes at this show, and many others, for many decades to come. (*London Standard*, 1840)

2002: Broomhill Pool in Sherrington Road closed on or about this day, which was towards the end of the summer season.

It had opened in 1930 and was built in the art deco 'moderne' style. It was 50m long and eight lanes wide – of competition size – and was complete with changing cubicles, sunbathing areas and a children's pool.

The year before it closed, the pool became a Grade II listed building, one of only twelve listed lidos in England at the time, with English Heritage describing it as a 'well-detailed and carefully integrated example of an urban lido which remains little altered in its principal features'.

When it closed, a campaigning group, the Friends of Broomhill Pool, was formed to stop it being bulldozed and to restore it so the public could use it again. The group was still active in 2014 and campaigning for Heritage Lottery funding. (Friends of Broomhill Pool; English Heritage)

— September 18th —

2011: A replica First World War battlefield, painstakingly created on a farm just outside Ipswich, was seen across the country when the ITV hit drama *Downton Abbey* returned for a second series. The programme followed the loves and lives of the Crawley family. Season two opened with Matthew Crawley, heir to the family fortune, dodging muck and bullets at the Battle of the Somme.

These First World War trench scenes were filmed at Rise Hall Farm, Akenham near Ipswich. Taff Gillingham spent thousands of pounds building trenches identical to those used by British and German troops in the First World War. He said:

> There's 10 acres of film set battlefield there and we push for historical accuracy. The trenches have been built exactly as First World War trenches were. When filming takes place there's a huge amount of local industry that benefits from it and I have up to 100 local extras who come and help us.

Rise Hill Farm trenches were also used for other TV programmes and played a starring role in the film *Private Peaceful*, based on the best-selling First World War novel by Michael Morpurgo. (*East Anglian Daily Times*, 2011)

~ September 19th ~

1272: John le Black, town clerk, fled from Ipswich. Suspected of various crimes (probably including embezzlement), he took off with some of the town's records. Among these was le Domesday, Ipswich's manuscript record of its own customs and laws. Neither the man nor the records were ever seen again.

All was not lost, though: twenty years later, the town authorities asked a panel of the most knowledgeable burgesses to write down the customs and laws from le Domesday as best they could remember them. Although the parchment roll they compiled was also lost over time, several copies were made, and six survive to the present day: three at the Suffolk Record Office and three at the British Library. (Robert Malster, *Ipswich: an A to Z of Local History*; Ipswich Borough Archives, compiled by David Allen)

1885: Conservatives in Ipswich held a garden fete. Reporting on it the following week, the *Ipswich Advance*, a radical newspaper, said: 'the fireworks were perfectly emblematic of Tory policy, being noisy, flashy, calculated to make fools gape, and not altogether successful.' (Thanks to Pip Wright)

1979: The first production at the Wolsey Theatre opened. It was *The Servant of Two Masters* and the audience 'laughed in all the right places – and sometimes even in the wrong ones'. (*East Anglian Daily Times*, 1979)

~ September 20th ~

1570: Over-large codpieces were condemned by the town authorities. They noted 'the common and meaner sort of people' were wearing excessive stuffing in their hoses, which was viewed as 'sinful, illegal and a cause of displeasure to God'.

The authorities ordered that no member of an Ipswich trade guild, nor anyone working for them, should pad out their hose with hair, wool 'or other stuffing therein laid'. Men were only allowed to line their hose with one layer of cotton and another of wool or linen. Constables were to arrest men sporting offending codpieces and bring them before the bailiffs for a stiff warning. If offenders were caught again, they were to be imprisoned until they had 'reformed their excess'.

Well-stuffed codpieces were all the rage in Henry VIII's time, but were generally frowned upon by this part of Queen Elizabeth's reign. (Nathaniell Bacon, *Annalls of Ipswich*)

1963: The *Evening Star* reported that Marjorie Flurrie, aged 22, of Ipswich, had been crowned Miss Lambretta International in Southend. She had to drive her scooter around the arena to be judged on her riding ability, her personality and her looks. Miss Flurrie was the first Ipswich girl to win the competition. (*Ipswich Evening Star*, 1963)

— SEPTEMBER 21ST —

1959: Novelist Ian McEwan, enrolled at Woolverstone Hall School on or about this day.

Woolverstone Hall was a remarkable post-war school. Founded in 1950 on the banks of the Orwell, it was run as a boarding school by the London County Council to educate bright but disadvantaged boys. It became known as the public's public school. Looking back at his school days, McEwan wrote:

> When I was 11, I was sent from north Africa, where my father was stationed, to attend school in Suffolk. By any standards, Woolverstone Hall was a curious place, a rather successful experiment by a left-wing local authority in old-fashioned embourgoisement. It had the trappings of a public school – Adam style country house, huge grounds, rugby pitches, a genially Philistine headmaster – and so on. But this ethos was rather stylishly undermined by the intake of mostly grammar-school level working-class lads from central London. There were also some army brats like me … as well as a tiny smattering of boys from bohemian middle-class backgrounds.

Other notable former students included Phill Jupitus (comedian), Peter Donaldson (BBC newsreader) and Peter Alexander, who held the unusual distinction of having appeared in all the main British TV soaps of the past twenty-five years. (*Mother Tongue*, by Ian McEwan)

~ September 22nd ~

1878: The *Brisbane Courier* reported incredulously that in the 'modern town of Ipswich in Suffolk, England', a Mrs Edwards of No. 14 Berners Street was offering a baby's caul for sale for £4 10*s*.

A caul, a piece of membrane covering a new-born's head and face, was traditionally valued as a talisman, particularly by sailors, who believed it protected them from drowning.

Although the *Brisbane Courier* was scathing about the superstitions surrounding cauls, belief in their powers lasted well into the twentieth century in some parts of Britain. (*Brisbane Courier*, 1878)

———

1998: Kerenza Peacock from Ipswich founded the successful all-female Pavao Quartet. With the quartet, Kerenza plays the traditional string quartet repertoire, but she also appears as a freelance violinist on prime time TV shows such as *Later … with Jools Holland*, *The Graham Norton Show* and even *The X Factor*.

At one point, glamorous Kerenza was playing on each of the top three albums in the pop charts at the same time as playing on the number one in the classical charts. (Thanks to Helen Hayes, Potton Hall Concert Hall and Recording Studios; Kerenza Peacock's website: kerenzapeacock.com)

‒ September 23rd ‒

1960: Ipswich man, Samuel Harvey (1881–1960), died. He was a recipient of the Victoria Cross.

The VC had been awarded to honour his 'conspicuous bravery' in the Battle of Loos (1915) when he repeatedly clambered over corpses and through machine-gun cross fire to bring ammunition to his comrades. He was 34 years old and a private in the York and Lancaster Regiment. Harvey also received the French Legion of Honour and the Russian Cross of St George. Comrades-in-arms said that his stubborn bravery in battle was 'not out of character'.

Harvey liked a drink. When approaching George V for his medal, so the story went, Harvey turned towards the queen, who was standing by the king's side, grinned broadly, winked and said in a loud voice: 'Mine's a pint.' Queen Mary's reaction was not recorded.

In later life he worked as a stableman in Ipswich, before retiring in relative poverty with his wife. At some point he lost his medal – rumours were that he had swapped it for a pint.

Harvey died penniless in 1960. His only possession was his VC miniature medal group, which was next to his pillow. He was buried with his wife in an unmarked grave in the Old Cemetery in Ipswich. Forty years on, the Western Front Association raised money for a memorial to him. (Steve Harvey, *Samuel Harvey VC* at Suffolk Record Office; Great War Forum: 1914–1918. invisionzone.com/forums/index.php)

─ September 24th ─

1326: Queen Isabella, estranged wife of Edward II, came ashore on the banks of the Orwell with an invading army, determined to seize power from her husband and his lover, Hugh Despenser.

Her mercenaries had gathered near Rotterdam and came over in a fleet of nearly a hundred ships. She gambled that she would only need a small force with her and that English people would rally to her as she made her way across the country – which they did.

It took three hours to unload the men, horses and provisions on to Suffolk soil. The queen's attendants made her a tent out of carpets, open at the front, where she sat by a great fire, writing letters to London and other cities to gain their support. That afternoon, her ships returned to Rotterdam and Isabella was welcomed for the night at Walton-on-the-Naze Castle.

The next day, wearing widow's weeds and with banners flying, she set off with her army for Ipswich, where 'she found all the houses amply and well-furnished with provisions, but all the people fled'.

Within four months, Isabella's husband had abdicated and her teenage son was on the throne, but it was Isabella and her lover who were the real rulers. Her invasion was a success. (Thanks to Matthew Thompson; Alison Weir, *Isabella, She-wolf of France*)

~ September 25th ~

1900: A locomotive on its way to Felixstowe stopped at a signal on the Ipswich side of the Westerfield level-crossing. Without warning, the boiler suddenly exploded, killing the driver, John Barnard, and his fireman, William Macdonald. The boiler was thrown forwards, over the level-crossing and on to the opposite platform.

The two men were buried in Ipswich. Their headstones were engraved with a picture of the train they were in charge of on this fateful day. (Thanks to Simon Knott)

1941: Clifford Grey, lyricist and entertainer, died in Ipswich. Among his best-remembered songs are 'If You Were the Only Girl n the World' and 'Another Little Drink Wouldn't Do Us Any Harm', both written in 1916. Later hits included 'Spread a Little Happiness'.

In 1941, Grey was in Ipswich appearing in an ENSA concert for servicemen when the town suffered a serious bombing raid. He had a heart attack, and died two days later. Grey was buried in the Old Cemetery in Ipswich. The inscription on his gravestone nicely summed up his career: 'He spread a little happiness'. (Thanks to Simon Knott)

— SEPTEMBER 26TH —

1534: The Tudor fire service in Ipswich was enhanced when the town authorities ordered that every free man in Ipswich must bring a leather bucket of 2 gallons' capacity to the Moot Hall. These leather buckets, known as bobbets, were used for fighting fires in the crowded wooden buildings lining the streets of the town centre. The Town Treasurer played his part by supplying each parish with ladders and long rakes for pulling burning thatch off buildings. (Nathaniell Bacon, *Annalls of Ipswich*; Ipswich Transport Museum)

1898: On this Tuesday afternoon, one of the first motoring accidents in Ipswich took place. A trap, driven by Mr Hewitt of Bishop's Hill, and a light carriage were passing each other by the Maypole Inn in Whitton, when a motor-car went 'scorching' past. Frightened by the strange noise, the horse pulling the carriage reared up and plunged into the back of the trap. The trap overturned and Mr Hewitt was thrown out. Fortunately, no one was hurt, only shaken. By all accounts, the car driver sped off unscathed in rather a 'Toad of Toad Hall' fashion! (*Ipswich Journal*, 1898)

— September 27th —

1867: A formal civic farewell was given at the Crown & Anchor to mark Henry Footman's departure to Cambridge. Footman worked for his father's firm — the draper's Footman, Pretty & Nicholson in Westgate Street — but he was also a well-known public figure. He taught at the Mechanics' Institute and was a co-founder of a Working Man's College in a room at the town hall. He was a Liberal town councillor and helped set up the Ipswich Penny Bank. Footman was leaving Ipswich to become an Anglican clergyman.

Nearly 20 years later, he was still in touch with Ipswich life. He heard that 250 'navvies' had arrived in the town to work on the docks and dig the sewers. Most public figures threw their hands up at the thought of this influx of reputedly hard-living labourers, but Footman wrote to encourage Ipswich churches to set up a mission for them. After all, he argued, they would leave some good work in the town, so they should be given the opportunity to receive the Christian Gospel. (*Ipswich Journal*, various dates)

— September 28th —

1658: Bell ringers and trumpeters were paid 15*s* for their part in the Ipswich celebrations held when Oliver Cromwell's son, Richard, was proclaimed Lord Protector of the Commonwealth of England, Scotland and Ireland. (Ipswich Borough Archives, compiled by David Allen)

———

1866: General Tom Thumb, his wife, Commodore Nutt and Minnie Warren – all 'wonders of littleness' – appeared on stage at the Ipswich Lecture Hall. (*The Eastern Counties' Chronology or Book of Dates*, 1906)

———

1895: John Ellor Taylor (b. 1837) died. He was a botanist, geologist and the curator of Ipswich Museum.

With the help of Edward Packard, founder of Packards & Fisons, Taylor created one the best museum collections of local geology in the country. He regularly gave lectures on scientific topics to audiences of up to 500 (free to the 'labouring classes'). He also made lecture-tours of Africa and Australia, and wrote several popular scientific books, including the curiously titled *The Sagacity and Morality of Plants*.

The inscription on his gravestone in the Old Cemetery sums up Dr Taylor's considerable contribution to public education in Ipswich: 'By knowledge, by humour, by rare and excellent gifts of speech, he opened the eyes of many to the order, variety and beauty of nature.' (Thanks to Simon Knott)

~ September 29th ~

1913: Did he jump or was he pushed? The distinguished German engineer Dr Rudolf Diesel (b. 1858) set sail from Antwerp to visit his factory in Ipswich. His hat and neatly folded coat were found the next morning in the stern of the ship, but despite a search no trace could be found of the man himself. Ten days later, a decomposed body was found by fishermen off the Belgian coast. There was a heavy storm and they were unable to bring it to land, although they did manage to retrieve a diary and eyeglass, later identified by Diesel's son as belonging to his father.

Conspiracy theories began in the press almost immediately: 'Inventor Thrown Into the Sea to Stop Sale of Patents to British Government' read one headline; another claimed 'British Secret Service Eliminates Diesel.'

Enquiries soon suggested that Diesel had been suffering from insomnia. Then, a meeting of his creditors revealed that he was bankrupt. Nothing was left of his fortune. However, the circumstances of his death remained – and still remains – a mystery. Did he commit suicide? Was he murdered? There was never an official investigation or trial. (Robert Malster, *Ipswich: An A to Z of Local History*; Greg Pahl, *Biodiesel: Growing a New Energy Economy*)

— September 30th —

1888: Harry Frank Bloomfield was born in Ipswich on or about this day. He grew up in the slums of St Clement's where he saw real poverty at first-hand. Looking back years later, he told the oral historian George Ewart Evans:

> I remember when I was about five they used to have a candle-factory in the alleyway in Fore Hamlet in Ipswich – at the back of the Earl Grey Inn. They used to make candles there, and they used to boil the mutton fat and then the candles were dipped. They made them by dipping the wicks into the mutton fat. Well, on a Saturday evening when the factory was practically being closed the children used to come round and get the scraps from the mutton. They used to enjoy that because they were very good to eat.'

(George Ewart Evans, *Where Beards Wag All*)

—

1973: A.S. Neill's funeral was held in Ipswich. He was the founder of Summerhill, the famous radical boarding school in Leiston, at which children were free from adult coercion and ran the community themselves. His nickname at the school was 'Orange Peel'. Pupils would chant 'Neill, Neill, Orange Peel' as he walked by, and so he used their words as the title of his autobiography. (A S Neill, *Neill, Neill, Orange Peel*)

~ OCTOBER 1ST ~

1588: John Robinson, an elderly Yorkshire widower, was hanged, drawn and quartered on Ipswich Cornhill.

Three years earlier he had been ordained as a Roman Catholic priest at Douay College in northern France – a major centre for English Catholics escaping persecution. When he arrived back in England at the port of Ipswich he was arrested straightaway and taken to London for interrogation. He was thrown into the Clink, a notorious prison in Southwark. A court found him guilty of being a Roman Catholic priest and denying the queen's supremacy in matters of religion. He was sent back to Ipswich for execution, a long journey which he walked barefoot.

John Robinson was beatified in 1929 and given the title 'Blessed'. His life is celebrated by the Catholic church on October 1 every year. (St Pancras Catholic church, centenary souvenir and guide)

1982: Cor Visser died in Ipswich on this day or thereabouts.

He was a Dutch artist who had sailed across to the English east coast in 1937. At the outbreak of war, he was on the Orwell and was unable to return to Holland. He moored in Ipswich and, with the exception of a few years in London as official war artist to the Dutch Government in Exile, he spent the rest of his life in the town. He lived in Fore Street for twenty years – a blue plaque marks the spot.

His paintings – many of them watercolours of the Orwell – are exhibited in Ipswich, the Rijksmuseum Amsterdam, the Victoria and Albert Museum and at the National Portrait Gallery in London. (Ipswich Society)

― OCTOBER 2ND ―

1902: On this day, William Gocher (1856–1921), a butcher's son from Ipswich, became a pioneer of sea-bathing in Sydney. He had emigrated to Australia as a young man and was keen to challenge the local government regulations which banned sea-bathing in daylight hours. The issue was one of public decency, as there were no changing rooms and swimming costumes were rare. On this day and on the two following Sundays, Gocher – wearing a neck-to-knee costume – swam at midday in the glare of self-created publicity. A year later, the reluctant local council agreed to allow all-day bathing provided that a neck-to-knee costume was worn. (*Australian Dictionary of Biography*)

―――

1971: The Purple Shop, on the corner of Fonnereau Road and Crown Street, opened as the Curiosity Shop. If you asked anyone who lived in Ipswich as a teenager, they would certainly know where it was. When the owners painted the outside purple, people started calling it the Purple Shop and the name was formally changed in 1984. The shop sold gifts, jewellery, legal highs, 'vaguely forbidden drug-related ephemera' and alternative clothes. Many thousands of local people had their ears pierced there and in the mid-1990s they started to offer body piercing too.

Paradoxically, but somehow appropriately, they had a branch in Felixstowe for a short time which was also called the Purple Shop, even though it was not purple! (Thanks to Simon Knott)

— OCTOBER 3RD —

1939: When Siegfried Feitlowitz's name was posted on the dining hall notice board at Barham House, Claydon, he learned at last where he was being sent next.

Siegfried, known in England as Sigi Faith, was born in Hamburg in 1928, and had escaped from Nazi Germany in December 1938. By the following May, he found himself with 700 other refugee boys, living in a disused workhouse in Claydon. It had become a transit camp for Jewish boys waiting to be placed with British families. A list of names would appear every day and the fate of those concerned decided. Sigi learned that day that he and another boy were going to Oswestry in Shropshire.

While his companion was delivered to a farm there to become a labourer, Sigi was taken to enrol at Oswestry School as a non-paying boarder. Although he hardly spoke a word of English at first, Sigi felt comfortable and did well.

Lack of funds prevented Sigi studying to become a doctor, as he had wanted. Instead, he trained as an accountant and in 1964 he opened a shoe shop. His company, Faith Footwear, grew to become a national brand with 365 branches and a staff of 2,200. Up until his death in 2010, Sigi was renowned for going to work every working day. (Association of Jewish Refugees)

~ October 4th ~

1811: Thomas Colson's boat was seen by a fellow fisherman, foundering in deep water at the mouth of the Orwell. The fisherman hailed Colson to come on board, but he resolutely refused. The next morning, the boat was found sunk. Colson himself was never found.

Colson was an eccentric, locally known as 'Robinson Crusoe'. As well as being a fisherman, he was an ingenious mechanic, having in the past made a working loom, a barrel organ with a set of puppets and his own fishing boat.

Unfortunately, from youth, he had believed in witchcraft and the powers of darkness. Thinking that he was tormented by wizards and imps, he covered himself with charms. Bones and stones with holes dangled from his body and he fastened his arms down with whalebone and wire. He must have cut a strange figure, but with these amulets for protection Colson was sure he could never be in danger, whatever the circumstances. And so it happened, when it came to real danger, Colson simply did not believe he needed to be rescued. And then, presumably, he was so weighed down with all his talismans that he had no chance of swimming to safety. (*Ipswich Journal*, 1811)

— OCTOBER 5TH —

2008: This Sunday saw the annual Gathering of the Griffin – a get-together of Scania truck drivers and other enthusiasts at the Orwell Crossing, a lorry stop on the eastbound A14 near Ipswich. Vehicles came from as far afield as Scotland and the West Country.

Over 100 lorries pulled into the park that afternoon for the drivers to meet up and have a look round at one another's trucks, which were individually decorated inside and out. Scanias of all ages and types were there and prizes were awarded for each series.

Scania driver Tom Shelby said:

> I come here quite often for work anyway. It's the best truck stop between Cambridge and Rotterdam. Sometimes I have a full English – this place has actually won awards for its breakfasts. But the atmosphere here for the Gathering of the Griffin is a bit special. It's nice to see my mates and their families and we raise a bit for charity. At 4.30 the trucks leave in chronological order and we create a massive convoy westwards along the A14.

(Thanks to Paul Field)

~ OCTOBER 6TH ~

1919: Field Marshall Allenby received the honorary freedom of Ipswich. He was one of the commanders of the Suffolk Yeomanry in the First World War and had led them through the Sinai Desert. On one occasion, they marched a gruelling 550 miles in thirty-eight days.

Allenby's army nickname was 'The Bull', because of his sudden bellowing outbursts of explosive rage, combined with his powerful physical frame.

To this day, his memory is alive in Egypt: his effigy is still burned in some villages. (Ashraf Khalil, *Revolt of Egypt's Canal Cities: An Ill Omen for Morsi*; www.firstworldwar.com/bio/allenby.htm)

1928: Alfred Hickman, second-class boy, was killed at HMS *Ganges* when he fell from the top of the training mast. As a bit of fun on this Saturday afternoon, he had climbed to the top for the first time. He slipped, grabbed a rope and swung to the ground but landed wide of the safety net. He was killed instantly. Hickman was just 15 years old.

At 143ft high, the mast was nearly as tall as Nelson's column. It had been erected in 1906 and thousands of boys had trained on it. This was the first fatality. Alfred's inquest took place in the sick quarters at HMS *Ganges* and a verdict of 'Death by Misadventure' was given. (Godfrey Dykes' website: www.godfreydykes.info)

~ OCTOBER 7TH ~

1853: On this Friday, and on the same day each week for hundreds of years, elderly people living at Tooley's Almshouses in Foundation Street enacted a little scene which could have come straight from a Trollope novel:

> The vicar of St Mary-at-the-Quay was also chaplain to the residents of the almshouses and, under the instructions of Tooley's will, a service took place every Friday morning, which all residents had to attend.
>
> At its close they proceeded to Tooley's tomb, where an official in livery read the roll-call of their names and handed to each one the little packet containing his or her dole money for the week. This was placed upon the tomb and then picked up by the recipient, and the worn surface of the slab shows where this took place.

The ceremony, which began in the mid-sixteenth century, continued until the church was closed in the 1940s. (Roy Tricker, *Church of St Mary-at-the-Quay*)

———

1920: The first female magistrates in Ipswich were sworn in. They were Marguerite Jefferies, daughter of John Jeffries of Ransomes Sims & Jefferies, and Caroline Bird, a member of the Labour Party. Both women were also town councillors at the time. (R.L. Cross, *Justice in Ipswich*)

~ OCTOBER 8TH ~

1838: Frank Flory (a village ne'er-do-well) and John Osborne were drinking all morning at the Cock in Bramford. They were spotted at one point behind a high-backed bench which was in front of some stairs leading up to the landlady's bedroom. They knew that £50 belonging to the Bramford Friendly Society was kept up there. It was locked in the money drawer of a wooden box. During the morning, one of them was heard to say to the other: 'Don't go up stairs – there's somebody up there'. And Frank's wife, who was in the pub with them, was overheard to say: 'Frank, don't be a fool.' Later that day the landlady heard knocking from the shed. She went out to investigate and found the inept Frank lying in a drunken stupor with a hand in the Friendly Society's box. The locked money drawer had not been damaged so the cash was safe. She said: 'Good God Frank, what are you doing of?' He muttered: 'I don't know.'

Frank was remanded at Ipswich Gaol and then sentenced to seven years' transportation to the hulks. His slightly more well-to-do companion, John, was let off with 'a suitable admonition'.

On his return to Bramford, Frank killed his wife one night in a drunken brawl. Whereas he had been sentenced to seven years for theft, his punishment for manslaughter was just one year in jail. (Author's own family history research)

~ OCTOBER 9TH ~

1860: The young Francis Hindes Groome (1851–1902) from Monks Soham enrolled at Ipswich School on or about this day. During his time there he developed a life-long interest in Romanies, encouraged by one of his schoolmasters. Groome went to Oxford University but he left before graduating to live with Romanies and study their way of life. He fell in love with a married Gypsy woman, Esmeralda Locke, and they eloped together to central Europe. They travelled from place to place, Esmeralda working as a traditional singer and dancer and Groome collecting Romany folklore.

When they returned to England, Groome continued his literary career, writing for various encyclopaedias and other reference works. He also published scholarly books about Romanies and their language, including *In Gypsy Tents* and *Gypsy Folk Tales*. Meanwhile, Esmeralda made a name for herself on the London stage. The couple became well-known in literary and artistic circles and Esmeralda frequently modelled for Dante Gabriel Rossetti.

In time, Groome and his wife parted and she returned to life on the road. Groome died in London in 1902 and was buried next to his parents in Monk Soham churchyard. (Romany Wales Project – the Locke family: www.valleystream.co.uk/romany-welsh%20.htm; Tony Copsey, *Suffolk Writers Who Were Born Between 1800–1900*)

— OCTOBER 10TH —

1838: The first Roman Catholic church in Ipswich since the Reformation was consecrated on this Wednesday. It was on Albion Hill (Woodbridge Road) and dedicated to Saint Mary.

How did it come to be built in such a Protestant town as Ipswich? It was the inspiration and work of the Abbé Simon who had arrived in Ipswich from revolutionary France in 1793. When he first arrived, he had lodged in Silent Street with Margaret Wood, a Catholic woman. At that time, any Catholic in Ipswich wanting to attend Mass had to travel to Bury, or to one of the homes of the landed Catholic families. Eventually, the Abbé bought a piece of land on Woodbridge Road and had a house with a small chapel built there where he said Mass for several years. The chapel was enlarged and became St Mary's church in 1838. Abbé Simon died the year after St Mary's opened. (St Pancras' Catholic church, centenary souvenir and guide)

———

2012: This intriguing headline appeared in a local newspaper: 'Pope Loses Temper In Ipswich' – disappointingly, it in fact refers to Richard Pope, an Ipswich town councillor. (*Ipswich Star*, 2012)

~ OCTOBER 11TH ~

1838: There was a shocking case of animal poisoning at Ashbocking Hall. Someone had managed to mix arsenic in with the bean meal which Farmer Stanford fed to his cattle. Nine bullocks ate the poisoned fodder and three died.

When the first bullock died, Mr Stanford had not realised it had been poisoned, so he threw its entrails on to the dung-heap. Unfortunately, two fine sows and seven pigs rooted around in the muck, with fatal consequences. Mr Stanford had the contents of their stomachs analysed. Large amounts of arsenic were found, and over the next few weeks, more animals suffered the same fate. Ex-employees Thomas and Rebecca Mallet were charged with the poisoning. Thomas had been Farmer Stanford's head horseman until he was sacked earlier that year – so he had a possible motive.

In court, the Mallets' neighbour gave evidence against the couple. His cottage adjoined theirs and he had climbed into a cupboard on several occasions and claimed he could hear them scheming through the wall. However, medical evidence showed that, on the dates that Thomas was accused of plotting, he had been too ill with smallpox to even speak. It also became clear that the neighbour held a grudge against the Malletts. In the end, the couple were acquitted and their nasty neighbour was charged with perjury. No one ever knew who the poisoner was. (*Ipswich Journal*, 1838)

~ OCTOBER 12TH ~

1568: Seventeen 'fysshes called grampasses' (probably killer whales) were found on the foreshore of the Orwell. As they were so 'verye huge and gret', it was decided to send one to Queen Elizabeth and another to Sir Nicholas Bacon, the Lord Keeper. A messenger was sent down to London to get expert advice on how to dispose of the rest. It was decided to bring the whale carcasses up to the town quay. They were cut up and the tails and fins disposed of. All in all, the town authorities spent just over £8 dealing with them. In the end, though, the Ipswich authorities made a tidy profit, as they sold the remaining carcasses to a group of local burgesses for £20. (John Webb, ed., *Town Finances of Elizabethan Ipswich*)

1790: As an old man, John Wesley, the co-founder of Methodism, visited Ipswich – but not to preach. He just needed to change horses between giving sermons first in Colchester and then in Norwich. He wrote: 'We set out early, but found no horses at Copdock; so we were obliged to go round by Ipswich and wait there half an hour. Nevertheless, we got to Norwich between two and three. In the evening I preached at Norwich.' Thus, not for the first or last time, Ipswich found itself playing second fiddle to Norwich! (John Wesley's Journal, 1790)

~ OCTOBER 13TH ~

1874: The *East Anglian Daily Times* was first published on this day. It was bank-rolled by James Jeremiah Colman – the Norwich mustard magnate. Its office, opposite the old Woolworth's in Carr Street, had a distinctive corner turret and was quite a local landmark. The newspaper moved to Lower Brook Street in 1966. (Robert Malster, *Ipswich: An A to Z of Local History*)

———

1880: A new transport service opened to the public on this day. Horse trams were the latest innovation in urban transport and Ipswich's first route ran between the Cornhill and the railway station. The service, run by the Ipswich Tramway Company, consisted initially of two single-deck tramcars, each pulled by a horse. Individual tramcars could carry about fifty passengers. Journeys were much smoother and faster than any other forms of transport but were still pretty bumpy, as the tracks were laid onto the cobbled roadways. The tramway service expanded from the depot in Quadling Street. More routes, more horses and more vehicles were added until the service closed in 1903, when the network was rebuilt for electric trams. (Ipswich Transport Museum)

~ OCTOBER 14TH ~

1341: On this day or thereabouts, Nicolas Soweband – a man accused of murder – claimed sanctuary in Ipswich when he 'fled to the church of St Mary de Caye'. St Mary-at-the-Quay church was then right at the water's edge, which made it a popular place for claiming sanctuary. Nicholas would have clutched the strong iron ring on the south door, claiming his right to remain safe in the church for forty days so a that a proper trial could be arranged. If the officers of the law managed to persuade Nicolas to leave sanctuary before a trial, they would have dressed him in a white robe or sackcloth, given him a wooden cross to carry, and forced him on board the first available ship out of Ipswich. Tantalisingly, no one knows how Nicholas' story began or ended. (Clive Fewins, The Church Explorer's Handbook; Roy Tricker, Church of St Mary-at-the-Quay)

2009: Building started on or about this day at the Seven Hills Crematorium near Nacton, beside the old road from Ipswich to Felixstowe.

Fittingly, this area was already associated with death. It was said to be where a bloody battle between Danes and Saxons was fought in the eleventh century. There were at least seven ancient burial mounds on the site, traditionally thought to be the graves of Saxons who had died in battle.

The Crematorium opened for business in 2010. (Seven Hills Crematorium website: www.sevenhillsnacton.co.uk; *White's History, Gazetteer & Directory of Suffolk* ,1885)

- OCTOBER 15TH -

1859: On this day, the *Ipswich Journal* reported on Charles Dickens' recent readings in the town. The newspaper said that, as the 'most successful fictitious writer of the present day', he drew a large, fashionable crowd to the old Corn Exchange. The article continued:

> The pieces chosen for reading were his *Christmas Carol* and The Trial from *Pickwick*.
>
> Mr Dickens is undoubtedly a good reader. His voice, at first, was perhaps somewhat to his disadvantage, but as he warmed in his subject the apparent gruffness wore away. His acting powers are high and his sense of the ludicrous is keen …
>
> [he carried] his willing listeners with him, whether he drew into light the gloomy recesses of Scrooge's office, or sat beside the more pleasant and healthful fireside of Bob Cratchit and Tiny Tim.
>
> The Trial from *Pickwick* was a great success. Indeed so great a treat as these Readings has scarcely ever been brought before an Ipswich audience.

Dickens was no stranger to Ipswich. He had visited previously to report on the 1836 general election, later using the corruption and bribery he witnessed here for the famous Eatanswill Election in *The Pickwick Papers*. He also used the Great White Horse as the setting for Mr Pickwick's inadvertent entry into a lady's bedroom in the same book. (*Ipswich Journal*, 1859)

~ OCTOBER 16TH ~

1839: The Times reported that 16-year-old Elizabeth Gossett had nearly lost her life in an accident in her parents' yard in Coddenham.

She had climbed on to the curb-stone of their well to reach up for some overhanging pears but had lost her balance and tumbled 90ft down. She clung on to the well rope and managed to put one foot in the bucket until her neighbour, John Offord, arrived to attempt a rescue. After a huge struggle, John managed to get Elizabeth out. She was badly bruised but no bones broken.

The Times reported that John Offord, a pump-maker, was an industrious fellow with a large family to support, so it was all to his credit that he had put his life in danger to rescue someone else. By huge coincidence, twenty-five years previously a young man had fallen into the same well and had been rescued by another Offord – John's father! (*The Times*, 1839)

1970: A hefty neck-ring of twisted gold was unearthed in a garden in Belstead, almost certainly part of the same hoard that had been discovered in nearby Holcombe Crescent a year or so previously. These Iron Age neck ornaments, called torcs, all came to light as ground was prepared for new housing. They were made about 75 BC and may well have been worn for some years before being buried together. They were extremely valuable and were acquired by the British Museum. Copies can be seen at Ipswich Museum. (British Museum; Ipswich Museum)

~ October 17th ~

1910: Mabel Hackney and Laurence Irving, husband and wife actors, appeared at the Lyceum Theatre, Ipswich. The play, *Margaret Catchpole*, was of local interest and was such a success that they promised audiences they would return to the theatre one day.

It was not to be. In May 1914, they both drowned in the St Lawrence river as they were leaving Canada after yet another successful tour. As their ship, the *Empress of Ireland*, collided with another vessel and began to sink, they got separated from each other. Laurence was safe, but he knew Mabel was in the river and could not swim so he jumped into the water to rescue her – but they both drowned. Over 1,000 people died or were reported missing on that terrible day. (Roy Hudd Music Hall Archive; Empress of Ireland: www.theempressofireland.com)

1936: Mrs Wallis Simpson was granted a *decree nisi* from her second husband, Ernest Simpson, at the Ipswich County Court in St Helen's Street. She had been living in Felixstowe for the six weeks before that, which allowed her to claim residential status in the area. The hearing was held quietly in Ipswich, to keep the whole thing out of London. The press, however, got wind of what was afoot and swarmed into Ipswich on the day of the court case.

After a short hearing, Mrs Simpson was whisked away back to London. Just two months later, the new king – Edward VIII – abdicated the throne and married Mrs Simpson the following year. They lived together overseas in virtual exile for the next 50 or so years. (www.planetipswich.com)

– OCTOBER 18TH –

2003: John Alderton, one of the stars of the hit series *Upstairs Downstairs*, was at school in Suffolk for a date with his own history. John and his wife, fellow actor Pauline Collins, were guests of honour at Amberfield School near Ipswich.

The grounds of the independent school were once the site of Nacton Workhouse. Among the men, women and children who died there in the depression of the 1780s was the actor's 3x great-grandfather, Joseph.

John Alderton, who had spent years researching his family history, stumbled across an ancestor's autobiography, written in neat copperplate handwriting at the end of the nineteenth century. This gave John clues about previous generations and eventually he discovered that Joseph's final resting place was Nacton Workhouse. John visited the area where the paupers' graves would have been. They were in a nearby copse of trees and marked by a large granite stone engraved 'To The Poor of Nacton'.

Some years later, after the 2006 Ipswich Murders, John realised that it was the exact spot where the body of one of the five victims was found. Her name, chillingly, was Amelie Alderton. (*Ipswich Evening Star*, 2003. Thanks to John Alderton)

~ OCTOBER 19TH ~

1468: Every butcher in Ipswich was ordered to be fined 12*d* if he sold beef from animals that had not been baited by dogs at the bull stake in the Cornhill. It was thought that baiting – which involved dogs harassing the cattle with barks and snarls – improved the meat in some way. The last recorded bull-baiting in Ipswich was held in 1805 in Fleece Yard off St Matthew's Street. (Nathaniell Bacon, *Annalls of Ipswich*; *The Eastern Counties' Chronology or Book of Dates*, 1906)

———

1867: The provision market (on the site of the modern-day Buttermarket Shopping Centre) was relaunched after several years of decline. The *Ipswich Journal* gave it a hearty welcome, and boys from the Ragged School played their part by working as porters, in uniforms of loose bright red shirts and corduroy trousers. The streets were decorated and there were crowds of shoppers.

One of the new features of the provision market was the availability of fresh goods, such as butter, cheese, eggs and vegetables, shipped over from Holland. The Dutch produce was welcomed by the *Ipswich Journal* correspondent 'even though the Dutch market women are not exactly models of feminine beauty'. No doubt the journalist was a bit of a Greek god himself and well qualified to comment! (*Ipswich Journal*, 1867)

~ October 20th ~

1587: John Betts and four other musicians were appointed as the new town waits by the Ipswich authorities. They were required to patrol through the town from 2 a.m. until light, perhaps waking the townsfolk on dark winter mornings by playing under their windows. Their other major duties were to welcome prestigious visitors at the town gates and to lead the mayor's procession on civic occasions, wearing their distinctive blue uniforms. John's band were offered an annual salary of £4 and they were allowed to earn more by playing in the mystery plays and pageants that were put on in the town.

The town authorities had bought a stock of suitable musical instruments just a few years previously. These would have included early versions of bassoons, oboes and trombones, all suitable for making a loud, penetrating sound which could be heard out of doors.

John Betts' appointment on this day turned out to be a successful one. There are records of his contract with Ipswich being renewed yearly for at least the next decade. (Nathaniell Bacon, *Annalls of Ipswich*)

~ October 21st ~

1916: On or about this Saturday, and for several years running, Helmingham School held a clothing club for villagers. It was always attended by Frederick Fish & Son, linen drapers of Ipswich, and here is how it worked:

Village children paid a weekly contribution to the club and this was recorded on a card at school. The cards were totalled each October and a bonus of 3s was added for each child by the Dowager Lady Eliza Tollemache of Helmingham Hall.

To save villagers the fare to Ipswich, a shop was opened for the whole of one Saturday at Helmingham School, stocked with van-loads of textiles brought along from Frederick Fish's shop. Village women would buy material to sew clothes themselves rather than buy ready-made garments. Four assistants from the shop usually attended, and all clothing cards were redeemed during the day. The assistants said they enjoyed their day out in the country, and especially appreciated the beer provided for them by the Tollemache family.

With the advent of the bicycle and then the bus, villagers could visit the Ipswich shops themselves, and so the school shop was closed. (George Ewart Evans, *Where Beards Wag All*)

─ October 22nd ─

1870: This Saturday's issue of the *Ipswich Journal* reported that Sir Shafto Adair of Flixton Hall in north Suffolk had recently invited several gentlemen to come and witness his new bridge being tested. The bridge, spanning the River Waveney, was in the small village of Homersfield, and was the first concrete bridge in Great Britain. It was designed by an Ipswich architect, Henry Eyton, who worked closely with Sir Shafto on the project.

For the first test, a five ton roller was drawn over the 48ft bridge by four horses. They went back and forth several times just to make sure it would bear the weight. Then a wagon laden with sacks of flour was pulled across it. The bridge held.

When it was restored over a hundred years later, the work cost £85,000. Seven administrative boundaries converged in the middle of the bridge and so, at the re-opening, seven representatives, all wearing their chains of office, cut the ribbon with seven pairs of scissors. Each piece of ribbon was saved for posterity. (*Ipswich Journal*, 1870; notice board at Homersfield Bridge)

~ October 23rd ~

1964: Anna Airy, artist and first female President of the Ipswich Art Club, died in Playford at the age of 82.

She was a talented and versatile artist. She had worked throughout the First World War as one of the first women war artists. In particular, she had four large canvasses accepted by the Imperial War Museum, all of munitions factories. 'Each provided a remarkable insight into the diversity of Britain's wartime production and, as one, captured the vast scale, the noise, the heat and energy of the nation's industrial effort.' Her work at the shell forge in Hackney Marshes was particularly difficult, as the factory floor became so hot that her shoes were burned off her feet!

Anna moved to Playford in 1933 and was elected president of Ipswich Art Club in 1945, a post she held until she died. This was the first time for many years that the president was a professional artist. (*The Daily Telegraph*, 2013)

~ October 24th ~

1785: Mary Pack, daughter of one John Pack, was born on this day, the earliest birth recorded at the first Baptist church in Ipswich. Later known as Stoke Green Baptist church, this meeting house was established in 1773 by Baptists who originally worshiped together at the Cat House in Woolverstone and were baptised by full immersion in the River Orwell. (Joseph Ivied, *History of the English Baptists*; Peter Bishop, *History of Ipswich*)

1957: Dingle Foot (1905–78) was elected MP for Ipswich. Dingle was a lawyer, brother of Michael Foot, and had formerly been a Liberal MP in the West Country. He had joined the Labour Party in 1956 and found a niche within the 'champagne socialist' tendency. His wife, Dorothy, was one of the Elliston family from Ipswich. Her social style contrasted somewhat with Dingle's Methodist background and she was nicknamed 'Dingle's Tory wife' within the Foot family.

A popular MP in Ipswich until 1970, Dingle lost by just thirteen votes to his Conservative opponent, Ernle Money.

Despite changing his party, Dingle Foot never really embraced socialism; he began his political life as a Liberal, and there his heart remained. Dingle Foot died in 1978 after choking on a chicken bone in Hong Kong (Liberal Democrat History Group: www.liberalhistory.org.uk)

1594: An early street lighting scheme was introduced in Ipswich. All townspeople were ordered to hang lanterns and candles outside their houses from November to February. A beadle was also appointed to make the cry 'lanthorne and candle' every evening to remind inhabitants to put their lights up. If they failed, householders could be sent to prison. On the same day, Ipswich shopkeepers were ordered to hang signs outside their shops. (Nathaniell Bacon, *Annalls of Ipswich*)

1983: Ruth Watson, hotelier and television presenter, bought Hintlesham Hall, about 5 miles from Ipswich.

She explained:

> When my husband, David, suggested we bought Hintlesham Hall from Robert Carrier I thought he was mad. He told me that if we didn't buy the hall I was never to mention the idea of having a restaurant again. So we bought it. We then turned it from a restaurant to a hotel with thirty-three bedrooms and an eighteen-hole golf course.

In 1990, the Watsons also purchased the Fox and Goose Inn at Fressingfield, and launched it as the one of the first gastropubs in England. Subsequent ventures included a hotel and a pub in Orford and a 120-acre organic farm.

Ruth Watson was made an Honorary Graduate of University Campus Suffolk in Ipswich in 2010. (University Campus Suffolk; http://ruthwatson.co.uk/)

~ October 26th ~

1866: William Ranson, known as the 'Suffolk Stag', was challenged to walk from St Peter's parish to the Bull Inn in Aldgate and back in thirty-six hours – a round trip of about 150 miles. William set off from the Crown Inn in Ipswich, accompanied by his father and another companion riding together in a cart. When they arrived in Aldgate, William ate a couple of chops and had a bath. Then they all hit the road again for the return leg of the journey. William successfully completed the walk in thirty-five hours and forty-three minutes. (*The Eastern Counties' Chronology or Book of Dates*, 1906)

2006: The *East Anglian Daily Times* announced that an Ipswich edition of the board game, Monopoly, had hit the shops. Traditional squares like Park Lane, Old Kent Road and Mayfair were replaced with some well-known locations from around the town, including Portman Road, the Waterfront and the Cornhill. Christchurch Mansion scooped the prestigious Mayfair spot, with the borough council's new Grafton House headquarters given the dubious honour of being the town's Old Kent Road – the cheapest slot on the board!

Former Monopoly world champion Jason Bunn was in Ipswich to mark the launch of the new game, which was unveiled in Debenhams. (*East Anglian Daily Times*, 2006)

~ October 27th ~

1891: The *Star of the East* newspaper carried the shocking details of an inquest into the death of 42-year-old George Stannard of Mount Pleasant, a slum off Back Hamlet. He had died from eating toadstools. A widower, 'addicted to drink', Stannard had previously been imprisoned for neglecting his five children, who were discovered 'in a most filthy condition covered with vermin and matted hair. The only furniture in the house was a damaged table, three chairs, a knife and spoon and a thin straw mattress.' The children had survived by running errands for neighbours who gave them coppers for them to buy bread and herrings. (Thanks to Pip Wright)

1940: On this night, the tenth Luftwaffe raid on Ipswich took place. Several hundred butterfly bombs – designed to kill anyone who touched them – were dropped on Ipswich and a further eleven fell on Nacton shore. Ten people were killed that night (including six men on the night shift at Ransomes & Jeffries). Others were seriously injured as they tried to move the bombs to prevent further harm.

A poster campaign was launched to warn people not to go anywhere near these new explosive devices as the slightest vibration could set them off. Ipswich was the first British town to be attacked with them. (Ipswich Museum)

~ October 28th ~

1940: Towards the end of the Battle of Britain, there was an international encounter in a remote part of the Shotley Peninsula. Here is how it was reported in the *Aberdeen Journal*:

> Hearing someone banging at the door and calling out in a foreign language this morning, Mr Sidney Wrinch of Erwarton, grabbed a shotgun and went to the door.
>
> Outside he found a Nazi airman, apparently an officer, plastered with mud from head to foot.
>
> 'He appeared to be asking if he was in Holland,' said Mr Wrinch. 'When I told him he was in England he looked very dejected, gave a cry of despair and drew one hand across his throat.'
>
> As the Nazi did not speak English, it took Mr Wrinch and his family an hour to persuade him that they were not going to kill him.
>
> The airman was one of the crew of five of a plane which crashed in flight near Mr Wrinch's farm during the night. He was taken away by the police. His companions were also captured.

(*Aberdeen Journal*, 1940)

~ October 29th ~

1804: Lord Chedworth, the amiable, eccentric Shakespearean scholar and magistrate, died at his home in Brook Street. He was aged 50.

He had moved to Ipswich as a young man and became well-known for his distain of fashionable circles. He made 'unsuitable' friends in theatrical circles and at racecourses, and scandalised his social equals by haunting the parlour of The Griffin Inn in Westgate Street. Contemporaries described him as a strange-looking man, awkward and ungainly, 'an odd fox', 'very singular, and negligent in his dress'.

Chedworth never married. He was publicly accused of homosexual behaviour when he was 27. He refused to defend his honour by duelling. Instead, he successfully sued for damages, but the episode made him even more wary of society.

He was buried, as he had directed, beside his mother in St Matthew's churchyard.

Chedworth's will caused a sensation. He generously remembered many of his friends, including his theatrical and drinking pals. In particular, he left £4,000 to the cheesemonger at the town quay who played whist with him. The cheesemonger was to share the bequest with his wife, as Chedworth had often enjoyed talking to her.

Chedworth's family tried to have the will overturned on the grounds of insanity, but failed. (*Oxford Dictionary of National Biography*)

~ October 30th ~

1893: Leonard Squirrell (1893–1979) was born in Spring Road, in a house since marked with a blue plaque.

As a schoolboy, Leonard won a national art competition with a drawing from the top of Holy Trinity tower looking down on dockside roofs. After that, there was never any doubt that he would be an artist.

Squirrell studied at Ipswich School of Art and then in London, interrupted by war work at the drawing office at Ransomes Sims & Jeffries. He was a great draughtsman, which is clear in his art work. During the war, Squirrell exhibited at the Royal Academy. This was the first of forty-six consecutive years when his paintings – often of Suffolk subjects – were shown there.

He was prolific, and in addition to his fine art, he produced pictures for calendars for local companies, such as R&W Paul and Compair.

For many years, Squirrell lived in Crabbe Street, later moving to Witnesham. He was a quiet, reserved man with a stammer. He left behind a collectable body of work, some of which is in national collections like the Victoria & Albert Museum, the British Museum and the Fitzwilliam Museum in Cambridge. (Ipswich Society)

2008: Kirsten Rausing, one of the richest women in the world, was made an Honorary Graduate of University Campus Suffolk in Ipswich for her services to thoroughbred racing and breeding in Newmarket. (University Campus Suffolk)

1789: The *Ipswich Journal* reported that two noteworthy visitors had arrived in the town on the previous Monday night. They were Lord and Lady Mazarone, who had fled from revolutionary Paris where, the newspaper explained in a later issue, anyone with an aristocratic name was in danger from the 'mob'.

Far from living the life of an idle aristocrat, Lord Mazarone had been imprisoned in the stinking Grand Chatelet prison in Paris for nearly thirty years until the prison was liberated by revolutionaries. His crimes were not reported. Lord and Lady Mazarone stayed at the Great White Horse in Ipswich for two nights. Lord Mazarone had a bit of a busman's holiday in the town: he spent the Tuesday visiting local prisons before setting off for London the next morning. (*Ipswich Journal*, 1789)

1863: A substantial hoard of coins was discovered in an earthenware pot, buried a full 10ft beneath the doorstep of the house on the corner of the Buttermarket and White Hart (later St Lawrence) Lane in the town centre. One hundred and fifty silver pennies came to light, some minted in London and others struck in Ipswich. The coins dated from the time of King Aethelred 'the Unready' (*c.* 968–1016). Some of them found their way into museum collections; others were snapped up by private buyers. (*Bury & Norwich Post*, 1863; William Conder, *Conder Family Ipswich*)

1783: The *Ipswich Journal* reported on the inquest of Mrs Simpson of Shotley. It said that she had died in agony earlier that week after breakfasting on her usual Bohea (or black) tea. Her husband was seriously ill for several hours after the same drink, but he recovered. A 14-year-old boy and four servants were also sick after drinking some, and one nearly died.

The teapot was, unfortunately, emptied before the physician and surgeon arrived, but they took the tea canister back with them to Ipswich for investigation. The inquest recorded a verdict of accidental death 'from a quantity of tea taken, of some poisonous quality'.

As there was an implication that the tea had been smuggled into Shotley, the *Ipswich Journal* took the opportunity to warn its readers as follows:

> The above melancholy accident should caution persons against the use of smuggled tea, as it is well known that the hawkers of that article frequently make use of a very pernicious drug, in order to give the tea a finer colour, and if unskilfully made use of, may, as in the above instance, prove fatal.

(Thanks to Pip Wright)

1989: The first patient was admitted to St Elizabeth's Hospice, Ipswich. (Hospice volunteers' newsletter, winter 2013)

– November 2nd –

1319: The Ipswich authorities made two rulings relating to the town bailiffs (the most senior civic officials): when a new bailiff was needed, the election must be held on the Feast of the Our Lady's Nativity (September 8). The bailiffs should each be given an annual payment of £5 plus 'fish, herrings, onions, garlic and gorse', as this was the ancient custom and practice. Gifts of gorse might seem strange to modern ideas, but it was used at the time as fuel and animal feed. (Nathaniell Bacon, *Annalls of Ipswich*)

1886: Eight families were invited to tea by the mayor to say goodbye and good luck. They were the first party of emigrants leaving Ipswich to settle in Western Australia. The men were unemployed and had found work there as railway navvies. The Ipswich Emigration Committee had lent them their fares.

The Magistrates' Room at the town hall was festooned with bunting and packed with well-wishers. Mr Elliston, surgeon, had given the emigrants a free medical examination and each family was provided with a Bible to take with them.

The emigrants left Ipswich a few days later to join the cargo ship *Elderslie*, which departed from London, bound for Freemantle. (*Ipswich Journal*, 1886; *Star of the East*, 1886)

— November 3rd —

2011: June Brown received an honorary degree from University Campus Suffolk. June was the Ipswich girl who became famous playing the role of the archetypal Cockney, chain-smoking 'Dot Cotton' in EastEnders.

June was born in Needham Market in 1927, and her family moved to Ipswich when she was a toddler. She was one of five children, but only three survived childhood. Her parents, Harry and Louisa Brown, were of Irish, Scottish and Jewish heritage, and they were new to Suffolk. Appropriately, June also had Cockney roots – her 3x great-grandfather was a champion bare-knuckle boxer from the East End!

June went to St John's Church of England School and then won a scholarship to Ipswich High School for Girls. She disliked the snooty headmistress, who liked to put the scholarship pupils in their places by saying that for girls, birth was more important than brains. June said in later life that, although the public assumed she spoke like Dot Cotton, her Ipswich teachers had always insisted on correct grammar and good diction, and these had become a lifelong habit for her.

In the Second World War, she was evacuated to Wales, but she finally left Ipswich when she was 17 and joined the Wrens – and that was where she got the acting bug. (IMDB biography: www.imdb.com; BBC News: http://news.bbc.co.uk/1/hi/entertainment/7452896.stm)

~ November 4th ~

1834: There was an unusual exhibit among the usual chrysanthemums, grapes and garden veg at the Ipswich Horticultural Show on this Tuesday. Dr Pennington, surgeon of Needham Market, displayed 'a fine specimen of opium, extracted and prepared from poppies grown by himself'. (*Ipswich Journal*, 1834)

2010: David Croft was made an honorary graduate of University Campus Suffolk at a ceremony at Ipswich Town Hall. He was noted for producing and co-writing a string of hit BBC sitcoms, including *Dad's Army*, *Are You Being Served?*, *It Ain't Half Hot Mum*, *Hi-de-Hi!* and *'Allo 'Allo!*

Croft, who lived in a farmhouse near Bury St Edmunds, knew Suffolk well, and several *Dad's Army* episodes were shot in the county: Honington Primary School was used for exterior shots of the church hall where Mainwaring and his men would meet up; Bardwell Green was used for a parade of Russian visitors; Brandon, Sapiston, Santon Downham and the sugar beet factory in Bury all had cameo roles; and Drinkstone Mill was the setting for Corporal Jones getting caught up in windmill sails.

As a producer, Croft's trademark was to signal the end of an episode with the caption 'You Have Been Watching ...' (University Campus Suffolk; *Suffolk Magazine*, 2010)

– November 5th –

1854: The Battle of Inkerman was fought on this day – a major engagement in the Crimean War which involved an alliance of Britain, France and the Ottoman Empire on the one hand, and Russia on the other.

In the years leading up to the war, companies of hussars and other cavalry had been garrisoned at the barracks in north Ipswich off Anglesea Road. Several streets and a pub nearby were later given names to commemorate their part in the conflict: Inkerman Pub was named after the battle which was a major defeat for the Russian army; Redan Street was named after one of the large Russian fortifications that ringed the city of Sebastopol; Cardigan Street was named after Lord Cardigan, commander of the 11th Hussars; Paget Road was likely named after Lord Paget, who was in command at the Battle of Inkerman; and Anglesea Road was probably named after the Pagets' family title, the 'Marquises of Anglesey'.

Many of the men who had been barracked in Ipswich before the Crimean War never returned to England. Some were killed in action, but even more died of diseases like cholera and never got anywhere near the battlefields. (Carol Twinch, *Ipswich Street by Street*)

~ NOVEMBER 6TH ~

1874: On this day or thereabouts, Isabella Brett died in Ipswich. Isabella kept a diary, of which three volumes survive – 1867, 1873 and 1874 – leaving a unique record of the life of a middle-class woman in Ipswich in the mid-nineteenth century. The diaries recorded trips to London (the family were seasick on the voyage from Ipswich), shopping, spring-cleaning, illnesses (her husband's alcohol-related maladies) and financial matters. Isabella lived for most of her married life at No. 163 Woodbridge Road. (Ipswich Women's History Trail)

———

2010: For the first time, the Ipswich Hindu community were able to celebrate Diwali (the Festival of Lights) at their new premises in the Thoroughfare. They had only moved there a couple of days before, having taken over the lease from the Buddhist Centre. Up to this point, Ipswich Hindus had not had their own premises for meetings and worship.

In the early 1980s, a group of five Hindu families used to gather in one another's homes to worship once a month. They would light a sacrificial fire with purified butter, sandalwood and small pieces of wood and then sprinkle samagri (nuts, fruits and spices) on it as they chanted. Over time, the group increased in numbers and needed their own premises. By the end of the first decade of the twenty-first century, there were just over 1,000 Hindus in Ipswich, some British citizens and others here from India to work on projects for companies like British Telecomms.

A few weeks after Diwali, marble statues of Lord Krishna and his consort, Radha, were installed at the Ipswich Temple. (Ipswich Hindu website: www.ipswichhindusamaj.org.uk)

— NOVEMBER 7TH —

1849: Richard Dykes Alexander and other philanthropists set up the Ipswich Ragged School in a cottage in St Clement's Lane. Within a year there were 290 children on roll, necessitating a move to bigger premises in Waterworks Street.

The pupils were some of the poorest in Ipswich: many worked for a living in the daytime; some were the children of 'worthless or drunken parents'; some had parents who were honest but poor; and others were children whose clothes were so tattered that no other school would admit them.

Lessons included scripture, reading, writing and rug making. Boys also learned carpentry, cobbling and how to chop and bundle firewood.

As well as being one of the founders of the school, Alexander was a pioneer photographer. He took several fascinating photographs at the Waterworks Street school, which showed the teacher with his classes of destitute boys. The girls' classrooms were further along the same street. For their photograph, Alexander sat them under a Bible text which summed up the Ragged School ethos: 'Deliver the Poor and Needy and Rid them out of the Hand of the Wicked.' (*Ipswich Journal*, various dates; *Ipswich Remembered 2*, photographs selected and prepared by SRO)

~ NOVEMBER 8TH ~

1851: Mrs Henry Knight and her daughter lectured on 'dress reform' wearing 'full Bloomer Costume' at the Temperance Hall in Crown Street. A capacity audience packed the Hall that night, eager to be entertained by something unusual.

Mrs and Miss Knight were late on stage. The crowd whistled and stamped impatiently. Then, as the door under the gallery opened, the 'Two Bloomers' emerged to great applause mingled with laughter. Some disappointed members of the audience were heard to say 'Oh, that's all, is it?' which caused more hilarity.

The gas lights were turned up full to give a good view of the women's costumes. They wore broad-brimmed hats trimmed with pink ribbons, black velvet jackets over white blouses, and pink satin skirts to 6in below the knee with matching pantalettes tied at the ankles. Mrs Knight explained that it was essential for women to be able to dress comfortably, as current fashions 'were among the evils that beset the present condition of women'.

The 'Two Bloomers' left the stage after about an hour to a noisy mixture of applause and hissing – which was better than the following week in Yarmouth, where they were met with whole-hearted 'ridicule, disgust and contempt'. (*Ipswich Journal*, 1851; *Bury & Norwich Post*, 1851)

— NOVEMBER 9TH —

1800: Admiral Nelson spent the night at Bamford's Hotel in Ipswich. He was travelling from Yarmouth to London with a party that included his mistress, the notorious Lady Hamilton. The plan had originally been to stay at his Ipswich house, Round Wood, which his wife had bought while he had been abroad. He had hardly ever visited it, although his wife and his father had lived there for some time.

When his wife heard Nelson was coming back to England, she invited him and his whole travelling party to dine there with her and stay the night. She may have wanted to meet him and his mistress on her own turf. But when she heard nothing from him, she thought it best to close up the house and go to London and wait for him there.

Nelson knew nothing about his wife's departure. When the party arrived at Round Wood, they found it empty and unprepared. He had a brief look round then promptly took his friends to find rooms in town.

When Nelson left Bamford's Hotel the next morning, he was greeted by an enthusiastic crowd who uncoupled his horses from the carriage and carried it aloft through the town.

He never visited Round Wood again. (Sheila Hardy, *Frances, Lady Nelson*)

— November 10th —

1606: Nearly 500 loaves of bread were given to the poor of Ipswich to celebrate the failure of Guy Fawkes' Gunpowder Plot. (Nathaniell Bacon, *Annalls of Ipswich*)

1838: Hezekiah Brown, a boy of about 14 from Ipswich, was barred from giving evidence in a trial because he did not understand what an oath was:

> Magistrate: Do you know the nature of an oath?
> Hezekiah: No I don't.
> Magistrate: Are you aware of the penalty of taking a false oath?
> Hezekiah: No I ain't.
> Magistrate: Do you know where you will go when you die?
> Hezekiah: No I don't.
> Magistrate: Have you never been at church or chapel?
> Hezekiah: I should like to go if I had clothes, but they won't let me into the church with these clothes.
> Magistrate: I never met a lad of your age in such pitiful state of ignorance.

Mr Brame, the prison governor, suggested that the lad could be given some instruction at the gaol if he would agree to spend a few days locked up, but after a further brief exchange, a local clergyman kindly offered to take the boy under his wing and give him some instruction. (Thanks to Pip Wright)

~ November 11th ~

1918: Olive Turney, a professional driver, described Armistice Day in Ipswich in her diary:

> Armistice Treaty signed at 5 a.m. Hostilities ceased from 11 a.m. Ransomes closed for the day. Ipswich extremely crowded all day. The streets quite impassable. Thanksgiving services in the evening.
>
> Kaiser fled to Holland. Socialist government proclaimed in Germany.

Olive was from Barsham near Beccles and she had moved to Ipswich to help with war work. She became a lorry driver for Ransomes Sims & Jefferies and delivered aircraft as they were finished at the factory. She also worked as a private chauffeur and as a taxi driver for Eggertons of Ipswich. She loved the freedom her driving jobs gave her.

In her subsequent diary entries, Olive wrote that Ransomes did not open for two more days after Armistice Day and when it did, no one felt like working. In Ipswich, church bells rang, flags flew and public clocks were once again allowed to strike at night after a long silence.

She summed up that historic week: 'Everyone rejoicing in this Town, standing around in throngs and not quite knowing what to do with themselves.' (Olive Turney's diary and journal, SRO; John F. Bridges, *Early County Motoring*; Ipswich Women's History Trail)

– November 12th –

1555: 'Two Egiptians' (gypsies) were married in St Mary's church, Bramford. It was one of the first official Romany weddings in the country. (Bramford Parish Registers, SRO)

1961: The film *The Angry Silence* won a BAFTA for Bryan Forbes for best British screenplay of the year. With a gritty, documentary-like approach unusual at the time, it had been partially shot on location at Clifford Road School and at Reavell's engineering works in Ranelagh Road. Local amateurs, plus a young Oliver Reed and workers from Reavell's all appeared as extras, while the starring role went to Richard Attenborough.

Attenborough played the part of a worker who was 'sent to Coventry' when he refused to take part in an unofficial strike. The theme provoked controversy – some saw it as the story of a man daring to fight to keep his individual freedom; others as an attack on trade unions. Ipswich Trades Council passed a motion of boycott against it.

Attenborough attended the premier at the Ritz Cinema in the Buttermarket, and greeted the Reavell's workers there who had taken part. (*Ipswich Evening Star*, 2006; John Hassard and Ruth Holliday, eds, *Organisation-Representation*)

~ November 13th ~

1976: The first Women's Aid refuge in Ipswich opened near the town centre to support and rehouse women and children escaping the horrors of domestic violence. The first woman and child moved in just a couple of weeks later.

It was set up by local Labour Party women to respond to an urgent need. It was also a practical way of commemorating International Women's Day.

This first hostel acted as an advice centre and office as well as a refuge. It ran as a collective with residents and workers (all volunteers) sharing all responsibilities. There was just one phone – a payphone in the hall – for calling the DHSS (as it was then) and the Borough Council for help and advice. Sometimes the volunteers used to go themselves to collect desperate women wanting refuge, occasionally taking a police escort with them.

In the first year or so, a total of 65 women and 131 children, mostly from Suffolk, were given refuge.

By 2014, Ipswich Women's Aid had expanded: it ran two refuges in confidential locations and a women's centre in Berners Street, and it had changed its name to Lighthouse. (Lighthouse website and annual reports)

– NOVEMBER 14TH –

1905: The first fatal motor accident in Ipswich was recorded:

> Seven year old Allan Staines was knocked down by a car in Wherstead Road and died almost instantly. He had been running along behind a carrier's car and for some reason had darted out in front of the car, which had no chance of stopping. The coroner said that it was the first death caused by a motor car that he had investigated.

(John F. Bridges, *Early Country Motoring*)

1925: Young men arrived at a labour camp in Suffolk for the unemployed:

> A group of men jumped off a lorry and walked into Barham House, in the Suffolk village of Claydon. All were young, single and unemployed, and the majority had travelled by train from coalmining areas. They were among 200 recruits to a new six month training course in basic farming techniques, before sailing on an assisted passage to Canada or Australia.

One of the first to arrive was a young unemployed miner from Sheffield. He was keen about everything, especially the food (he had put on 11lbs) and the 'jolly evenings' listening to music, live at the piano or on the radio or gramophone.

Not all recruits were as enthusiastic, though, because no one was given a choice about joining this scheme – they were all conscripted. (John Field, *Exporting People of British Stock*)

‒ November 15th ‒

2006: Ipswich enjoyed the premiere of the new James Bond film, *Casino Royale*, at Cardinal Park. When *Casino Royale* had opened in London all eyes were on Daniel Craig to see how he would shape up as the new leading man. In Ipswich, though, there was an extra local interest: Bond's classy yacht (the *Spirit 54*) was made by local boat builders Spirit Yachts, of New Cut West.

The *Spirit 54* was needed by the film-makers for several months. The first two days' filming were in the Bahamas (doubling for the Med), with Bond and his latest conquest flirting onboard. Then it was over to Venice for some helicopter shots of Bond sailing into the lagoon and suavely motoring up the Grand Canal to St Mark's Square.

Mick Newman, Director of Spirit Yachts, summed it all up: '2,000 miles of sailing, two transatlantic crossings, 1,500 miles on trucks, a dozen airfares or so ‒ for about three or four minutes in the film!' (Spirit Yacht's website: www.spirityachts.com)

‑ November 16th ‑

1896: Ipswich witnessed its first motorised vehicle: 'Charles Berners of Woolverstone Park drove his De Dion powered tricycle into town to visit Mr Popplewell's cycle shop in Woodbridge Road. Mr Berners had bought his machine in Paris several months earlier, but had only been able to use it in his private grounds.'

When the 'Red Flag Act' was repealed in this year, Mr Berners was then allowed to take his motor carriage on the highways at speeds up to the national limit of 14mph! (John F. Bridges, *Early Country Motoring*)

———

1971: Led Zeppelin played at St Matthew's Baths on the corner of Civic Drive and St Matthew's Street. Tickets were £1 and the set included the classic hits 'Whole Lotta Love' and 'Stairway to Heaven'.

The concert hall, opened in 1924, doubled as a swimming pool in the summer. This was drained in the autumn and covered with a sprung wooden floor.

Other world famous bands appearing at the baths included the Yardbirds, Cream, The Animals, John Mayall, the Spencer Davis Group, Georgie Fame and 'local' blues and soul man Geno Washington, a GI from RAF Bentwaters.

St Matthew's Baths closed when Crown Pools opened. The building remains, now with listed status and complete with its original glazed roof lantern, but surrounded by ugly modern shops. (David Kindred's website: kindred-spirit.co.uk; Ipswich Historic Lettering website: ipswich-lettering.org)

— NOVEMBER 17TH —

1896: Henry Miller, whose stage name was 'King of Horse Educators', married Matilda Peck in Ipswich on or about this day. He was born in 1870 in New York and had learned how to break horses using techniques developed by mustang-riding Native Americans. As a young man, Henry came to England in a cattle boat to seek his fortune. He spent some years touring with circuses and working the music halls where audiences paid to see him billed as 'Professor' Henry Miller. His act involved mastering untameable stallions with skill and showmanship – his style being more of a horse dominator than a horse whisperer.

When Miller married and settled in Ipswich, he worked as a colt breaker. He kept ten horses – carriage horses, not shires – in Britannia Road and many more in Crabbe Street in the stables of a big house. His children had to clean them out and feed them before school.

During the First World War, Miller served in the Army Veterinary Corps, but by the time he was discharged the world had changed. Transport was now motorised and there was hardly any call for his horse skills.

Miller died in Ipswich in 1939. (George Ewart Evans, *Horse Power and Magic*)

~ NOVEMBER 18TH ~

1819: *The Times* gave a remarkably impartial account of a gathering in Ipswich which had been held to protest about the brutality used to break up a political meeting in Manchester (known later as the Peterloo Massacre).

It reported that ninety Ipswich householders had petitioned magistrates for permission to hold the meeting. This was refused but the meeting went ahead anyway. Upwards of 2,000 people gathered and *The Times* described them as respectable and well-behaved. It said that the orderly meeting was ably chaired by Mr Ransome senior, a factory owner and Quaker who was known for his progressive views.

In contrast, the equally Tory *Ipswich Journal*, reporting the same meeting, was antagonistic. It described how the small crowd, never more than 600 in number, was made up entirely from 'people drawn there by curiosity, women, and boys' and all from the 'labouring classes'. It explained that the meeting – opened by a band from Needham playing 'Ça ira' (the unofficial anthem of the French Revolution) – was held in a field off Woodbridge Road and speakers jumped up on to wagons to 'harangue' the crowd.

Both papers reported the resolutions passed at the meeting, which were: the right of English people to assemble; disgust at the way the authorities had dealt with the Manchester meeting; and a call for an inquiry. (*Ipswich Journal*, 1819; *The Times*, 1819)

~ November 19th ~

1854: The Patriotic Fund was set up this year to support the wives and children of soldiers serving in the Crimean War. By this day, funds raised in East Anglia were: Ipswich £826; Thetford £234; Debenham £52. (*Lloyd's Weekly Newspaper*, 1854)

1972: Bernard Reynolds, local artist and teacher at Ipswich Art School, won the prestigious Sir Otto Beit Medal for Sculpture on or about this day.

His award-winning piece was *The Ship*, a semi-abstract sculpture made of aluminium, steel and fibre-glass. The internal structure of steel tubes and aluminum castings was made by Ipswich firms, finished and assembled by Reynolds himself with the help of two of his students.

He presented it to the town and it was first installed at the foot of the Civic Centre (later demolished), moving to the Civic Drive roundabout in 1996.

Reynolds described his winning sculpture as 'an arrangement in 3D of five units each based on a shape suggesting sails or hulls. It aims to symbolise ships and shipping of all periods, and therefore Ipswich's long history as a port.' (Ipswich Borough Council; Bernard Reynolds' website: www.bernardreynoldssculptor.co.uk)

– NOVEMBER 20TH –

1336: Horsewade (Handford) Mill sat on a channel off the River Gipping by what later became the recreation ground on Alderman Road. When it burned down, John Haltebe, the miller's son, was given permission on this day to rebuild it at his own expense. The town authorities also gave him an eight-year lease on the land and allowed him to use Oldenholme meadow nearby. John's rent was a single red rose to be 'paid' every year at midsummer. (Ipswich Borough Archives, compiled by David Allen; Nathaniell Bacon, *Annalls of Ipswich*)

1802: Sarah Rolfe reassured customers that, contrary to rumour, her family fellmongery was still in business, dealing in animal hides and making gloves and breeches. She also promised local bricklayers a continued supply of animal hair for strengthening plaster – available from the Buttermarket or at her riverside yard by Stoke Bridge. (*Ipswich Journal*, 1802)

1918: After the first group of German submarines surrendered to the British off Felixstowe on this day, at least 100 more of them gathered off Shotley, making an 'avenue' of subs a mile and a half long in the mouth of the Orwell. (The Eastern Counties' Chronology or Book of Dates)

― NOVEMBER 21ST ―

1681: At this time, there were two attempts to set up cloth-weaving businesses in Ipswich, both of them involving Huguenot (French Protestant) refugees who were fleeing to England in great numbers.

One scheme was launched under the auspices of the Royal Lustring Company, which was founded by Ipswich-born philanthropist and merchant Thomas Firmin to give work to paupers and other impoverished people. He brought skilled Huguenot weavers to Ipswich to make glossy silk fabrics. Their families came with them and their children were housed, partly at public expense, at Christ's Hospital.

The other weaving initiative in Ipswich at this time was led by a Frenchman named Bonhomme. He was financed by the French Church in London to employ fellow Huguenots to produce good quality sailcloth in the French style.

Unfortunately, both the silk weaving and sailcloth enterprises were short-lived and the Huguenot community in Ipswich found themselves having to move elsewhere for work. (Samuel Smiles, The Huguenots; Vincent Redstone, *The Dutch and Huguenot Settlements of Ipswich*)

~ November 22nd ~

2004: The *East Anglian* reported that a new print of the film *Akenfield* had been shown recently at Ipswich Film Theatre to two rapturous houses.

Originally filmed in 1974, *Akenfield* was shot on location in a number of East Suffolk villages around Charsfield. Adapted by author Ronald Blythe from his own best-selling novel, it told the story of three generations of the Rous family on the day that old Tom Rous was buried in the village churchyard. It was the age-old story of youngsters wanting to get away, while their roots pulled them back towards home.

Director Sir Peter Hall wanted to capture the autobiographical atmosphere of the book and insisted that 'ordinary people' should be cast. They had to improvise the dialogue as they went, guided by Hall who was working from Ronald Blythe's minimalist twenty-page script.

The film made a local celebrity of Peggy Cole. She was cast as young Tom's mother, although she had turned up for the first day's shooting thinking she was just going to make the tea!

Dave Gregory, films officer at the Ipswich Film Theatre, enthusiastically welcomed the reprint as the previous print of the film had degraded so badly that it could no longer be shown. (*East Anglian Daily Times*, 2004)

– NOVEMBER 23RD –

1903: Electric trams came into public service in Ipswich, replacing horse-drawn trams. They ran on tracks and had over-head cables.

On this Monday morning, the first passengers got on at Whitton, heading for the Griffin in Bath Street. They were three staff from the *East Anglian* newspaper and a labourer. Although it was only 5.30 a.m., the tram driver clanged the bell as they went and people came out of their houses in their nightwear to have a look.

The first electric tram route ran from Whitton to Bourne Bridge via the Cornhill and the railway station. A connection also ran to the GER river steamer via the spur along Bath Street.

Within a year, Ipswich had routes operating all over town and had thirty-six double-deckers in service, all in their livery of dark green and cream. Each tram had room for twenty-six passengers downstairs and twenty-four 'on top'. The top deck was open to the elements as the Board of Trade did not allow covered-over carriages on the upper deck on narrow gauge track – and, at 3ft 6in, the Ipswich gauge was one of the narrowest in the country. (Ipswich Transport Museum; Robert Malster, *Ipswich: An A to Z of Local History*)

~ November 24th ~

1908: Suffragette Sylvia Pankhurst (1882–1960) was the first of the Pankhurst family to come to Ipswich to speak. She appeared at the Public Hall in front of a large audience and, writing later about the meeting, said that she thought that the building had been packed with people whose tickets had been bought for them by anti-suffragette protesters.

When she rose to speak, there was an almighty commotion – shouts, yells, rattling of tin cans and ringing of bells. People started singing a hostile song which had been especially composed for the occasion – the words were printed out on sheets and distributed. Several fights broke out in the hall, and walking sticks and other missiles were thrown. Stink bombs were let off.

When the organisers saw the damage that was being done, they asked the police to come and restore order. However, the chief constable claimed he had no power to act. Looking back, Sylvia wrote that she thought this claim was strange – she had attended many meeting where the police had used their powers to eject suffragettes when they were the ones doing the interrupting. (The Eastern Counties' Chronology or Book of Dates; Sylvia Pankhurst, *The Suffragette*)

— NOVEMBER 25TH —

1801: Lieutenant Stoddart of the Inniskilling Dragoons, quartered in Ipswich, appeared at the Court of the King's Bench, London, on a charge of assault.

He had accompanied his commanding officer to a ball at the Ipswich Assembly Rooms when a doorman had told them that their subscription fees were overdue. Stoddart took offence, immediately sought out the Master of Ceremonies, and publicly pulled his nose – an ungallant insult. The gentlemen present in the Assembly Rooms were scandalised and insisted the case be sent to court.

Stoddart was found guilty and sentenced to four months in the Marshalsea. A wigging from the judge condemned him for his lack of courtesy to the 'Inhabitants of the Town of Ipswich' and their rules. (*Bury & Norwich Post*, 1801; *Ipswich Journal*, 1802)

1848: This Saturday's issue of the *Ipswich Journal* reported on the brilliance of the Northern Lights which had been visible in the Ipswich skies the day before.

> In the early part of the evening, the usual spires of light were observed rising in the northern hemisphere from north-east to south-west. But towards nine o'clock the lights increased in brightness, and presented the appearance of an irregular arch of crimson light across the sky, while from a point south-east of the zenith, rays of light were diverging in all directions.

All contemporary accounts agreed that a more magnificent display of the Northern Lights had seldom been witnessed across the country. (*Ipswich Journal*, 1848)

– November 26th –

1948: On this Friday night, Peggy Walker from Leeds met her future husband, an American serviceman from Texas, at the Arlington Ballroom in Museum Street.

Just after the end of the Second World War, Peggy had joined the Women's Land Army and was posted to Suffolk. For the next few years she worked on various farms around Ipswich. She shared a dormitory at Hope House Hostel in Foxhall Road with four other city girls. She had never even seen a cow before, let alone milked one, and quickly had to learn to ride a bicycle so she could travel between farms. She wore the Land Army uniform of green jersey, brown breeches and a brown felt hat. Peggy's jobs were many and varied: weeding, stone picking, hay making, stacking corn, milking, trapping rats, loading carts and leading horses for ploughing. Like lots of the girls, she hated planting potatoes and beets and pulling them on frosty or rainy days.

Lots of the Hope House Hostel girls enjoyed going to dances at weekends. There was always the chance of meeting GIs who came into town from the USAF bases, and everyone's favourite was the Arlington Ballroom. The girls had to go in uniform, which Peggy said was an absolute passion-killer, but on this Friday night she met her man! (Thanks to Peggy Miller, *née* Walker)

— NOVEMBER 27TH —

1899: Eley Went was born in Ipswich on or about this day but moved to Ufford with his family as a boy. He was a self-taught fiddler, although he did take a few lessons from a violinist at St Audrey's Asylum in Melton.

In 1917 he went into the army and played in a fife and drum band. After seeing action in France, he returned to Suffolk and started playing in local 'singing' pubs, like the Blaxhall Ship. This was usually with fiddler 'Spanker' Austin and melodeon player Reuben Kerridge. They also performed in churches and for servants' balls.

Eley, known as 'Fiddler' Went, had a reputation for his prodigious improvisation skills.

He died suddenly in 1976 and, as people said: 'Eley Went and thar he goo'. (Sleeve notes from CD: *A Story to Tell: Keith Summers in Suffolk 1972–79*)

1926: The Ipswich Psychic Society was founded in the ground floor of a large, spooky Victorian house in Anglesea Road. It was visited soon afterwards by the creator of Sherlock Holmes, Sir Arthur Conan Doyle, who had turned to spiritualism after several deaths in the family. Regular events included trance addresses, symbolic clairvoyance, psychic demonstrations and the Healing Circle. In the 1950s, the Society changed its name to Cedars Spiritualist church. (Cedars church: www.cedars-spiritualists.co.uk; Ipswich Psychic Society leaflet, SRO)

- November 28th -

1772: The *Ipswich Journal* carried an advertisement for Freston Tower, which had just opened as an isolation hospital for people with smallpox and also as an inoculation centre. These services were first offered by Messrs Goodwin and Sparkes and then by Mr Bucke, surgeon of Holbrook and Ipswich.

Patients staying at the tower were offered a beautiful prospect across the Orwell and opportunities to go fishing and fowling, with boats and nets provided. Fees were charged on a scale up to 5 guineas, exclusive of tea, wine and washing.

These were the early days of inoculation in Great Britain. Edward Jenner, the pioneer of smallpox vaccine, was not to complete his investigations for several years, and inoculation against the disease was still a risky procedure. (*Ipswich Journal*, 1772)

2009: This unappealing headline appeared in the *Ipswich Evening Star*: 'Mouse Seen on Sausage Roll' (*Ipswich Evening Star*, 2009)

2012: Waxwings – plump, pretty birds, slightly smaller than starlings, with brightly coloured plumage and prominent crests – were seen in great and unusual profusion in the Ipswich area. They had come south because of extra-cold conditions in Scandinavia where they usually spent their winters. (Thanks to Paul Field)

~ NOVEMBER 29TH ~

1735: The *Ipswich Gazette* told the tale of an unusual highway robbery:

> On Monday last, a butcher was robbed near Romford. He was accosted by a woman mounted on a very good horse who threatened him with a pistol and demanded his money. The butcher was amazed to see she was a female highwayman. He played for time, and told her that he did not know what she meant.
>
> But then her partner in crime rode up. He told the butcher how rude he was to deny a lady what she had asked for and threatened to shoot him in the head. 'At the sight of the gentleman's pistol, the butcher thought it proper to grant the lady six guineas, some silver and his watch', and then they all parted amicably.

(Thanks to Pip Wright)

1948: At this time, about eighteen families were still living in temporary buildings vacated by the USAF at Nedging Tye near Ipswich. These plywood huts were broken into and squatted very soon after the end of World War Two but such was the housing crisis that local families were still living there in 1948. Each hut sat on chunky wooden piers and had two bedrooms, a kitchen, a toilet (no bathroom) and a living room. None of the dwellings had ceilings – each room opened into the roof void, so were often freezing cold. The site was enclosed by a 10ft barbed wire fence.

Eventually the squatters moved out, mostly returning to Hadleigh and the surrounding villages where they had originally come from. (Council Hutments – Site 3, Nedging Tye, SRO)

~ November 30th ~

1805: As it was St Andrew's Day, troops from the Scots Greys garrisoned in Ipswich held a ceremony to honour their patron saint and 'introduce' him to Ipswich.

> A soldier of the regiment represented the venerable Saint, who was mounted on a fine grey horse, and wore a bear-skin cloak and a long white beard. He had a roll of paper in his right hand and a cross affixt to his breast. Two men led his horse and a guard of 12 soldiers in Highland dress with their broadswords drawn, kept off the crowd. The procession was preceded by the band of the regiment who played several national airs.

The day was rounded off back in the barrack yard when the regiment paraded in new clothes.

This ceremony went on for many years but petered out by the mid-1840s – not a bad thing, according to the *Ipswich Journal*, as it had deteriorated into 'irregularities among the soldiers'. It was replaced by a Benefit Fund to help demobbed soldiers into civilian life.

No similar celebrations were held in Ipswich for the other 'home' saints – David, Patrick and George. (*Ipswich Journal*, 1805)

— December 1st —

1849: The new Ipswich Freehold Land Society issued a prospectus of its aims and objectives on this day, and the following year members took part in the first ballot for its freehold building plots.

The Society had bought the Cauldwell Hall estate and divided it into suitably sized plots, each costing £23. The Society had a high moral purpose, believing 'the effort involved in saving for an allotment, followed by the physical labour of developing the land would help to make responsible citizens'. And owning the necessary 40s worth of freehold land would give these 'responsible citizens' the right to vote in local and national elections. On ballot day, the draw for plots took nearly two hours, such was the interest.

There followed a period of intense activity on the estate with the new owners laying out roads, cultivating their land and building cottages for themselves, often using the flints and stones they found on site. This area was soon known as 'California', with its promise of a better life to come.

The rural appearance of streets like Crabbe Street and Cowper Street persisted for many years. Over 150 years later, Wendy Hazelwood said: 'I love my flint cottage. It doesn't look out on to any street – it just has a gate on to Crabbe Street and then a long path past my small, higgledy-piggledy garden plots. It's secluded. You'd never think you're in the town.' (Muriel Clegg, The Way We Went'. Thanks to Wendy Hazelwood)

‐ December 2nd ‐

1838: On or about this day, Ipswich-born Henry Carter (1821–80) set off for London with a heavy heart. His father was sending him to work for his uncle in the glove trade. Young Henry did make his fortune – but not in London and not in gloves.

Ever since he had seen skilled men working in a silversmith's shop in Ipswich, Henry had wanted to be an engraver. He saved up quietly to buy himself a set of tools and set about learning how to use them. Under the alias 'Frank Leslie', Carter started to work secretly as an engraver and quickly built up enough of a reputation to be taken on by the Illustrated London News.

Then, in 1848, Carter set off for the USA to seek his fortune. He changed his name legally to Frank Leslie and set up his own publishing house. Business boomed. His illustrated family journals, like *Chatterbox*, were popular across the States.

In 1874 Frank Leslie married. However, the couple routinely squandered money, living in an enormous house and lavishing hospitality on friends. Eventually his business went bust. In 1880, Leslie died at their New York apartment, owing $300,000. (*New York Times*, 1880; Tony Copsey, *Suffolk Writers Who Were Born Between 1800–1900*)

– December 3rd –

1807: Clara Reeve (1729–1807) died at home in Fore Street and was buried in St Stephen's churchyard. She was a well-known novelist who published more than twenty books in a career spanning over three decades.

Clara was born in Ipswich, one of eight children of a bookish, clerical family. She was in her 40s when her first book was published – an English translation of a seventeenth-century novel originally written in Latin.

Her most famous novel, *The Old English Baron*, came out in 1778 and was an immediate success. It became a major influence on the development of Gothic fiction and, in all likelihood, was known by Mary Shelley, author of *Frankenstein*. (Ipswich Women's History Trail; Sir Walter Scott, Lives of the Eminent Novelists and Dramatists)

1932: The Nobel Prize for Physiology and Medicine was presented to Charles Sherrington (1857–1952) for his work in neurology – one of many awards in a glittering career.

As a boy, Sherrington lived in Anglesea Road and attended Ipswich School where he only learned a little science. Despite that, he graduated in medicine from Cambridge University and became an eminent neurologist. He did groundbreaking work in mapping areas of the brain and studying synapses and reflexes. He also wrote the standard neurology textbook of his time.

Sherrington retired to Valley Road in Ipswich in 1936 and died in 1952. (Ipswich Society; *Oxford Dictionary of National Biography*)

‒ DECEMBER 4TH ‒

2008: Art dealer and celebrity 'sleeper spotter', Philip Mould, bought a painting of Ipswich for £50,000 at Sotheby's, where it was simply catalogued as 'English School, C18th'. The painting, called *A View of Ipswich*, showed Christchurch Mansion against the background of the town, the river and the countryside beyond. Mould thought it could be an early Gainsborough.

If his theory was correct, Mould estimated that Gainsborough had painted it in Ipswich in the late 1740s. At that time Gainsborough was travelling between London, Sudbury and Ipswich looking for commissions from wealthy patrons. He painted Holywells Park, Ipswich (home of the Cobbold family) during those years ‒ his only authenticated landscape of the town. For most of the 1750s, Gainsborough and his family lived in Foundation Street, Ipswich, but Philip Mould believed that the Christchurch Mansion picture belonged to the late 1740s. Following authentication by several experts, Mould offered the painting to the Gainsborough's House museum in Sudbury for £750,000 but it was too expensive for them.

There is a nineteenth-century gouache version of *A View of Ipswich* by the artist Paul Sandby on display at Christchurch Mansion, on permanent loan from Norwich Castle Museum. (Extremegroundhopping, Ralph Morris' blog: http://extremegroundhopping.wordpress.com)

‒ DECEMBER 5TH ‒

1412: The first recorded headmaster of the borough school (the forerunner of Ipswich School) was Richard Penyngton. Early in December of 1412 he was sued for assault by a local butcher. When Penyngton failed to appear in court to answer the charges, his goods were ordered to be seized, including his 'togas' (academic gowns) and grammar books. (I.E. Gray and W.E. Potter, *Ipswich School 1400–1950*)

‒•‒

1877: At a regular weekly meeting of the Caxton Literary Society in St Stephen's Church Lane, Mr Frederick Daking delivered an interesting lecture about a new invention: the telephone. When he had explained how it worked:

> … various experiments were made with the instrument with successful results.
>
> The room in which the lecture was delivered was connected with a house on the opposite side of the lane, and conversation was carried on. One or two members sung some songs, and these were heard most distinctly by those at the other end of the wire. One or two selections were played upon a harmonium in the society's room, and the selections recognised.

Mr Daking was thanked for introducing this new invention to Society members, but it was agreed that the telephone would never supersede the telegraph. (*Ipswich Journal*, 1877)

− DECEMBER 6TH −

1996: Memorable Cheeses, a specialist cheese shop, opened this Thursday in an old dairy in The Walk.

The owners, Sarah and Peter Forster, had the idea of opening it one day when they were walking on Felixstowe beach. Sarah said:

> We decided to sell cheese because there were no other specialist cheese shops in Ipswich or nearby. We opened in time for the Christmas trade that year and it went so well that we ran out of cheese by the New Year.
>
> We didn't know about the bad reputation of Suffolk cheese till customers told us. Traditionally, local cheese was exceptionally hard and made from very thin, skimmed milk. It was called 'Suffolk Bang' and was considered only fit for servants, labourers and members of the armed forces.
>
> These days, Suffolk cheeses are much better quality. The most popular one we've sold is Shipcord, made at Rodwell Farm Dairy in Baylham.
>
> Thinking about the cheese we have sold over the years, the smelliest one was undoubtedly Stinking Bishop which was used to revive Wallace from the dead in the film Wallace & Gromit: The Curse of the Were-Rabbit.
>
> And the weirdest cheese we heard about was made from breast milk, but we decided not to stock that one!

(Thanks to Sarah and Peter Forster)

‒ December 7th ‒

1895: The *Ipswich Journal* announced the death of the Rev. George Drury, who had been the Anglican rector of Claydon for most of the second half of the nineteenth century. He was one of the 'great High Church eccentrics' and a controversial local figure.

Ipswich and its villages were not well disposed to anything 'Roman' and local low-church Protestants were scandalised by him. Simon Knott, the Suffolk Churches historian, later described how 'in the 1870s, Father George's congregation would parade through Claydon with banners of the Blessed Virgin flying, kneeling down with them in a field while singing the "Ave Maria". High Mass was accompanied by incense, vestments and candles.'

Father George established a convent in Claydon which was attacked by a mob, and he only worsened his reputation by mishandling the burial of an unbaptised infant in his churchyard (the Akenham Burial Case).

He protected himself and his rectory by erecting a 9ft wall but that soon became covered with anti-Catholic graffiti.

Simon Knott described Drury's funeral: 'It was carefully documented by ritualism-watchers, who noted the robed choir, the cross carried in procession, the incense and the sign of the cross. His large grave is guarded by railings in the south-east corner of the churchyard, beneath the great yew tree.' (*Ipswich Journal*, 1895. Thanks to Simon Knott)

~ DECEMBER 8TH ~

1841: By this day, young Edward Byles Cowell (1826–1903) of Ipswich had begun teaching himself the Persian language. He had become interested in it when he found a Persian grammar book at the Ipswich Literary Institution library. He was 15 and a pupil at Ipswich School. It was said that he woke himself up to study early every morning by getting the milkman to pull a string attached to his foot! When Cowell was obliged to leave school the following year to run the family business, he carried on studying in his own time. He was now helped by Major Hockley, an old Bombay hand, whom he had met through the Ipswich Literary Institution.

In 1847 Cowell married Elizabeth Charlesworth of Bramford. By then, he had also begun to teach himself Sanskrit and Arabic, and she encouraged him to study for a degree in oriental languages at Oxford University.

After graduation, the Cowells lived in Calcutta for several years and Edward held various posts at the University there, adding Hindi and Bengali to his repertoire of languages.

They moved to Cambridge in 1864 and Cowell, by now a noted translator and academic, became the first Professor of Sanskrit at the University there. (M.G. Smith, *'Twixt Potteries and California*)

– DECEMBER 9TH –

1824: The Suffolk Medical Book Society held its first formal meeting. It was set up to run a small medical library of texts and journals from the back room of an Ipswich bookshop. Subscribing members and apprentices had the right to visit, borrow books or have them sent by post. At this first meeting, members voted to buy a core stock of fourteen books covering topics such as poisons, burns, indigestion and 'female diseases'. At least fifty-eight surgeons and apothecaries signed up as members and a few years later, military surgeons stationed in Ipswich were also allowed to join. (Sally Irvine, *Surgeons and Apothecaries in Suffolk: 1750–1830*)

1835: A meeting was held at the Ipswich Arms in Lower Brook Street to support the wives and families of the Tolpuddle Martyrs: farm labourers from Dorset who had been transported to Australia for banding together to protect their meagre wages. £200 had already been collected in Ipswich and more was needed. Similar meetings were held up and down the country to collect donations and raise awareness of what had happened to these men.

In 1838, the British government relented and the Tolpuddle Martyrs returned home as heroes with free pardons. Five men from Ipswich went as a deputation to London to welcome the men back and to discuss how the lot of agricultural labourers could be improved. (Robert Ratcliffe, *History of Working Class Movement in Ipswich*)

– December 10th –

1666: 'Dorcas Woodwarde a maide that lived at our Angell died of the plague, and was buryed' in Bramford. Three other plague deaths were recorded that year in the village. Across England, the Great Plague killed an estimated 100,000 people. (Bramford parish registers, SRO)

1815: Cuffee and Amber Cross, negro slaves of Silent Street, had their son baptised by Rev. Milesom Edgar at St Nicholas' parish church. The child was given the Christian name Thomas. Cuffee was the name given by white slave owners to men originally called Kofi, a common name in what is now Ghana. His owner was probably a merchant with trade connections in the West Indies, where people from that part of Africa were exported to.

After the baptism at St Nicholas church, the family disappeared from the Ipswich records. (Parish registers of St Nicholas' church, Ipswich, SRO)

1902: The first Aswan Dam was opened. Its sluice gates, designed to control the Nile's flood waters, were made in Ipswich by Ransomes & Rapier. (Robert Malster, *Ipswich: An A to Z of Local History*)

~ December 11th ~

1745: A cutter secretly landed cargo at Sizewell Gap and about fifty armed men of the Hadleigh Gang were waiting there to pick it up. They were members of one of the most successful smuggling bands in Suffolk and carried out at least seven major operations this year.

The gang could always call on plenty of horses and men, especially as unemployment was high. They loaded their horses with dry and wet goods, mostly tea and brandy. When there was a lot of brandy to move they would use wagons, escorted by a dozen or so armed men.

As their headquarters was at Hadleigh, over 40 miles from the coast at Sizewell, they must have relied on warehouses and discreet customers to make their way back safely. Once safely back in their home territory, one of their secret locations was in the village of Semer.

Without a regular coastguard service or police force, the Hadleigh Gang could operate more or less as they chose, with only the occasional Dragoon patrol to challenge them.

The loss to the Revenue in 1745–46 from smuggling on the Suffolk coast was estimated at over £100,000. (Leonard P. Thompson, *Smugglers of the Suffolk Coast*, *Ipswich Journal*, 1869)

~ DECEMBER 12TH ~

1795: Rev. David Edwards died in Gloucestershire. He had been the minister at Tacket St Congregational church in Ipswich for some twenty-six years but was forced to leave after an incident at Christmas in 1791.

The story went that he had two daughters of marriageable age and that some of his congregation thought they were altogether too familiar with men from the local barracks. One day, the girls were accosted by a prim young chapelgoer who pointed at a portrait of her own grandfather hanging on the wall and asked what he would have thought of their behaviour. One of the Edwards girls answered that she was sick of hearing about the old man and poked her umbrella through the canvas. The incident divided the congregation. Edwards and his family left Ipswich and a splinter group moved to set up their own church in Dairy Lane (later known as Fonnereau Road). (Peter Bishop, History of Ipswich)

1837: A meeting was held at the Admiral's Head in St Margaret's Street, at which 'sixty intelligent and independent men' formed a local Working Men's Association. They were early Chartists who advocated secret ballots, universal male suffrage and short fixed-term parliaments, and they were active in and about East Suffolk over the following years. (Robert Ratcliffe, *History of Working Class Movement in Ipswich*)

⟶ December 13th ⟵

1755: On or about this day, 14-year-old Sarah Kirby (1741–1810), moved from her home town of Ipswich to London when her father became tutor to the future George III. Under her married name of Sarah Trimmer she became a prolific writer and was one of the founders of the Sunday School movement.

Sarah's books were so popular that she became one of the best-selling authors of her time. Her children's story, *Fabulous Histories*, inspired numerous animal stories and remained in print for over a century. Her periodical, *The Guardian of Education*, was the first critical review and history of children's literature. Her writing was admired by Samuel Johnson and other notables of the day.

Sarah also founded several Sunday and charitable schools, and wrote manuals for other women who wanted to start their own schools or write for children and the poor.

Sarah's writing promoted a rigidly conservative and hierarchical world view. She died in Brentford in 1810 but her work remained influential throughout the nineteenth century. (Ipswich Women's History Trail; Marion Ann Taylor and Heather E. Weir, eds, *Let Her Speak for Herself*)

– December 14th –

1941: By this day, several British Restaurants had opened in Ipswich. Local authorities were funded by central government during the Second World War to set up communal kitchens for people who had been bombed out, run out of ration coupons or otherwise needed help. They were called British Restaurants, as Winston Churchill thought the phrase 'Communal Kitchens' had too much of a socialist ring to it.

Ipswich had British Restaurants in Arcade Street, Ranelagh Road, Clarkson Street, Tower Ramparts and in Whitton. Meals cost a maximum of 9*d* for three courses. The meals were cooked and served by volunteers, usually members of the Women's Royal Voluntary Service. The fare was straightforwardly plain and cheap, with the rule that customers could not have two proteins together on one plate. In Ipswich, as elsewhere, Woolton Pie made a frequent appearance. This was a meatless, dry and, some said, inedible combination of carrots, parsnips, turnips and potatoes covered in white sauce and wrapped in pastry. One of the Ipswich managers admitted that it was 'one dish which was not a favourite'.

British Restaurants survived the end of World War Two by a couple of years and were disbanded in 1947. (BBC: www.bbc.co.uk/history/ww2peopleswar/stories/84/a4264184.shtml; Norman Longmate, *How We Lived Then*)

— December 15th —

1828: Robert Fitzroy, a Suffolk aristocrat, was made Captain of HMS *Beagle* on this day when it put into port in Rio de Janeiro. The *Beagle* was engaged in carrying out a survey – mapping and naming a huge area around Tierra del Fuego and the Straits of Magellan.

A few weeks later, the *Beagle* was to the far south-west of Chile when it came across a prominent island with a number of islets and rocks. Captain Fitzroy named it Ipswich Island and wrote in his diary:

> Landing was dangerous and ascending the hill extremely difficult, on account of thick tangled brushwood which grows about three or four feet high on every part of the east side and is so matted together as to be almost impenetrable.

There was a larger island nearby, which he named Grafton Island. These Suffolk names were chosen in honour of Fitzroy's own ancestry: his family titles included the Duke of Grafton and Viscount Ipswich.

A couple of years later, in the 1830s, Fitzroy captained the *Beagle* again. This second voyage lasted five years, during which time the naturalist Charles Darwin was on board, laying down the scientific groundwork for his theory of evolution. (www. planetipswich.com)

~ DECEMBER 16TH ~

1903: A memorial in Christchurch Park was unveiled. It commemorated nine Protestant martyrs who had been burned to death in the town. It was erected by public subscription in response to a series of newspaper articles by the local archaeologist Nina Layard, who was proud of her own Huguenot (French Protestant) descent.

These Ipswich martyrs were killed in the purge of Protestants during Mary Tudor's reign. Three of them were women: Agnes Potten, Joan Trunchfield, and Alice Driver.

Agnes Potten and Joan Trunchfield were both young mothers. They spent several months in prison for taking food to a jailed clergyman before they were burned together at the stake on the Cornhill.

Alice Driver, from Grundisburgh, was arrested for helping a Protestant weaver from Woodbridge. At her trial, her ears were cut off for comparing Mary Tudor to Jezebel, the wicked Old Testament queen. On the day of her martyrdom, Alice was chained by the neck on the pyre before it was lit. Her last recorded words were: 'Here is a goodly neckerchief, blessed be God for it.'

Unveiling the Martyrs' Memorial on this Wednesday, the Dean of Canterbury said that his sincere hope was that the Church of England would always remember the martyrs of the 'reformed faith' and remain free 'of the domination of Rome'. (Ipswich Women's History Trail; N.F. Layard, *Seventeen Suffolk Martyrs*)

~ December 17th ~

1982: The Orwell Bridge opened, carrying the A45 over the Orwell estuary. Originally a tunnel had been considered to reduce the impact on such a beautiful landscape but, as that option was so expensive, architects were commissioned to design a bridge to 'the highest aesthetical standards'.

It was nearly 1 mile in length, with eighteen spans, one of which was among the longest pre-stressed concrete spans in use in the world at the time (190m). The bridge was strong enough to carry three lanes of traffic in each direction.

The construction took about three years. The workforce numbered approximately 300 and was mainly recruited locally. One of the construction workers later wrote: 'I helped construct the Orwell Bridge from start to finish. Pleasant memories mostly. We would often pause when news from the Falklands War came through on the radio in the works canteen.' Sadly, two construction workers died during the project.

The Transport Secretary of the time, David Howell, opened the bridge and cut the ribbon. The bridge succeeded in taking traffic out of Ipswich and improving access to the Port of Felixstowe – as local people are reminded to this day whenever the bridge has to be closed. (Stevin Construction BV)

– December 18th –

1788: Organist and composer Joseph Gibbs (1698–1788), was given a full civic funeral at St Mary-le-Tower on this Thursday, with music played by the Scots Greys and the East Suffolk Militia. He had been the church organist for nearly forty years.

Born in north Essex, he followed in his father's footsteps and became a professional musician. In 1748, he was appointed organist of St Mary-le-Tower in Ipswich, and there he stayed for the rest of his life.

Gibbs was a friend of Thomas Gainsborough, who painted his portrait. They were both members of the Ipswich Musical Society and a lost Gainsborough sketch of one of its meetings apparently featured Joseph in the audience, asleep!

Gibbs was best known for his 'Eight Sonatas for Violin and Continuo' – a composition in which the solo violin was accompanied by a harpsichord or bass violin. It was published in London with a subscription list that included the most famous musicians of the day, as well as many Ipswich figures.

His effects, including music, instruments and two Gainsborough paintings, were sold at auction the year after he died. (*New Grove Dictionary of Music and Musicians*; Here of a Sunday Morning website: www.hoasm.org)

~ DECEMBER 19TH ~

1835: In this Saturday's issue, the *Ipswich Journal* reported that there had been riots at two Ipswich workhouses that week – firstly at St Clement's, and then at St Margaret's.

The Riot Act was read and hussars were called in from the Ipswich cavalry barracks to enforce order. Four paupers were arrested and sentenced to death at the March Assizes the following year. They were James Burgess, aged 24, Daniel Folly (a sailor), 52, Michael Terry, 19 and Robert Hurren, 19. All their sentences were commuted to twelve months in prison. (*Ipswich Journal*, 1835; www.ancestry.com)

2006: Simon Knott described how it felt to be in Ipswich at the end of the month in which five women's bodies had been found, but no murderer identified:

> It is December 19, 2006, at 4.30 p.m. The temperature has just fallen below freezing, and Ipswich waits for night under a blood-red sky …
>
> For us, the last few weeks have been an assault on our town; not only the murders, but the media circus that has followed in their wake.
>
> As you'd expect in this warm-hearted east coast industrial port, there has been a pulling together, a sense of Ipswich looking after its own. Not once have I heard a single word of condemnation or blame for any of the five murdered women. In almost every church in the town, five candles have burned on the altar, five photographs in simple frames beside them. Ipswich knows that, above all else, these were Ipswich people.

(Thanks to Simon Knott)

~ December 20th ~

1832: Priscilla Wakefield (1751–1832) was buried at the Quaker Meeting House in Ipswich. She had died at her daughter's house in Woodbridge Road. As well as being the aunt of prison reformer Elizabeth Fry, Mrs Wakefield was influential and interesting in her own right.

Originally from Tottenham, she started writing to support the family when her husband's money-making schemes failed. She wrote on a range of subjects and, in 1796, she published the first comprehensive survey of botany to be written by a woman. Mrs Wakefield was also an active philanthropist. She founded a maternity hospital, 'lying-in' charities to support women who had recently had a baby and a children's 'penny bank', which developed into England's first savings bank.

She moved to Ipswich in 1813 to be with her daughter, but already knew many of the figures in local society, including the painter Gainsborough and the Cobbold family. (*Oxford Dictionary of National Biography*)

1913: An unusual strike took place at Pretty's corset factory about pay over the Christmas period. The women 'purchased rattles, miniature flags, trumpets, and so on and made plenty of noise' as their delegates went in to negotiate. The girls won! (Robert Ratcliffe, *History of Working Class Movement in Ipswich*)

~ December 21st ~

1882: A book of poems by Jean Ingelow (1820–97) was given to the winner of the upper-school prize for arithmetic at Ipswich School for Girls. This award was apt as the poet had a strong Ipswich connection. As a girl in the 1830s and 1840s, she had lived at 2 Elm Street over her father's bank, in large first-floor rooms.

In the 1850s, the Ingelows left Ipswich for London, where Jean spent the rest of her long life. She had already started her writing career in Ipswich and by the 1870s she had become a best-selling author of poetry and children's books, highly regarded by the likes of John Ruskin. She was especially popular in the USA, where American readers petitioned Queen Victoria to make her Poet Laureate when Tennyson died in 1892. In character, she was said to be reserved, dignified and conservative.

In the twentieth century her popularity nosedived. Her writing was thought to be overcooked and sentimentally religious. Although her children's tale *Mopsa the Fairy* was reissued in 1972 and again in 1992, her books fell out of favour with the times and she dwindled into obscurity. (Tony Copsey, *Suffolk Writers Who Were Born Between 1800–1900*; Ipswich Society; *Oxford Dictionary of National Biography*)

– December 22nd –

1660: On or about this day, John Darbie was busy installing a complete ring of six bells in the tower of St Clement's parish church. He was originally from Kelsale near Saxmundham and had established a bell foundry in Ipswich. His work had a good reputation and during his working life he cast 158 bells for Suffolk churches. Many of his bells had his name inscribed on them. Other Ipswich churches have bells from the Darbie foundry, including: St Mary-at-the-Elms (three bells, 1669); St Mary-le-Tower (three bells, 1671) and St Peter's (one bell, 1682, and another in 1683). (Robert Malster: *Ipswich: An A to Z of Local History*)

1962: Ralph Fiennes, actor, was born in Ipswich Hospital. Cousin of the Prince of Wales and the adventurer Ranulph, Ralph Fiennes is probably most famous as Lord Voldemort in the *Harry Potter* films. He won numerous prestigious awards for films like *The English Patient* and *Schindler's List* and for his Shakespearian stage performances. In 2007, he was awarded the accolade of Most Vile Villain for his role as Harry Potter's arch-enemy. (Viacom Entertainment Group website: www.spike.com)

– DECEMBER 23RD –

1895: The *Sydney Morning Herald*'s special correspondent published an account of his recent trip to Ipswich, which was no doubt fascinating for the thousands of Australians originally hailing from Suffolk:

> The drive through the old town along narrow but well-kept streets is more than ordinarily interesting. Some of the buildings date back for hundreds of years. Many of the shops and inns are exactly of the character described in the works of Strype and Camden [who were seventeenth-century historians and writers].
>
> But the modern perambulators now assist in blocking the narrow ways, the cobble stones are displaced by wood pavements, and plate-glass and flaring gaslights are gradually asserting their right to occupy the chief centres where business is transacted.
>
> Would it be believed that on the day of my visit, about 10,000 of Ipswich inhabitants were assembled on the village green to see two professional teams of lady footballers [yes, really!] give what was but a slender exhibition of the great national game.

(*Sydney Morning Herald*, 1895)

1943: The Rev. Winifred Brown (b. 1919) became the first woman church minister in Ipswich on this day or thereabouts, when she was appointed by the Ipswich Unitarian congregation to lead them. When she came to Ipswich, she was only in her mid-20s and her first task was to unify a congregation which was bitterly divided on the issue of pacifism. She remained in Ipswich for three years and then left to become a schoolteacher in Leicestershire. (Ipswich Women's History Trail)

~ December 24th ~

1194: On or about this date, the surname 'Hadley' was first recorded. It belonged to a 'Matilda de Hadlega', a woman from Hadleigh in Suffolk and wealthy enough to be mentioned in the financial records of the time. Other places near Ipswich giving rise to surnames include Washbrook, Baylham (Baalham, Balaam etc.), Brightwell, Tuddenham and Freston – but not Ipswich (nor its old form, Gyppeswick). (D.M. Stenton, ed., *Great Roll of the Pipe for the Sixth Year of the Reign of King Richard the First, Michaelmas 1194*)

1831: The Consistory Court of Norwich arbitrated between Moses and Michael Levy, two Jewish brothers from Ipswich. Their children had fallen out and the row had escalated until the brothers exchanged public insults about each other's wives. In particular, Michael had called Moses' wife a whore.

At this point, the law became involved. Cases of defamation were dealt with by Church of England courts and so the Levy brothers were called to attend the Consistory Court, 50 miles away in Norwich.

The court found that Michael was more at fault than Moses. His sentence was quite inappropriate for a Jew. He was ordered to go to St Margaret's parish church in Ipswich, where he had to ask for God's pardon and Michael's forgiveness and recite the Lord's Prayer. (S.M. Waddems, *Sexual Slander in Nineteenth Century England*)

~ DECEMBER 25TH ~

1858: On Christmas Day, Mary Ann Girling revealed that she had seen a vision in her Ipswich bedroom. Christ had appeared to her to say that she was to lead the children of God to the Promised Land.

Mary Ann left her husband and children and gathered together a group of followers to move with her to Hordle in the New Forest. Over 150 people joined her, many from the villages around Little Glemham where she had been born. They must have cut strange figures: a community of believers who performed frenzied dances and shook with religious fervour. Mary Ann banned them from any sexual activity. They were also prohibited from selling anything they made or grew and they were not allowed to work for wages. Mary Anne was revered and called 'mother' by her followers. But she was feared by local people and was threatened with being burned as a witch.

In the 1881 census, the Children of God all stated their occupation as 'prefers to live by faith'. Their address was given as 'The Shakers House and Tents' in the New Forest. By this time their numbers were dwindling.

After the death of Mary Ann in 1886, the community quickly disintegrated. (Carol Twinch, *Little Book of Suffolk*; *Oxford Dictionary of National Biography*; www.ancestry.co.uk)

~ December 26th ~

1863: Mr Robert Seager of St Peter's Street was praised in the *Ipswich Journal* for his:

> ... splendid display of pork and ham, cured upon his own principles. Mr Seager contrives to prevent the carboniferous particles of the wood affecting the meat he cures, and the consequence is, that his hams and bacon have a rich red appearance, instead of the sooty colour which earned for hams and bacon in past times the title of 'blackened meat'. The flavour is also greatly improved.
>
> The meat cured by Mr Seager will keep for any length of time, and is consequently in great request for exportation to the West Indies.

(*Ipswich Journal*, 1863)

1980: During the nights of December 26th and 27th 1980, American servicemen stationed at RAF Woodbridge and RAF Bentwaters (about 12 miles from Ipswich) reported mysterious lights in nearby Rendlesham Forest. A team of airmen went to investigate and one of them voiced a running commentary into a dictaphone. About a fortnight afterwards, the men filed top-secret witness reports, which were strictly classified. They claimed that they had encountered an alien craft deep in the forest which had flown off when they approached. However, their secret tape-recording was leaked and the incident attracted international attention, which has prompted much speculation over what actually happened ever since. (MoD files on Unidentified Flying Objects, The National Archives, Kew)

— December 27th —

1872: The Guardians of Ipswich Workhouse in Whip Street held a heated meeting to decide whether they should send the bodies of dead 'unclaimed' paupers for anatomical examination.

The argument had been precipitated by a letter sent from the Professor of Anatomy at Cambridge University requesting the corpses of paupers who died alone in the world (i.e. 'unclaimed'). He needed them for dissection and, if the pauper was friendless, who was there to mind? The bodies would be buried in Cambridge, all expenses paid. Such schemes were quite legal – an attempt, on the one hand, to prevent body-snatching but, on the other, to maintain a supply of cadavers to surgeons.

As a medical man, Dr Chevallier was keen to send corpses to Cambridge. Opponents, he said, were impeding scientific progress and pandering to the feelings of the poor. Five other board members agreed with him. The six men opposed to Chevallier felt that this was not a way to treat the poor – it would do a great 'violence to their feelings' and their bodies would be treated worse than criminals' bodies.

The Chairman challenged Chevallier to 'leave your own bones' for dissection 'if you are so anxious about scientific examinations' and he used his casting vote to throw the proposal out. (*Ipswich Journal*, 1872. Thanks to Mark Mower for background to this story)

– DECEMBER 28TH –

1540: On this day, the 'boy bishop' of Ipswich preached a church sermon, as was the custom. It marked the end of his term of office. Every year a boy was appointed to be the 'bishop' of Ipswich, to serve from St Nicholas Day (December 6) until Holy Innocents' Day (December 28). The practice was banned in 1541 as Protestant ideas spread through the English church. (Robert Malster, *Ipswich: An A to Z of Local History*)

1993: British customs officials seized £70 million of Colombian cocaine which arrived on a ship at the Port of Felixstowe. They had been preparing for it since anti-Mafia investigators had tipped them off.

A container adapted to hide drugs was unloaded on the dock and three men were arrested when they went to the docks to pick up the cocaine. Two were remanded in custody at Ipswich magistrates' court and charged with smuggling. The third man was released on police bail.

A Customs and Excise spokesman said that this was the first confirmation that the Mafia were smuggling drugs into the UK. He believed that the haul had originated from one of the world's largest drug cartels – the Medellin in Colombia – but that, worryingly, the Mafia had moved in on their operation, so extending their grip on the world drug trade. (BBC News: http://news.bbc.co.uk/onthisday/hi/dates/stories/december/28/newsid_2546000/2546979.stm)

~ December 29th ~

1914: Early in the First World War, Witnesham man Sergeant Clement Barker wrote to his brother from the Ypres trenches and told him about the Christmas armistice he had just witnessed:

> A German looked over his trench – no shots – our men did the same, and then a few of our men went out and brought the dead in (69) and buried them. The next thing that happened – a football was kicked out of our trenches and Germans and English played football.
>
> Night came and still no shots. Boxing Day the same, and has remained so up to now…
>
> We have conversed with the Germans and they all seem to be very much fed up and heaps of them are deserting.
>
> Some have given themselves up as prisoners, so things are looking quite rosy.

Sgt Barker grew up at the Barley Mow in Witnesham. He enlisted as a cook in the Grenadier Guards in 1901.

When the letter came to light on the BBC's *Antiques Roadshow* in 2012, it was described as important evidence of the 'last bit of chivalry of the First World War'. (*Daily Mail*, 2002)

— December 30th —

1154–89: Henry II was so fond of one of his minstrels' party tricks that he rewarded him with the gift of Hemingstone Manor near Ipswich. The rent was cheap – the entertainer and his heirs just had to repeat the special routine in the royal presence every Christmas.

When we learn that the minstrel was known as Roland le Fartere and that the trick was to leap, whistle and fart, we can understand why Roland's descendants eventually left Hemingstone rather than pay the rent! (Juliet Barker, *Agincourt: The King, the Campaign, the Battle*)

1748: In this Saturday's issue, the *Ipswich Journal* announced that about 250 sick British soldiers had just arrived in the town from the Netherlands. They had been fighting France and Prussia in the last months of what became known as the War of Austrian Succession. These new arrivals joined injured soldiers already housed at Christ's Hospital, which was being used as a military infirmary. A week later, six of the soldiers were buried in Ipswich.

The following year, in 1749, many more soldiers and seamen found themselves in Ipswich when the war ended and more troops were shipped home. The rapidly disbanded men often faced unemployment and destitution. (*Ipswich Journal*, various dates; L.J. Redstone, *Ipswich Through the Ages*)

~ December 31st ~

1835: The first mayor of Ipswich was elected. He was Benjamin Brame, solicitor of Lower Brook Street and a Whig (or a 'Destructive', as the *Ipswich Journal* called them). He was elected by his fellow local politicians and served a year in office. New legislation had created a new administration structure for towns – a mayor, high steward, recorder, aldermen and councillors – in an attempt to rid local politics of corruption. (*Ipswich Journal*, 1835; Ipswich Borough Council)

1854: Sister Mary Bernard (1810–95), born in Ipswich as Julia Dickson, arrived on or about this day to work at Scutari Hospital on the Asian side of Constantinople. When she had heard that Florence Nightingale had taken forty nurses there to care for troops fighting in the Crimea, she volunteered to join them. As an experienced nurse herself, Sister Bernard was one of five nuns assigned to work directly under Nightingale. They found that poor care for wounded soldiers was being given by overworked medical staff. Medicines were in short supply, hygiene was neglected and mass infections like cholera were common. Before long, Sister Bernard contracted severe fever herself and was invalided home in July 1855.

Later, the courageous nun set out with five other sisters for New Zealand where she founded the first community of Roman Catholic nuns on South Island. (*Te Ara: Encyclopedia of New Zealand*)

— December 30th —

1154–89: Henry II was so fond of one of his minstrels' party tricks that he rewarded him with the gift of Hemingstone Manor near Ipswich. The rent was cheap – the entertainer and his heirs just had to repeat the special routine in the royal presence every Christmas.

When we learn that the minstrel was known as Roland le Fartere and that the trick was to leap, whistle and fart, we can understand why Roland's descendants eventually left Hemingstone rather than pay the rent! (Juliet Barker, *Agincourt: The King, the Campaign, the Battle*)

1748: In this Saturday's issue, the *Ipswich Journal* announced that about 250 sick British soldiers had just arrived in the town from the Netherlands. They had been fighting France and Prussia in the last months of what became known as the War of Austrian Succession. These new arrivals joined injured soldiers already housed at Christ's Hospital, which was being used as a military infirmary. A week later, six of the soldiers were buried in Ipswich.

The following year, in 1749, many more soldiers and seamen found themselves in Ipswich when the war ended and more troops were shipped home. The rapidly disbanded men often faced unemployment and destitution. (*Ipswich Journal*, various dates; L.J. Redstone, *Ipswich Through the Ages*)

– DECEMBER 31ST –

1835: The first mayor of Ipswich was elected. He was Benjamin Brame, solicitor of Lower Brook Street and a Whig (or a 'Destructive', as the *Ipswich Journal* called them). He was elected by his fellow local politicians and served a year in office. New legislation had created a new administration structure for towns – a mayor, high steward, recorder, aldermen and councillors – in an attempt to rid local politics of corruption. (*Ipswich Journal*, 1835; Ipswich Borough Council)

1854: Sister Mary Bernard (1810–95), born in Ipswich as Julia Dickson, arrived on or about this day to work at Scutari Hospital on the Asian side of Constantinople. When she had heard that Florence Nightingale had taken forty nurses there to care for troops fighting in the Crimea, she volunteered to join them. As an experienced nurse herself, Sister Bernard was one of five nuns assigned to work directly under Nightingale. They found that poor care for wounded soldiers was being given by overworked medical staff. Medicines were in short supply, hygiene was neglected and mass infections like cholera were common. Before long, Sister Bernard contracted severe fever herself and was invalided home in July 1855.

Later, the courageous nun set out with five other sisters for New Zealand where she founded the first community of Roman Catholic nuns on South Island. (*Te Ara: Encyclopedia of New Zealand*)